*Publications of the Committee on
Taxation, Resources and Economic Development*

8

*Proceedings of a Symposium Sponsored by the
Committee on Taxation, Resources and
Economic Development (TRED)
At the University of Wisconsin—Madison, 1973*

Other TRED Publications

1 *Extractive Resources and Taxation*
   Mason Gaffney, editor

2 *Property Taxation—USA*
   Richard W. Lindholm, editor

3 *The Property Tax and Its Administration*
   Arthur D. Lynn, Jr., editor

4 *Land and Building Taxes*
   Arthur P. Becker, editor

5 *The Assessment of Land Value*
   Daniel M. Holland, editor

6 *Government Spending and Land Values*
   C. Lowell Harriss, editor

7 *Property Taxation and the Finance of Education*
   Richard W. Lindholm, editor

Property Taxation
Land Use
&
Public Policy

Edited by

Arthur D. Lynn, Jr.

Published for the Committee on
Taxation, Resources and
Economic Development by
THE UNIVERSITY OF WISCONSIN PRESS

Published 1976
The University of Wisconsin Press
Box 1379, Madison, Wisconsin 53701
The University of Wisconsin Press, Ltd.
70 Great Russell Street, London

First printing
Printed in the United States of America

For LC CIP information see the colophon
ISBN 0-299-06920-6

Publication of this book was made possible in part
by support from the Schalkenbach and the Lincoln foundations

Contributors

Kenneth Back
: Director of Finance and Revenue, Government of the District of Columbia

George F. Break
: Professor of Economics, University of California—Berkeley

Glenn W. Fisher
: Regents Professor of Urban Affairs, Wichita State University

Mason Gaffney
: Professor of Economics, University of Victoria

C. Lowell Harriss
: Professor of Economics, Columbia University, and Economic Consultant, Tax Foundation, Inc.

Daniel M. Holland
: Professor of Finance, Alfred P. Sloan School of Management, Massachusetts Institute of Technology

Douglas N. Jones
: Congressional Research Service, Library of Congress

Helen F. Ladd
: Department of Economics, Wellesley College

Dick Netzer
: Dean, Graduate School of Public Administration, New York University

John M. Payne
: Professor of Law, Rutgers University Law School

John Shannon
: Advisory Commission on Intergovernmental Relations

Frederick D. Stocker
: Professor of Economics and Public Administration, The Ohio State University

v

Contents

List of Tables and Figures

Preface

One reviewer of an earlier volume in the TRED series noted that the group had once again "rushed in where angels fear to tread." Such may again be the case here where, despite the natural and obvious limitations that a relatively brief conference imposes upon both the breadth and depth of consideration possible, property taxation, land use, and public policy are explored in order to ascertain at least in a preliminary fashion the impact of the interrelationship of property taxation and land use patterns upon present and prospective public policy.

Recent years have witnessed a growing national debate about appropriate public policy designed to enhance the quality and style of life in a technological society. One conference, which considers only a particular subset of that debate, can at best make only an incremental contribution to the range of understandings conducive to formation of the consensus necessary for effective agreement about appropriate public policy. Nonetheless, given that caveat dictated by what might be termed becoming modesty, we are convinced of the cumulative value of such contributions to the process of long-run policy determination.

Property taxation has been much considered by TRED as well as by many other observers and analysts. The tax has been roundly criticized time out of mind, and certainly the phrase *natura non facit saltum* is descriptive of the process of adjustment and improvement of this ancient levy. Nonetheless, positive development occurs. Ronald Welch recently noted five significant changes in the property tax during the past four decades. These included its virtual elimination as a source of state revenue, a relative decline as a source of local government general revenue, a substantial increase in total revenue dollars produced, a tendency to become less general in coverage due to the development of both increased exemptions and additional classification of property categories for ad valorem tax purposes, and, finally, distinct improvements in property tax administration.* His summary comment serves to remind us that change occurs even if sometimes only at a glacial rate. Even so, concern continues

* "The Way We Were: Four Decades of Change in the Property Tax," *The Property Tax in a Changing Environment,* Advisory Commission on Intergovernmental Relations, Washington, D.C., March, 1974, M83, p. 29.

about the effect of the tax upon land use and resource allocation as well as the character and results of the tax in terms of received criteria such as economic neutrality and distributional equity. Similarly, while classification or exemption have often accorded preferential treatment to farm land, household personalty, and business inventories, significant analytical and policy questions remain concerning possible partial or complete untaxing of improvements and the classification of land for ad valorem tax purposes.

While property tax change has progressed at a rather slow and uneven pace, a congeries of other developments have generated increased interest in both urban and rural land use policy, especially the former. Many concerned with land use improvement potentials have concluded from their examination of the evidence that land use planning must be strengthened and improved, especially at the state level. In this connection, the possibility of adjustment of the property tax base from land and improvements to heavier taxation of land has received renewed attention not merely in terms of traditional justifications but also in relation to the presumed land use effects of such a policy change. Accordingly, it seemed appropriate for the Committee on Taxation, Resources and Economic Development (TRED) to consider the impact of the interrelationship of property taxation and land use patterns upon public policy, including but by no means limited to the potential untaxing of improvements.

This book contains the papers presented and the summarized discussion recorded at a conference entitled Property Taxation, Land Use, and Public Policy conducted by TRED, an association of academic economists concerned with natural resource taxation. The conference took place on the campus of the University of Wisconsin at Madison during the period October 19-21, 1973. Eleven papers and the summary discussion at the end of the conference are included in these proceedings, which are presented in four sections as follows: (1) The Property Tax, A Current Appraisal; (2) The Property Tax: Land Use Effects; (3) Property Taxation: Public Policy Alternatives; and (4) Summary Discussion. Brief introductions are provided at the beginning of each of the first three of these subdivisions.

Part 4 reports the conference discussion period and captures in substantial part the reflective consensus of the participants in the 1973 TRED conference. By design, the conference group was not limited to fiscal economists, in order that current views derived from both actual administrative practice and the political aspects of tax policy formation and implementation might be included. On balance, in my opinion, this has proved to be a constructive element in conference planning and execution.

The Twelfth Annual Conference presented in this eighth volume in the TRED series derives from the continuing program of the Committee on

Taxation, Resources and Economic Development. This result of the ongoing activity of this group is intended to provide one element of a basis for increased understanding of property taxation and its multiple effects upon our economy and polity. One hopes that this volume will have a useful, if necessarily modest, effect upon the development of rational and productive public policy in this area of perennial, yet nonetheless significant, fiscal concern and that it, like its predecessors, will be a one more forerunner in an extended exploration of these matters.

I greatly appreciate the effective assistance of my fellow members of TRED—the Committee on Taxation, Resources and Economic Development—in the design and implementation of the 1973 conference on Property Taxation, Land Use, and Public Policy which gives rise to the papers in this eighth volume of the TRED series on property tax concepts, problems, and potentials. This group of academic economists concerned with natural resource taxation has become a happy and productive fraternity during the gestation period of these several volumes.

I register my very real debt to the authors and discussants who made the conference sessions both pleasant and instructive. In particular, I am grateful to Weld Carter for his continuing assistance and tolerant forbearance, to Daniel M. Holland and Eli Schwartz for handling the Conference Hour and the summary of that discussion which results and, most fundamentally, to Barbara L. Barnhart for her editorial assistance and for preparation of the index. It should also be recorded that The Ohio State University has been helpful; that the tolerant forbearance and effective cooperation of my colleagues Edward H. Bowman and Clinton V. Oster are recognized and much appreciated; and that the good ladies of my family quite rightfully disclaim any and all responsibility for what follows, although their sustained good humor and creative patience have been not without substantial value in this undertaking.

On behalf of the TRED group, I express appreciation to the Robert Schalkenbach Foundation and to the John C. Lincoln Foundation for the support of both the 1973 conference and this publication.

ARTHUR D. LYNN, JR.

Columbus, Ohio
April 1974

I. A CURRENT APPRAISAL

Introduction

Part I, "A Current Appraisal," includes four chapters which as a group provide a current vista of contemporary property taxation. In the first chapter, "Property Taxation and the Political System," Glenn W. Fisher considers the stability characteristics of the tax from the point of view of political systems theory rather than from the somewhat more conventional approach of the fiscal economist and in so doing explains in considerable part the glacial rate of property tax change. Fisher explains in political terms what virtually every veteran tax administrator knows intuitively and what many economists have not inconsiderable difficulty in understanding, namely, when we know or think we know what needs to be done to improve the property tax, why it is so difficult to achieve the application of such knowledge in the real world of policy formation and application.

In the next chapter, George Break reappraises the current state of knowledge about property tax incidence and notes certain of the policy implications of his analysis. Given the existing diversity of incidence theory, Break cautions policy makers against undue acceptance of any particular incidence analysis and suggests that present uncertainties in this area may lead to policy selection based in considerable part on other grounds.

The third chapter by John Payne examines the legal framework of potential property tax reform in the post-*Rodriguez* era and evidences cautious optimism about constructive judicially induced potentials.

Finally, rounding out Part I, Kenneth Back, a veteran tax administrator, notes the current characteristics of property tax administration and the progress that has been made in this area. After considering the evidence, Back indicates positive optimism about future administrative quality possibilities and offers the well-grounded opinion that technically there are no insurmountable barriers to effective, even-handed property taxation.

Thus, the four chapters in Part I set the scene for subsequent consideration of the property tax and land use effects.

3

1 *Glenn W. Fisher*

Property Taxation and the Political System

There is a very large literature dealing with property taxation in America. In this literature, one can follow the development of the tax from its earliest beginnings, find careful analyses of the legal aspects of the tax, or read detailed descriptions of administrative procedures. Sophisticated statistical analyses of the quality of the assessment process and of the distribution of tax burdens can be found in current literature. One can also read carefully worked out analyses of many of the economic aspects of the tax or an excellent technical literature regarding methods of assessment.

Much of this literature has been written by practicing or academic economists or public adminstrators; much of it is critical. Some authors provide detailed instruction for improving administration, some propose major changes in the whole system, and some advocate curtailing or eliminating the tax.

It would be too harsh to say that this published criticism has had no effect, but honesty forces us to admit that changes in the property tax system have been slow and not always in the direction recommended by those who have made impartial studies of the tax. Probably many of us here have attempted to shock our readers or listeners into an understanding of the slowness of change in the property tax system by quoting one of the classic criticisms of the tax, which read almost as if they were written yesterday.

This paper does not repeat the criticisms nor add proposed reforms. Its purpose is to suggest that political systems analysis can explain why the property tax has changed so slowly in the face of criticism by experts and a high level of unpopularity among the general public.

In the following section of the paper, it is noted that property tax experts, although aware of the system concept, have failed to apply it to the political aspects of property taxation. The political systems concept, as developed by David Easton, is described briefly. The second section is an attempt to apply Eastonian type systems analysis to the property tax system. It is argued that the property tax system has developed a number of features which are well adapted to dealing with political stress. These features contribute greatly to political survival of the system. It is also maintained that survival is aided because the property tax system has developed in a symbiotic relationship with the fragmented local governmental system. In the final section it is suggested that the political system approach may well lead to a reappraisal of the tax or to a change in the tactics of those who want to change the system.

The Systems Concept

Political scientists have not reached the consensus regarding the boundaries or the methodology of their discipline which economists have achieved. Political science still awaits its Marshall and its Keynes, and there is no Samuelson among its elementary texts. Nevertheless, there are a number of approaches to the study of a political phenomenon which can provide valuable insights as to the nature of the phenomenon. Several of these might be useful to the student of the property tax, but this paper restricts itself to a discussion of the utility of a systems approach.

Public finance economists have long understood the complicated nature of the economic interactions which result from tax and expenditure decisions. Partial equilibrium analysis of tax incidence clearly indicates the extent to which a change in tax policy causes a multitude of subsidiary changes throughout the economic system. Even though this kind of analysis requires *ceteris paribus* assumptions which assume away many interesting and important economic consequences of tax policy, partial equilibrium analysis does make it abundantly clear that the economic consequences of the policy under consideration often include changes which are remote from the original, observable impact of the tax. For example, it can be shown that a commodity tax affects not only the producers and consumers of the commodity, but also, depending upon the pertinent cross-elasticities of demand, results in changes in the output and prices of complementary or competing commodities. This, in turn, affects the distribution of income to entrepreneurs and employees in industries which the casual observer might expect to be completely unaffected by the tax policy in question.

Macroeconomics emphasizes that tax and expenditure policy not only affects the prices of particular commodities and factors of production, but also such aggregates as the general level of employment, prices, and output. Recent years have also seen considerable progress in attempts to develop general equilibrium models which account for changes in economic aggregates and, at the same time, make possible a more complete analysis of changes in prices and quantities of particular commodities or factors.

In contrast to the widespread appreciation of the complexity of economic reality, there is little reflection in the literature of public finance of the complex political interactions which are involved in public finance decision-making. Comments about the political aspects of the property tax are usually confined to references to political obstacles to reform which seem to imply that the main problems result from the ignorance or selfishness of those who make political decisions.

In the past, those students of public finance who became interested enough in the political aspects of public finance to inquire more deeply found that they could get little help from political scientists. In the years during which economists were forging the tools for precise analysis of economic effects, political scientists were largely involved in normative pursuits. One major branch of the discipline devoted itself to the theory of government, while another busied itself with describing structures of government and proposing reforms in these structures. The former was highly philosophical, and the latter was based upon a rather incomplete understanding of man's social behavior.

The rise of the "behavioral" school of political science has changed the situation. In the last few years, political scientists have produced an impressive body of theory, fact, and speculation about the way political decisions are made. Controversy abounds and methodology differs, but there is a common desire to develop a positive science which is centered around the question of how people behave in the political context, that is, with how political decisions are made.

Out of this concern for scientific analysis of political decision-making has come a considerable amount of literature which can shed light upon the question of how political decisions about public finance are made and upon the political interactions which proceed and follow such decisions. It behooves the students of public finance to study this literature carefully.

This paper explores a part of this literature in an effort to suggest a framework for analysis which might contribute to an understanding of political-economic interactions in the property tax field. It draws heavily upon the work of David Easton, but his analysis has been modified and simplified in an effort to adapt it to the purpose at hand.[1]

Basically, Easton attempts to develop the framework for a theory of how political systems persist whether the world be one of stability or change. The analysis is built upon four general premises:[2]

1. it is useful to view political life as a system of behavior;
2. a political system is distinguishable from the environment in which it exists and is open to influence from it;
3. variations in the structures and processes (responses) within a system may usefully be interpreted as constructive or positive alternative efforts by members of a system to regulate or cope with stress flowing from environmental as well as internal sources; and
4. the capacity of a system to persist in the face of stress is a function of the presence and nature of the information and other influences that return to its actors and decision makers (feedback).

The first and second premises are, at least implicity, common to a great many studies of political behavior, but the third and fourth emphasize the fact that Easton's analysis is concerned not only with how decisions are made within a particular system at a particular moment of time, but also with the way the system adapts itself so that it can continue to exist in spite of changing circumstances in the environment and within the system itself.

Easton emphasizes that a political system is not a constellation of human beings isolated for study, but that it is a set of interactions which are distinguishable from other kinds of social interaction in that they are oriented toward the authoritive allocation of values (valued things) for a society. Interactions which fall outside the political system are considered to be part of the environment.

Exchanges or transactions at the boundaries between the political system and its environment constitute the inputs and outputs of the system. Inputs may be in the form of demands or support.

Demands are expressions of opinion that an authoritive allocation should or should not be made by those who have the responsibility for doing so. They may take the form of a request for a specific action such as the construction of a new school building in a specific location or the form of a vague request for "better government" or "better education." Support can be roughly characterized as willingness to accept the system even though particular demands are not met. It may be generalized as in a general declaration of patriotism and love of country or it may be directed toward particular political objects such as "freedom of the press" or "the right to elect my assessor."

The output of the political system may be called "policy." It is the way in which the system acts back upon its environment, but output changes the environment, and often this creates or changes the demands being made upon the political system. The chain of events described as demand-output-environmental change-demand is a feedback loop which is a distinctive feature of the analysis. This approach focuses concern, not just on the output of a political system, but also upon the way the political system transforms itself to meet changing conditions and thus to persist through time. Easton points out that the capacity of the system to endure is always under stress. By their very nature, political systems are called upon to deal with relationships among members of a system which involve the sharpest kind of antagonism. In words which will strike a responsive note among students of taxation, he points out that scarcity is probably the most significant phenomenon of every society and that when differences over the distribution of scarce values cannot be adjusted privately (by the market mechanism?), resort to some sort of political allocation is inevitable. That political systems rarely collapse under the stress to which they are subject would, Easton suggests, be something to gaze at in wonder if it were so commonplace. On the other hand, political systems rarely maintain themselves unchanged for long. Instead, they persist because they constantly transform themselves in response to stress.

The Application of Systems Analysis to the Property Tax System

As a tax economist turned political scientist, the writer can testify that exposure to political science in general, and to the systems concept in particular, has a tendency to reorient one's thought processes. It becomes clear that a political system or a subsystem is an evolving, adaptive mechanism that has somehow managed to exist in a rapidly changing environment. The allocative type of question which the economist phrases in terms of resource allocation and the political scientist phrases in terms of the authoritive allocation of values is joined by another type of question dealing with systems coping or persistence. The former deals with who gets what, and the latter deals with the survival of the system under which the "who gets what" decision is made.

In an attempt to shed some light on the persistence question, I propose to consider the property tax as a system closely related to the local government system.[3] It will be assumed, without proof, that the property tax system has been maintained with little change for a long period of time.[4] This implies that there have been no significant demands for changes in the system or that such demands have been offset by support for the system. The former is clearly contrary to the facts, and we are left with the conclusion that in spite of the well-publicized unpopularity of the property tax, it must enjoy a considerable amount of support from politically influential individuals or groups.

Dealing with Stress

It has often been pointed out that the property tax was well adapted to an earlier time but is not suited to modern conditions. That statement is a judgment on the allocative aspects of the property tax. From a maintenance viewpoint, the ability of the system to maintain itself would suggest that is is very well adapted to modern conditions. In this section, an attempt is made to identify some of the features of the property tax system which explain this maintenance.

It should be noted, first of all, that local taxation is potentially the source of a great deal of conflict. The decisions involve the distribution of income—not in an abstract or macroeconomic sense but in a very personal, individual way. The decisions are made by persons who are often, literally, the friends and neighbors of the persons affected by decision. Given the tendency of persons to avoid personal vilification and general unpopularity, it can therefore be expected that mechanisms which diffuse the pressure and depersonalize the conflict will develop. In fact, it is possible to identify several common features of the property tax which serve these functions.

1. Fragmentation of Authority.—One of the most obvious of these mechanisms is the fragmentation of authority. Responsibility for the levy of the tax which a given taxpayer pays is divided among several multi-member boards. Assessment is carried out by another official using manuals prepared by a consulting firm or a state supervisor and reviewed by one or more boards of review and equalization. Computation of the tax and the enforcement of tax limits is the responsibility of another official and collection of the tax rests in the hands of still another. If foreclosure proceedings are necessary, at least two other elected officials are involved.

Such a diffusion of authority is often condemned by those who prize efficiency and believe that responsibility should be clearly established. It is argued below that centralization of authority for the levy of property taxes would be imcompatible with the present system of local government. Beyond this, however, even the attempt to centralize "purely administrative" functions such as the determination of value or interpreting tax rate limits is doomed to almost certain failure. Legislative action is made difficult by the opposition of those who want to keep privileged positions and who have multiple points of access to the legislative process. These are joined by many who might actually gain by the change but who, in the face of uncertainty, opt for continuance of the status quo.

If the pressures against such legislation are somehow overbalanced by the demands for "reform," it is highly likely that, at some point in the process, agreement will be purchased by ambiguity or that authority will be clearly vested in an individual or agency with inadequate staff and inadequate operating funds. These forms of symbolic output serve the function of reducing stress but have little impact on the real output of the system. Even in the unlikely event that unambiguous legislation vests authority for assessment supervision or administration in a well-staffed, well-financed executive agency, it is unlikely that the authority will be exercised for long. A governor, dependent upon local political leaders for electoral support and for cooperation in many other matters, is unlikely to back the head of one of his minor agencies in a dispute with local leaders over a complicated and controversial matter of property assessment. Even the occasional appearance of a governor with a passion for "doing right" and with no further political ambitions would have no lasting effect. The punishment which he would absorb over the matter would make it certain that his successor would be more amenable to the public will.

2. *Fractional Assessment.*—Except for brief periods following a rapid decline in property values, almost every study of property tax assessments has discovered that property assessments are well below the statutory standard. Almost invariably property tax experts condemn this practice as a violation of the law and as a hinderance to equitable assessment; John Shannon, one of the few writers to discuss this phenomenon from a political behavior viewpoint, has pointed out that there are very strong political forces which make it virtually impossible to maintain assessment at 100 percent or any other statutory level of assessment.[5]

Assessment at less than the statutory level makes it much less likely that a taxpayer will believe himself unfairly treated. An attempt to move to a 100 percent level would greatly increase the demands upon the system as many taxpayers would begin to demand assessment reductions. Failure of the assessing authorities to fully and promptly respond to these demands would very likely result in a great reduction in specific support for the property tax system.[6]

3. *Assessment Inequities.*—Although it is probably true that fractional assessment reduces the possibility of equal or equitable assessment, it is at least mathematically possible to underassess all property at an equal percentage of market price so that the tax bills of all taxpayers would be in conformity with the theory of a uniform general property tax. Inequity in assessment, in contrast, is the *relative* under- or overassessment of certain classes of property, property owned by certain classes of persons, or specific parcels of property. The particular properties or taxpayers involved and the mechanism by which the inequalities come about vary

greatly from locality to locality and from time to time. Examples include underassessment of the poor widow because the assessor feels sorry for her and the underassessment of the wealthy corporation because the assessor is paid off in money or political support. Examples also include deliberate, open classification of property, as in Cook County, Illinois, and secret underassessment of industry, as in many growth-oriented localities. Relative underassessment may be inadvertent, as when vacant lots are underassessed because value is not changed from the date of platting, or deliberate, as when the assessor decides that vacant lots are unproductive and should not be required to pay a large tax.

One thing that all patterns of discriminatory assessments have in common is that they grow out of, and are maintained by, the operation of the political process and the political pressures of the locality in question. Some have been deliberate responses to an actual or threatened political disturbance and many have been successful in quieting that disturbance. The defacto classification system of Chicago, for example, was adopted in the depression years when the property tax system was under great stress. The favorable treatment of the homeowner which is a feature of the classification system has value to the political incumbents and considerable support from those concerned about the physical develop- ment of the city. The resulting general discrimination against the large industrial and commercial properties creates pressure for relief and the strongest of these pressures appear to have been dealt with on an individual basis—in a way that served the interests of the controlling political organization. The result was a system within which a great number of those voters most aware of the property tax and most likely to move to the suburbs—the single-family homeowner—paid a lower tax. Owners of these kinds of property least subject to suburban competition had the choice of paying higher taxes or seeking special relief. These latter groups grumbled about the system but never in the thirty-five year period ever mounted a full-scale effort to challenge the system by litigation, legislation, or the electoral process. The reasons for this are complex. They include such factors as the participants' appraisal of their chances of success, possible reprisals if they failed, and the nontax consequences of success.[7] The fact that the Chicago system has some features which some tax experts would commend and some which all would condemn is almost or totally irrelevant to the fact that the system survived. In other words, the role of feedback from tax experts or others who place major emphasis upon such factors as economic efficiency, equity, or similar goals was not large enough to have a significant impact upon decision making.

The Chicago case is one of the better-known and more complicated examples of assessment inequalities which contribute to political survival of the property tax, but examples exist in every state and locality. Unfortunately, the facts are often difficult to discover, and those cases which have been analyzed by researchers have usually been considered from an economic rather than a political perspective.

There is, of course, a relationship between the difficulty of discovering cases of inequality and the survival of the system. The increase in the number of sales-assessment ratio studies conducted by states and by the U.S. Census Bureau undoubtedly has contributed to improvements in the equality of assessments of single-family houses. Exposure of inequities in the assessment of this class of property is likely to create feedbacks which operate to push the system toward more equal assessment. It should be remembered, however, that both accurate assessment and satisfactory sales-assessment ratios are most likely for this class of property. In the case of more complex properties, there are very real technical and theoretical problems of determining values. Feedback into the politcal system in these cases is greatly influenced by the availability of expert legal assistance and by economic conditions, the public attitude toward economic growth or toward a particular taxpayer, partisan considerations, and historic patterns. It is far less likely that the net result of the feedback dealing with complex properties will create movement toward equal assessment. Movement will be toward changes which are consistent with system maintenance, but it will be only by chance that greater equality results.

The history of iron mine taxation in Minnesota might provide an excellent case study.[8] When the high quality Mesaba ore had a strong advantage over all competitive sources of supply, the perplexing problem of how to tax such a resource was solved in a way which placed much of the local tax burden on the out-of-state mining companies. With the exhaustion of this ore, political forces quickly operated to bring about a change favorable to the taconite processing industry. The current concern for the physical environment has brought about another change in the environments which surround the political system, so that it is safe to predict that there are strong feedbacks favoring heavier taxes on the industry.

4. Fractional Rates.—The property tax is one of the few taxes for which rates are figured to three or four decimal points and for which rates normally change every year. This avoids concentrating the attention of opponents to rate increases. In contrast, most other tax rates normally are set at one-half or full percentage point intervals. In the case of low rate taxes such as a sales tax, this means that proposed rate increases come infrequently but often amount to a 20 or 25 percent increase. This attracts the attention of all opponents, who are often able to defeat the change.

Linkages with the Local Governmental System

The property tax system survives, in part, because mechanisms for dealing with stress, in a setting which is potentially very stressful, are highly developed. Another reason for its survival is that it exists in a symbiotic relationship with another system which has also shown a high degree of resistance to change—the local governmental system. In this section it will be argued that the maintenance of the existing property tax system is a necessary condition for the maintenance of the existing system of local government in the United States, and that demands for major changes in the property tax system are apt to generate support for maintenance of the existing system from those who are friends of the local governmental system.

The local governmental system is a series of interactions among officials and residents of some 78,000 local governments which vary tremendously in such characteristics as geographic area, population, and range of governmental functions performed. The geographic boundaries of these units overlay and overlie each other in such a way that it is common for any given geographic point to be within the jurisdiction of several governments. Members of the system have motives for defending it that range from the tax advantages of industrial enclaves to highly emotional attachments based on personal and family history.[9]

Property Tax as a Source of Revenue.—Probably the strongest linkage between the property tax system and the local governmental system results from the fact that the property tax is the major source of revenue for local government. This has come about because the property tax has evolved into a tax which is particularly well suited for financing a fragmented local government system. Replacement by any other revenue source would require a fundamental change in the system.

The stress-reducing features of the property tax have already been discussed. These are important in explaining the suitability of the property tax as a method of financing local government, but, in addition, jurisdictional and administrative features of the tax make it especially well suited to financing a fragmented system of local government. The base of the present-day property tax consists largely of property that has a fixed location and is highly visible. This eliminates serious jurisdictional disputes and makes the tax suitable for administration by small administrative units.[10] This fact makes the tax ideally suited to raising revenue for a system in which any geographic point is within the jurisdiction of several units of government. Every parcel of property has a physical location, units of government have geographic boundaries, and it is simple for the county clerk to add the rates imposed by the several units of government to determine the total tax rate in each "tax code area." Add to this the *in rem* character or real estate taxation and you have a method of raising revenue which is clearly well adapted to a difficult situation.

No other revenue source currently on the horizon could possibly finance the existing system of local government. The problems which would arise if such an attempt were made can be illustrated by briefly examining the most commonly suggested alternatives, local sales or income taxes, and grants from larger governments.

Both the sales and income taxes have proved themselves capable of producing revenue for local units of government, but together they produce only a small fraction of the revenue produced by the property tax. The most successful such taxes are administered by the state and confined to one or two nonoverlapping types of local governments in a given locality. The problem of jurisdiction, compliance, and tax competition which would result if a state like Illinois with 6,385 units of local government were to force those units to finance themselves with locally levied and locally administered sales or income taxes are so obvious that it is not necessary to detail them. A shift to local levy and state administration would solve a few of these problems and temporarily hide some others, but it is difficult to believe that it would be a viable system.

Another possible alternative to property tax finance would be to finance local governments by means of grants from larger tax collecting units of government, such as the state or, perhaps, a specially created regional government within the state. Usually it is assumed that the collecting government would obtain its funds from an income or sales tax and distribute the funds on the basis of a general formula.

Any proposal to finance local governments entirely (or largely) by grants faces two very great obstacles to political survival. One of these involves the distribution formula and the other involves the problem of maintaining the independence of the lower level government.

If local governments fully supported by grants are to be free to determine expenditure policy, it is necessary that revenue be distributed by means of a general formula which is independent of the past or future expenditure decisions of the government in question. An attempt to devise and implement such a formula faces two difficulties. The first of these is technical and the second is inherent in the political system of the superior level of government.

The technical problem is that it is not possible to devise a formula which would fairly distribute the funds necessary to completely support all existing units of government. Conditions and assignment of governmental functions vary so greatly, even within a single state, and data on tax needs and resources are so scarce for small units of government that it is unlikely that even disinterested technicians would be able to agree on a formula.

This problem can be illustrated by reference to the newly enacted federal, general revenue-sharing formulas. Even though these formulas distribute funds only to general, not special, units of government, there are a number of problems which have been given only scant attention. The formulas depend heavily upon income data—but it is well known that income data for small areas is unreliable. Furthermore, when such data is used for allocative rather than research purposes, there is an incentive to manipulate the data. Litigation and legislation dealing with the details of the allocation formulas and the statistics on which it is based will multiply. It should also be noted that general revenue sharing is distributed by formulas which utilize data concerning existing tax collections. If grants were to be used as the sole source of finance, these data would of course be unavailable.

Closely related to the technical problems with allocation formulas are the more narrowly political ones. The American political system contains many "veto points," and it is thus necessary that a great many groups and interests be satisfied to prevent their use of a "veto."[11] In the case of grant formulas, this is apt to mean that no significant number of local units of government and no functional area of expenditure can appear to be worse off than under existing arrangements. This almost invariably means that minimums must be guaranteed by some kind of implicit or explicit "grandfather clause." This, in turn, increases the amount of revenue that must be raised and provides very powerful ammunition for those who oppose the change. This process is clearly illustrated in the legislative history of federal revenue sharing.

The second major reason for arguing that grants cannot replace locally raised revenue is that they would erode the independence of local governments and change the local governmental system. This statement may strike some as "the same old bug-a-boo" which "reactionaries" have always raised to federal or state aid, but a careful analysis of how the political process works provides strong support for the statement that any unit of government which receives substantially all of its revenue from another unit is not likely long to remain independent. Raising tax revenue is a politically unpopular act which costs the responsible individual or unit support. This loss can be offset by politically skillful expenditure of the funds raised and by careful manipulation of political symbols. This may include expenditure for broadly popular programs and the creation of special benefits for powerful opposition groups. This must be accompanied by carefully worked out public relations programs to assign credit to the politician or governmental unit which needs the support. It is highly unlikely that a system which places the responsibility for the politically unpopular act of taxing upon one unit of government and gives other units of government complete control over expenditure could long endure. Inevitably, those charged with the responsibility for taxation will attempt to buy off opposition to tax increases by placing requirements or restrictions on the use of funds.[12]

Other Linkages.—The dependence of local units of government upon the property tax as a source of revenue may alone be sufficient to explain the mutual interdependence of the property tax and local governmental systems, but there are also other linkages, such as tax and debt limits, borrowing procedures, accounting procedures, and budget procedures.

Most local governmental units are subject to state imposed debt limits. In most cases these limits are stated in terms of assessed value or otherwise tied to property taxation. As a result, any proposal to reduce the property tax base reduces the borrowing power of local governments, so that local governments can be adversely affected even if the revenue is replaced. A similar result may stem from the fact that local government borrowing procedures are closely tied to the property tax base. Commonly, property tax levies provide security for local government bonds even though it is contemplated that they will actually be repaid from other sources. Bond attorneys and bond underwriters are frequently reluctant to approve general revenue bond issues without such security.

The budgeting and accounting procedures of most local governments are firmly rooted in the property tax system. The fund system of accounting, the earmarking and allocation of funds for particular purposes, and such things as the budget calendar are often based upon or closely coordinated with property tax procedures.

It must be stressed that none of the linkages between the property tax system and the local governmental system, except the revenue linkage, are likely to be strong enough to serve as absolute barriers to change. They are elements in a system of interaction which tend to prevent change. This can be illustrated by assuming that a blue ribbon commission recommends that certain kinds of property be eliminated from the local tax base and that revenue be replaced by the state according to a stated formula. Opposition to this proposal would arise from a number of sources. The governing board of local governments would fear, rightly or wrongly, that the formula would provide insufficient replacement revenue—now or in the future. If the proposed formula is complicated or requires data not readily available, the possibility that such a belief will be held is increased. Individuals with a financial or professional interest in the bond business would quickly point out that it would reduce the borrowing power of the local government—or at least result in higher interest rates on bonds. Those conversant with budgeting and accounting procedures would probably discover that some problems would be created or that other changes would be required. It might well be, for example, that state requires that expenditure for certain purposes be made only from certain property tax funds or that state grants are subject to some general restriction which is contrary to the purposes of the property tax funds being replaced. It is not unlikely that changes in several different state statutes might be required to correct this.

All of this is the setting for a complicated series of interactions that the proposal will set off. Those supporting and those opposing the change will include those occupying various positions of influence in the political structure—legislature, judiciary, local government councils, state executive department, political parties—and each will take action to obtain his ends. Local governing bodies will demand changes in the formula to protect their interest, organizations such as the state organization of accountants or municipal finance officers will establish a task force to study the implications of the proposal and to demand any needed changes in it. The financial community will do likewise with regard to the aspects of the proposal that might affect borrowing procedures, and those groups who expect to be hardest hit by replacement taxes may well organize to oppose the change or suggest a different replacement.

It is impossible to identify all the members of the system who will be involved in the interactions, but such interactions often involve a very large group that widens as the original proposal begets additional proposals and as the normal process of political bargaining results in the involvement of issues and actors which were remote from the original proposal. The net result, however, is likely to be that the proposal is killed or modified to the point that it is properly classified as symbolic output rather than real output.[13]

Implications of Systems Analysis

Most of the literature of property taxation has focused upon the allocative aspects of the tax. Most proposals for changes have stemmed from dissatisfaction with the results of the allocative process.

It may be that the methodology of the research has tended to obscure important realities. The process of social planning or public policy advice-giving requires that a goal be given (or chosen) and that logic be applied to available facts in order to determine the best way of reaching the goal. As a result, tax economists and other researchers have tended to concentrate upon the results or the administrative details of the property tax system rather than upon the broad maintenance-related aspects of the system. They often proceed as if the results of the research would be handed to a government tax manager who shares the stated or assumed goal and who has absolute (or at least considerable) power to impose his will with regard to tax policy. Frustration results when those to whom the recommendations are made ignore the advice or move timidly to make small changes which are often erroded away in a few years. Clearly, these same economists are aware that a single businessman cannot change the economic system. They would not advise him to try and would not be surprised at the failure of an occasional ideologically motivated attempt to do so.

It is probable that systems analysis can help those who study the property tax to understand that the property tax is a political system which involves interactions among many actors with different motives and with limited power over the system. In addition, such an approach results in emphasis upon the fact that the system has survived because it has adapted itself to a rather hostile environment.

There appears to be no evidence, however, that the system which survives will produce outputs which are optimum from the viewpoint of those interested in equity or economic efficiency. In short, political science has not produced a theoretical equivalent of the competitive economic system, which is always tending to an optimum allocation of resources.

The failure of political science to develop an equivalent concept is probably not due to any intellectual inferiority but rather to the wider range of human motivations and behavior which the political scientist must allow in his models. The actors in a political system have a wide range of rapidly changing goals of which the thrill of participation itself may be one of the most important.

The principal value of the systems approach is that it provides a systematic way of thinking about the many linkages and feedbacks which may occur and which may be remote from the effects which would normally be analyzed by tax economists. It has not developed to the point at which it can be said to be an operational model, and it is not possible to quantify the linkages or to state with precision just what the effects of a particular input will be upon system survival.

Nevertheless, it would not surprise a system analyst to discover that the *de facto* classification system of Cook County, Illinois, was constitutionally legalized in 1970 because such legalization was important to the Democratic organization whose support was necessary if a new constitution was to be approved. Nor would he be surprised to learn that under these circumstances neither the revenue committee of the constitutional convention nor the body of convention delegates wasted any time analyzing the equity and the economic effects of classification.

Political systems analyses in general and this discussion in particular are not directed specifically toward tax reform, but both have implications for the reformer. Awareness of the many linkages in the political system might well lead reformers to propose different tactics. John Shannon's recommendations with regard to assessment reform are examples.[14] In effect, he argues that the political obstacles to full value assessment should be recognized and that rather than adopt a coercive approach to force compliance, an attempt be made to change the information feedback loop so that new demands will be fed into the system. It is not possible to be sure that this approach will work. The new demands may induce counter-demands or threats to reduce support so that change will not occur. But, at least, it does represent an effort to take political system characteristics into account, and it avoids repeating the often unsuccessful recommendation to "enforce the law."

One can cite many other possibilities for change in tactics which might result from wider understanding of the nature of political systems. For example, it might be feasible to package proposals for reform of the local government system and of the property tax in a single package. It may well be, for example, that the obstacles to reorganization or elimination of certain types of local governments, such as school districts, are less strong than are the obstacles to proposals which threatens the financial support of several kinds of local government.

Another possible result of the increased awareness of the political systems aspects of the property tax is that it might lead to a broader appraisal of the property tax. The predominance of economists and administrators among those who have written about taxation has led to a tendency to appraise the property tax primarily upon rather narrow economic and administrative grounds. A political system approach might well lead us to take into consideration the merits and demerits of a tax system which permits the survival of fragmented local government systems and of the stress-reducing features of the tax.

Notes

1   David Easton, *A Framework for Political Analysis* (New York: Prentice-Hall, 1965), *Political Systems* (New York: Knopf, 1953), *A Systems Analysis of Political Life* (New York: John Wiley, 1965), and "An Approach to the Analysis of Political Systems," *World Politics,* 9 (1957), pp. 383-400. Much of Easton's work is abstract and, for the uninitiated, difficult reading. However, the first of the three volumes listed above provides a brief statement of the major elements of his analysis. For a brief summary and a general appraisal of the systems approach, see Oran R. Young, *Systems of Political Science* (Englewood Cliffs: Prentice-Hall, 1968).

2   Easton, *A Framework for Political Analysis,* Ch. 2.

3 Easton suggests that we need not be overly concerned with whether or not a given set of interactions constitutes a "system." He points out that there is nothing to prevent us from stating that everything in the world is related to everything else, thereby combining all social life into one grand system, but that such an approach would add little to our understanding of political behavior. What commands our attention, instead, is the need to decide what set of activities is an interesting one in the sense that it is relevant and helps us understand some theoretical problems (Easton, *A Framework for Political Analysis,* pp. 30-31).

The boundaries which we establish for a system will depend upon what we wish to examine in detail. What is left outside as part of the environment will be factors that we accept as givens (*ibid.,* pp. 65-66).

It is important to understand that a political system is composed of interactions, not persons or outputs. Later references to "mechanisms" or "features" such as fractional assessment or assessment inequalities should be understood to mean the interactions which create and permit the continuation of these results rather than the results as such.

4 In Easton's terminology *maintenance* is weighted with the notion of salvaging the existing pattern of relationships and directs attention to their preservation. *Persistence* signalizes the importance of considering, not any structure or pattern, but rather the life processes of the system themselves. In this sense, a system may persist even though everything else associated with it changes continuously and radically (*A Framework for Political Analysis,* p. 84).

In light of our assumption that the property tax system has changed little, it appears appropriate to speak of systems maintenance rather than persistence.

5 John Shannon, "Conflict between State Assessment Law and Local Assessment Practice," Richard W. Lindholm, ed., *Property Taxation: U.S.A.* (Madison: The University of Wisconsin Press, 1969), pp. 39-63.

6 The difference in the way a political scientist and an economist analyzes the effects of a fractional assessment system really turns upon the relevant assumption regarding taxpayer knowledge and rationality. The tax economists, well versed in the complexities of the tax, are apt to point out that taxpayers in general have nothing to gain by a fractional system and that with a proper educational effort the electorate could be sold on the advantages of a full-value system. The political scientist, aware of the many issues upon which political decisions must be made and of evidence which shows the relatively small impact that policy issues have upon electoral or legislative decisions, is not apt to put much faith in such an effort.

7 During the long incumbency of the present mayor, his organization has enjoyed a considerable amount of support from those with business and real estate interests in the Loop area. Tax relief obtained by bringing down the organization would have been considered by many to be a mixed blessing.

8 Clarence W. Nelson, "Broader Lessons from the History of Lake Superior Iron Ore Taxation," Richard W. Lindholm, ed., *Property Taxation: U.S.A.*

(Madison: University of Wisconsin Press, 1969); Warren Aldrich Roberts, *State Taxation of Metallic Deposits* (Cambridge: Harvard University Press, 1944), pp. 323-75.

9   Logically, the relevance of the argument that the symbiotic relationship between local government and the property tax system contributes to the maintenance of the property tax system would have to be established by analyzing the maintenance of the local governmental system. This is beyond the scope of this paper, but it can be noted that the historical record indicates that the local government system has been maintained for long periods with little change.

10 One of the major evolutionary changes in the property tax has been the *de facto* or *de jure* elimination of personal property, especially the more mobile, easily hidden kinds, from the tax base.

11 There is a large political science literature related to political pluralism. A recent, very readable exposition is Theodore Lowi, *The End of Liberalism* (New York: W. W. Norton and Co., 1969).

12 The official concerned would phrase this in terms of the moral responsibility of those who tax to insure taxpayers that the funds are used wisely. Whichever way it is phrased, the systems maintenance consequences are the same.

13 Murray Edelman's concept of politics as symbolic action, like the concept of political systems, may have much to add to our understanding of how public finance decisions are made. Murray Edelman, *The Symbolic Uses of Politics* (Urbana: University of Illinois Press, 1964), and *Politics as Symbolic Action* (Chicago: Markham Publishing Company, 1971).

14 Shannon, "Conflict," pp. 54-61.

George F. Break

Property Taxation: A Reappraisal of Burden, Incidence, and Equity and Their Policy Implications

During the past twenty years a new comprehensive, general-equilibrium framework for the theoretical analysis of tax shifting and incidence has been gradually developing. One of the early results of this development has been a considerable conceptual clarification that has provided the basis for a better understanding of the distinctive features of different government fiscal policies and of exactly where, in that very broad picture, the incidence of taxation fits. Still more important, though also more questionable, have been some new and different conclusions concerning the probable burden distributions of some of our most important taxes. Particularly prominent among these is the general property tax. Since that levy is currently in the midst of a major, and frequently agonizing, reappraisal of its proper role in the whole U.S. tax structure, it is important that these newly emerging, or in some cases reemerging, conclusions about property tax incidence be widely discussed before it is too late. This chapter will attempt to set the stage for that discussion.

Some Basic Elements of Modern Tax Incidence Theory

This is not the place to attempt a comprehensive treatment of all of the basic elements of modern tax incidence theory.[1] Those that are particularly relevant to the determination of property tax incidence, however, need to be reviewed briefly. They are seven in number.

1. The Sources and Uses of Funds Distinction.—It is now widely agreed that incidence means the effects of a given policy instrument on the distribution of private real incomes, and that these effects are the sum of those operating on the two sides of any household's budget. One is the sources-of-income side, for which wage, profit and interest rates, and land prices are the important parameters, and the other is the uses-of-income side, for which it is relative consumer product prices and rates of return on saving that matter. One of the most interesting aspects of this distinction is the frequency with which tax incidence on only one side of the budget is considered to be important.[2] Thus the analysis of a general sales tax tends to deal only with the uses side, while that of the corporate profits tax has favored the sources side. Whether the one side or the other dominates in the case of the general property tax is at the heart of the present controversy over its incidence.

2. Exclusion of Macro Policy Effects.—One of the hallmarks of modern incidence analysis is the proposition that incidence is a function only of relative, and not of absolute, price changes.[3] A sharp distinction, in other words, is drawn between the use of macro policy instruments, including taxation, to alter the level, throughout the economy, of aggregate private incomes, and the use of tax policy to alter the distribution of a *given* level of total private income. It is the latter that is the essence of incidence, and the effects of such redistributive tax policies on the absolute level of prices is regarded as both indeterminate and irrelevant (because they depend on separate, and independent, macro policies).

3. Differential Tax Incidence Context.—Given this strict delineation of the incidence concept, a comparative approach to the identification of tax burdens follows more or less automatically. Specific incidence analysis, which deals with one tax in isolation from any other fiscal actions, is unsatisfactory because it fails to separate macro policy from tax policy effects[4]; and a balanced budget model, in which the effects of equal changes in taxes and in government output are analyzed, is unsatisfactory because it fails to separate expenditure policy from tax policy effects. The differential incidence model, which compares the distributional effects of two equal-yield taxes, has two variants. In the first, the tax of particular interest, say *A*, is compared to a limited number of others, *B*, *C*, or *D*, for which it may be substituted, and in the second, tax *A* is compared with a hypothetical, distribution-neutral tax *Z*. Only the latter approach, of course, yields a unique burden-distribution pattern that may be spoken of as *the* incidence of tax *A*.[5]

4. First-Order and Second-Order Effects.—Implicit both in the construction of the theoretical models and in their application to actual tax policies is a basic distinction between those tax effects that are so important that they must be included in the analysis and those tax effects that may be disregarded with impunity. One such distinction that is important in the analysis of property tax incidence is the proposition that the incidence on the uses side of a general but nonuniform tax on capital (or on labor) is of only second-order importance.[6]

5. *Interactions with Nontax Policy Instruments.*—A bothersome difficulty with incidence analysis is that whenever one policy instrument is changed in order to move the economy closer to one particular social goal—for example, when tax policy is used to change the distribution of private real income—a number of other policy instruments will also have to be changed in order to keep the attainment of all other social goals at their original levels.[7] Strictly speaking, then, one should deal only with the incidence of alternative packages of policy instrument changes. Most tax incidence analysts, however, clearly prefer to place any accompanying changes in nontax policy instruments in the second-order category and thus to attribute all of the distributional effects of the package to the tax change alone.[8]

6. *Market Structure Assumptions.*—Not very surprising, given the failure of economic theory to deal very effectively with oligopolistic markets, is the standard assumption in formal incidence models that markets are either perfectly competitive or pure monopolies. Much of the controversy over the incidence of the corporate profits and general property taxes concerns the effects of tax changes in markets where prices are administered and profits are not necessarily maximized.

7. *Factor Supply Assumptions.*—Another important standard assumption of formal incidence models is that the aggregate supply of both labor and capital is fixed. This means that property tax incidence is dealt with in a world in which saving and investment are completely insensitive to any tax-induced changes in rates of return. Whether such substitution effects are of first-order or second-order importance, unfortunately, remains an unsettled empirical issue involving not only the amount by which aggregate saving and investment would eventually be changed by a given change in rates of return but also the speed with which the adjustment would occur. Most dynamic tax incidence models, for example, produce very slow speeds of adjustment and thereby strengthen the case of those who place rate-of-return substitution effects in the second-order category.[9] While for some tax comparisons only substitution effects matter, for others the possibility that disposable income would be redistributed among high and low savers must be taken into account. Here, too, there is

disagreement between permanent-income theorists and others as to the quantitative importance of these income effects.

Property Tax Incidence in the Extended Harberger Model

One's first impression of the Harberger incidence model, presented to the world in 1962 in an application to the corporate income tax,[10] is that it is too simple, and makes too many questionable assumptions, to be taken seriously as a basis for evaluating the distributional effects of tax policy in the real world. After all, it is only a two-factor, two-sector static equilibrium model with a very stylized view of even that simple kind of economy. The more one considers the available alternatives, however, the more one is likely to come back to the Harberger model as much the best starting point for incidence analysis.[11] Indeed, particularly as extended in both scope and application by McLure and Mieszkowski,[12] the Harberger model may yet turn out to be a brilliant exercise in the separation of first-order tax incidence effects from others of only incidental significance.

The extended Harberger incidence model, then, is well worth serious attention, especially in the present context because it has some rather radical suggestions to make about property tax incidence. The two taxes in the formal model that are relevant are a tax on one factor in all of its uses, the burdens of which are shown not to be shiftable regardless of the mobility of either factor, and a tax on one factor in one of its uses, which has predictable effects on product, but not on factor, prices.[13] The former hypothetical tax is relevant to the extent that local property taxes impose a uniform burden on all tangible capital assets in the country, and the latter hypothetical tax is relevant to the differentials that exist around that uniform tax either because different kinds of property are treated differently in most parts of the country or because different localities impose different tax rates on all kinds of taxable property. That the first part is an important, and perhaps the dominant, component of the general property tax is indicated by the nationwide scope of the tax and by the fact that its behavior represents a response to national economic developments as well as to purely local ones. This means, as Mieszkowski in particular has emphasized, that the incidence analyst should begin by considering the effects of a uniform nationwide property tax and then proceed from that base to deal with what he has called the excise tax effects of tax rate differentials around the average, nationwide property tax rate.[14]

The distributional effects of a uniform, nationwide tax on all tangible property are readily summarized. The rate of return to all receivers of capital income would be lowered by the tax, and in a closed economy no significant shifting of those burdens would occur unless the aggregate supply of capital were sufficiently sensitive to its lower rate of reward. This possibility aside, the tax burden would be on capital income generally, and its vertical distribution pattern, relative to total income, would be unequivocally progressive. Under such a tax landowners, both current and future, would simply bear their proportionate share of the total tax burden. This contrasts sharply with the long-accepted doctrine that a tax on land, even though part of a general property levy, is fully capitalized and hence borne only by those owning land when the tax is imposed.

The distributional effects of a nonuniform, nationwide tax on tangible property, though more complicated, are also well established. Resources would be shifted from high- to low-tax sectors, and product prices in the former would rise relative to those in the latter. Effects on wage and profit rates, however, would depend on the elasticities of substitution between labor and capital in production in the various sectors and on the extent to which high-taxed sectors were either capital or labor intensive relative to low-taxed sectors. All of these effects on the sources side of the incidence picture are systematically dealt with in the extended Harberger model, but their exact specification requires empirical estimation of the key determining parameters. On the uses side it is important to note the precise nature of the consumer burdens produced by a nonuniform property tax. Unlike the general consumer burdens of a retail sales tax, the present ones are not necessarily regressive in relation to income. Given the no-macro-effects context of incidence analysis, a more or less balanced pattern of price increases and price reductions should occur, with little or no change in the general consumer price level. The question then concerns the probable distribution of these specific price changes by family income level. Vertical incidence would be progressive on the uses side if consumption of high-taxed products were concentrated in the upper income groups and consumption of low-taxed products in the lower income groups; vertical incidence would be regressive in the opposite case and neutral if there were no systematically income-related product price changes.

The distributional effects of a uniform property tax levied at different rates in different parts of the country are the most difficult of all to analyze.[15] Among the new elements are potentially high sensitivities of both labor supplies and consumer shopping habits to intercommunity tax rate differentials, as well as the different taxpayer reactions induced by a high tax differential that finances valuable public service differentials and by one that does not. The result is a plethora of incidence patterns, all depending on specific local circumstances which are difficult to establish empirically.[16] Even so, two general propositions of first-order importance do stand out. Both apply to those property tax differentials that are unmatched by correspondingly great public service differentials.[17] The first is that the high interregional mobility of capital will bring about a complete shifting of property tax differentials, quickly in rapidly growing areas and less quickly in stagnant or declining areas, but sooner or later everywhere. In equilibrium, in other words, high-tax areas will have to pay relatively high before-tax prices to capital owners, low-tax areas will do the reverse, and net-of-tax rates of return to capital will be equalized everywhere for ventures of comparable risk. The second proposition is that the high mobility of workers, households, and shoppers within any given metropolitan area creates a strong presumption that intra-urban property tax differentials will be borne mainly by landowners and will be capitalized in the traditional fashion.[18]

These, then, are the most important aspects of the extended Harberger model that are relevant to the determination of property tax incidence in the real world. Three tentative, but important, propositions are thereby put forward for serious consideration by both fiscal experts and public policy makers. The first is that a significant, and quite possibly a major, portion of the total property tax burden in this country rests on recipients of capital income generally in the form of lower rates of return than they would otherwise receive. The second is that among recipients of different kinds of capital income landowners will bear an especially heavy burden. In addition to their share of the average, nationwide property tax burden on capital income, landowners are also seen as bearing a major portion of above-average tax rate differentials existing within large metropolitan areas. The third is that the consumer burdens of property taxation are much less important than they have traditionally been considered to be. In the extended Harberger model consumer burdens are not a function of the average nationwide tax rate but only of the above-average tax rate differentials that exist in particular industries or in particular parts of the country. Moreover, some of these high tax differentials may be borne by workers or landowners, and even those that remain on consumers must be compared with the consumer benefits created by below-average tax rate differentials before any general conclusions may be drawn concerning property tax incidence on the uses of income side.

There is no need to stress the sharp contrast between these three propositions and more conventional views of property tax incidence. Basically, the latter assign to landowners that portion of the tax that is assessed on land and to consumers all, or most, of the remainder. Since these opposing positions are not likely to be reconciled in the near future and since each has some strong a priori arguments to support it,[19] the best that the policy maker can do is to avoid relying entirely on either one of the two opposing theories and to be fully aware of the different policy implications of each. These are discussed in the next section.

The Policy Significance of Alternative Views of
Property Tax Incidence

For those who appreciate balance in a tax system the incidence question is a troublesome one indeed. The three widely recognized bases for ability-to-pay taxation are income, wealth and consumption, but it is extremely difficult to say exactly in what proportions these three are presently used in this country. At the state and local level the property tax still ranks first as a source of tax revenue, and as we have seen, professional opinion is widely divided as to whether it burdens mainly consumers or mainly wealth owners. Opinion is similarly divided over the incidence of the corporate profits and federal payroll taxes for social security. To indicate the quantitative significance of these differences of opinion, table 2.1 shows three out of the many possible allocations of U. S. taxes among the three possible bases, both for the state-local sector alone and for the entire U.S. tax system. The first allocation (a) resolves all of the incidence uncertainties in favor of burdens on capitalists, the second (b) resolves them in favor of burdens on consumers, and the third (c) has little to recommend it other than an even-handed resolution of the uncertainties in question. Clearly, there are substantial differences among the three allocations, and one's view of the equity of the U.S. tax system is likely to be much influenced by which of the three is viewed as coming closest to the true

TABLE 2.1
Alternative Percentage Allocations of U.S. Taxes, 1972

Allo-cation	State-Local Taxes Only[1]			Federal, State, and Local Taxes[1]		
	Income	Wealth	Consumption	Income	Wealth	Consumption
(a)	22	43	31	55	27	17
(b)	22	3	72	46	3	50
(c)	22	22	52	51	15	33

Source: *Survey of Current Business* (July 1973), pp. 30-31.

[1]Percentages do not add to 100 because of the omission of the unclassified category, which was 3.5 percent of state-local taxes but only 1 percent of total U.S. taxes.

Allocation (a) *Income:* personal income and social security taxes; *Wealth:* property, corporate profits, motor vehicle license, and death and gift taxes; *Consumption:* sales and excise taxes.

(b) *Income:* (a) minus one-half of federal social security contributions; *Wealth:* one-half of motor vehicle licenses; death and gift taxes; *Consumption:* sales and excise, property, corporate profits; one-half of federal social security contributions and of motor vehicle license taxes.

(c) *Income:* (a) minus one-quarter of federal social security contributions; *Wealth:* one-half of property, corporate profits; three-quarters of motor vehicle license taxes; death and gift taxes; *Consumption:* sales and excise; one-half of property, corporate profits; one-quarter of federal social security contributions and of motor vehicle license taxes.

picture of U.S. tax burdens. A not unimportant element in that big picture is the tax that is the subject of this paper.

Vertical Equity

The vertical distribution, by household income class, of property tax burdens depends critically upon whether the incidence of the tax falls mainly on consumers or mainly on capitalists. Table 2.2, derived from the Brookings Institution's MERGE income and tax file of 30,000 randomly selected family units, shows some of the quantitative dimensions of that distinction. At one extreme, given in the second column of the table, is a burden distribution that allocates the land portion of the tax to landowners and all the rest to consumers.[20] As will be noted, it shows the expected, uniformly regressive distribution up and down the income scale. At the other extreme, shown in the first column of the table, would be a tax whose burdens were entirely on capital income. Here the pattern is a little more complicated. Below a family income of $5,000 a year and between $20,000 and $25,000 the average tax burden is 2.6 percent of

TABLE 2.2
Effective Property Tax Rates under Alternative Incidence Assumptions, by Family Income Classes, 1966
(income classes in thousands of dollars; tax rates in percentages)

Adjusted[1] family income class	Effective property tax rate,[2] assuming the incidence to be	
	on property income in general	with land portion on landowners, remainder on consumers
0-3	2.5	6.5
3-5	2.7	4.8
5-10	2.0	3.6
10-15	1.7	3.2
15-20	2.0	3.2
20-25	2.6	3.1
25-30	3.7	3.1
30-50	4.5	3.0
50-100	6.2	2.8
100-500	8.2	2.4
500-1,000	9.6	1.7
1,000 and over	10.1	0.8

Source: Joseph A. Pechman and Benjamin A. Okner, *Who Bears the Tax Burden?* (Brookings Institution, 1974), p. 59. Computed from the MERGE file fo 30,000 family units.
[1]Adjusted family income is a broadly defined concept that includes accrued capital gains, interest on state-local bonds, and government transfer payments.
[2]Tax as a percent of income.

income, whereas between \$5,000 and \$20,000 it is only about 1.9 percent. For all practical purposes this is the only part of the burden distribution that matters, since the great majority of families are located there. Speaking very roughly, we may say that the burden distribution is regressive between the bottom quintile of income receivers and most other families, that it is roughly proportional over the middle three quintiles (though the use of much smaller income classes would clearly be desirable over this heavily populated income range), and that it becomes progressive in the top quintile and continues that way to the top of the income distribution.

Even a property tax borne entirely by capitalists, then, would have some regressive features in the lower ranges of the income scale. On the other hand, it will also be noted that the effective burden rates of the capitalist property tax are below those of the consumer property tax for all income classes below \$25,000. If capitalist burdens are the rule rather than the exception, in other words, the great majority of families would clearly find the present property tax less burdensome than any alternative equal-yield tax based mainly on consumption. Moreover, for home owner-occupants, who constitute the single most important property tax paying group, there are a number of well-established ways of eliminating the excessive tax burdens of the lowest income families, the most efficient of which is the Advisory Commission on Intergovernmental Relations' (ACIR) so-called "circuit-breaker" approach.[21] In mid-1973 ACIR reported that every state had adopted some form of property tax relief for elderly homeowners, that twenty-one of them were using the circuit-breaker plan, and that four of these plans applied to homeowners of all ages.[22]

Whenever property tax relief is proposed for home owners, a lively political issue ensues regarding the extent to which relief should also be authorized for renters. In mid-1973, for example, seventeen states had renter relief programs and thirty-three did not.[23] Here again the incidence issue is of critical importance. If property tax burdens fall mainly on landlords rather than on tenants, there is no economic case for renter credits; if property tax burdens fall mainly on tenants, there is no economic case for tax relief to home owners only. On this issue, fiscal economists are presently in the unpleasant position of either having to provide highly frustrating policy advice (if they reveal the full extent of existing incidence uncertainties) or of risking the giving of wrong advice (if they opt for one position or the other).

An even livelier local public finance issue concerns the vertical equity of the whole housing part of the general property tax. While the incidence question is obviously relevant to the rental housing segment and needs no further comment here, it also appears to matter for owner-occupants as well. If property tax incidence is primarily on the uses side, owner-occupant burdens should be distributed according to gross imputed rental expenditures, and from the empirical evidence now available, which unfortunately leaves a good deal to be desired, it appears that in this case the burdens would either be regressive or roughly proportional to household abilities to pay taxes.[24] With property tax incidence primarily on the sources side, however, owner-occupant burdens should be distributed either in relation to home market values or to imputed rental income gross of property tax liabilities, and in the former case there is empirical evidence that housing values, on the average, are progressively related to gross rentals.[25] Moreover, as long as the property tax is viewed as a general levy on capital income, there would seem to be no need to break out the housing portion and to consider it separately, since the vertical equity of the tax is determined by the distribution of its total capital income burdens.[26]

Horizontal Equity

One of the more worrisome aspects of a tax whose burdens are largely shifted elsewhere by legal taxpayers is whether or not the resulting pattern makes any sense among users of different consumer products or among providers of different kinds of factor services. If property tax burdens are mainly shifted to consumers, for example, would it not improve horizontal tax equity to replace it with a general consumption tax of either the retail-sales or value-added variety? Greater control could then be exercised over the interproduct allocation of tax burdens, and these gains could be obtained at little or no loss in vertical equity, since the vertical distribution of tax burdens would be very little affected by the tax substitution. On the other hand, if property tax burdens mostly remain on capitalists and if the goal sought is a uniform tax on all tangible capital assets, the main sources of horizontal inequities will be property exemptions[27] and uneven assessment practices.

A horizontal inequity that has received considerable attention from property tax critics is the above-average burden placed on housing, compared to other sectors of the economy. Rosenberg's detailed estimates for 1953-59, for example, showed that whereas for the nation as a whole property taxes were 14.2 percent of capital income, on nonfarm residential dwellings the average rate was 26.7 percent.[28] The discriminatory burdens of one tax, however, need not create horizontal inequities requiring policy action, since other taxes in the system may impose discriminatory burdens of an offsetting kind. The appropriate analysis of such potential offsets again depends upon views about property tax incidence. In the consumer burden case the relevant comparison is with sales and excise taxes and with whatever portion of corporate profits and employer payroll taxes is assumed to be shifted to consumers, since none of these taxes reach housing services to nearly the extent that they do other consumer goods. While to my knowledge no comprehensive study of this sort has been made, an interesting recent comparison by George Peterson and Arthur Solomon showed that apparent gross sales tax rates of 17 percent on housing and 6.4 percent on other commodities were reduced to net tax rates of 7.1 percent and 5.1 percent respectively when deductibility provisions under the federal individual income tax were taken into account.[29]

In the opposite case of capitalist property tax burdens, one important offset is the corporate profits tax to the extent that it imposes its burdens on capital income. When it is brought into the picture, Rosenberg's estimates show an average tax rate of 37.3 percent on all capital income, but one of only 27.9 percent on housing income.[30] A second important offset is provided both by the failure of the federal individual income tax to include the net imputed rental income of home owner-occupants in its base and by its allowance of property taxes and mortgage interest payments as itemizable personal deductions. Henry Aaron's estimates for 1966, for example, show that property tax and mortgage interest deductions saved homeowners $2.9 billion in that year, and that inclusion of imputed rentals would have added another $4.0 billion to their tax burdens.[31] Far from being a victim of excessive tax burdens, housing in this second case must be viewed as the recipient of very substantial tax subsidies.

Economic Effects

The differential economic effects of a property tax that burdens mainly consumers, compared to one that mainly burdens capitalists, appear to have received considerably less attention in the literature than differential equity considerations. Brief mention will be made here of only two potentially important differences.

The first concerns the supposed level of land prices under the two incidence theories. As already noted, in the consumer burden case property taxes on land are presumed to be fully capitalized, whereas in the capitalist burden case it is only interregional tax rate differentials, and particularly those existing within metropolitan areas, that are likely to be capitalized. It would appear, then, that land prices would be lower under a consumer burden property tax, other things equal, than they would be under a capitalist burden tax. These differences, in turn, can be expected to affect the behavior of both investors and housing consumers.

The second difference concerns the measurement of local government fiscal capacities, the design of intergovernmental grants, and the economic efficiency of local choices of government service levels. All of these important policy issues rest to some extent on the distinctive contribution, if any, that business property makes to local government tax raising capabilities. If burdens are on business owners and if most of these owners live outside of the taxing jurisdiction, it seems clear that business property has a special fiscal effect that approximates the receipt of an unrestricted matching grant from another governmental unit. This would be particularly true for school districts (where the addition of business property would add to fiscal resources without adding to school costs, and the substitution of business for residential property would both increase opportunities for tax burden exporting and reduce school populations). But it would also be true for other local government units to the extent that the cost of their services to business fell short of the property taxes collected from business.[32]

If business property tax burdens are mainly shifted to local residents in the form of higher consumer prices, however, the picture would be rather different. In this case, unlike the former, of two communities with the same per pupil residential property assessments, the one with a significant amount of business property as well would not have a higher taxpaying capacity. The relative treatment of the two communities in the design of equalizing intergovernmental grants, in other words, should depend on property tax incidence considerations, though this issue is seldom raised explicitly. Finally, the behavior of local residents, in their choice of levels of local public services, is likely to depend significantly on whether they perceive business tax burdens as falling mainly on others or as being shifted back onto themselves in the form of higher prices. Casual observation suggests the former to be the more plausible hypothesis, but it would be interesting to see some empirical testing of the two possibilities.

Conclusions

Property tax incidence, it would appear, is much too important a subject to be left entirely to the arcane deliberations of the experts. By ignoring the whole issue, or by giving unquestioning allegiance to one school of incidence thought or the other, policy makers risk the making of choices that will later turn out to have been very ill-advised. Facing up to existing uncertainties may not be a pleasant task, but it does seem a necessary ingredient for good fiscal decision-making at all levels of government. It would, for example, tip the scales in favor of policies that would be desirable regardless of what the incidence pattern of the general property tax turns out to be. One such policy would be the adoption of a federal negative income tax that varied benefit levels in line both with changes in national living costs over time and with differences in those costs in different parts of the country at any given time. Such an income-support program would improve the economic status of the lowest income groups regardless of the extent to which property tax burdens, or indeed any other tax burdens, are shifted to consumers.

Notes

1 See Peter Mieszkowski, "Tax Incidence Theory: The Effects of Taxes on the Distribution of Income," *Journal of Economic Literature,* 7 (December 1969), 1103-24. See also Charles E. McLure, Jr., "General Equilibrium Incidence Analysis: The Harberger Model After Ten Years," *Journal of Public Economics,* 4 (May 1975), 125-61; George F. Break, "The Incidence and Economic Effects of Taxation," in Alan S. Blinder et al., *The Economics of Public Finance* (The Brookings Institution, 1974), pp. 122-79; and Joseph A. Pechman and Benjamin A. Okner, *Who Bears the Tax Burden?* (The Brookings Institution, 1974), ch. 3.

2 On this point see John A. Brittain, *The Payroll Tax for Social Security* (The Brookings Institution, 1972), 52-53.

3 See, especially, Charles E. McLure, Jr., "Tax Incidence, Macroeconomic Policy, and Absolute Prices," *Quarterly Journal of Economics,* 84 (May 1970), 254-67, which develops a point made much earlier by Richard A. Musgrave "On Incidence," *Journal of Political Economy,* 61 (August 1953), 307.

4 The main exponent of the specific incidence approach has been Earl R. Rolph. See his *The Theory of Fiscal Economics* (University of California Press, 1954), chs. 6 and 7.

5 The classic treatment of these three alternative incidence concepts is by Richard A. Musgrave in *The Theory of Public Finance* (McGraw-Hill Book Company, 1959), 211-17.

6 One of the outstanding uses of these two distinctions to arrive at a definite conclusion concerning tax incidence is by John A. Brittain in *The Payroll Tax for Social Security,* ch. 2.

7 Carl S. Shoup, *Public Finance* (Aldine Publishing Company, 1969), 12-15.

8 See, for example, John Bossons, "The Economic and Redistributive Effects of a Value-Added Tax," in the *Proceedings of the Sixty-Fourth (1971) Annual Conference on Taxation* (National Tax Association, 1972), 254-65.

9 See the following four papers by Marian Krzyzaniak: "Effects of Profits Taxes: Deduced from Neoclassical Growth Models," in Krzyzaniak, ed., *Effects of Corporation Income Tax* (Wayne State University Press, 1966); "The Long-Run Burden of a General Tax on Profits in a Neoclassical World," *Public Finance* (1967:4), 472-91; "The Burden of a Differential Tax on Profits in a Neoclassical World," *Public Finance* (1968:4), 447-73; and "The Differential Incidence of Taxes on Profits and on Factor Incomes," *Finanzarchiv* (1972), 464-88. See also Martin Feldstein, "Tax Incidence in a Growing Economy with Variable Factor Supply," Harvard University, Institute of Economic Research, Discussion Paper No. 263 (December 1972), and

Kazuo Sato, "Taxation and Neo-Classical Growth," *Public Finance,* 22 (1967), 346-70.

10 Arnold C. Harberger, "The Incidence of the Corporation Income Tax," *Journal of Political Economy,* 70 (June 1962), 215-40.

11 An alternative, but very similar, model is that presented in Melvyn B. Krauss and Harry G. Johnson, "The Theory of Tax Incidence: A Diagrammatic Analysis," *Economica,* 39 (November 1972), 357-82.

12 See especially Charles E. McLure, Jr., "The Theory of Tax Incidence with Imperfect Factor Mobility," *Finanzarchiv* (1971), pp. 27-48, and Peter M. Mieszkowski, "On the Theory of Tax Incidence," *Journal of Political Economy,* 75 (June 1967), 250-62.

13 See McLure, "The Theory of Tax Incidence with Imperfect Factor Mobility," pp. 37-41.

14 Peter Mieszkowski, "The Property Tax: An Excise Tax or a Profits Tax?" *Journal of Public Economics,* 1 (April 1972), 73-96.

15 The relevant tax in the Harberger model is again a tax on one factor in one of its uses, the use in this case being in one particular region of the country. For detailed analyses of this sort see Charles E. McLure, Jr., "The Inter-Regional Incidence of General Regional Taxes," *Public Finance,* 24 (1969), 457-83, and "Taxation, Substitution, and Industrial Location," *Journal of Political Economy,* 78 (January/February 1970), 112-32.

16 These are discussed in more detail in Break, "The Incidence and Economic Effects of Taxation," pp. 154-68.

17 This distinction goes back at least to Alfred Marshall. See his analysis of the incidence of local rates, which are classified either as "beneficial" or "onerous," in appendix G of *Principles of Economics,* 8th ed. (Macmillan, 1930), 794-804.

18 For empirical evidence supporting this capitalization hypothesis see Wallace E. Oates, "The Effects of Property Taxes and Local Public Spending on Property Values: An Empirical Study of Tax Capitalization and the Tiebout Hypothesis," *Journal of Political Economy,* 77 (November/December 1969), 957-71, reprinted in Oates, *Fiscal Federalism* (Harcourt Brace Jovanovich, 1972); R. Stafford Smith, "Property Tax Capitalization in San Francisco," *National Tax Journal,* 23 (June 1970), 177-93; and John H. Wicks, Robert A. Little, and Ralph A. Beck, "A Note on Capitalization of Property Tax Changes," *National Tax Journal,* 21 (September 1968), 263-65.

19 Traditional theories of property tax incidence need no separate treatment here. For a thorough analysis see Dick Netzer, *Economics of the Property Tax* (The Brookings Institution, 1966), ch. 3.

20 The landowner portion of the tax burden distribution shown in the second column of table 2.2 must be interpreted with some care. Since the presumption is that in the consumer burden case of property tax incidence, land taxes will be fully capitalized, current landowners can be said to bear the tax only in the sense that they would be the gainers if it were removed today. The amounts in the second column of the table, accordingly, may be said to show the annual value of these potential capital gains from elimination of the tax.

21 See, for example, Advisory Commission on Intergovernmental Relations, *Financing Schools and Property Tax Relief—A State Responsibility,* Report A-40 (January 1973), ch. 5.

22 Advisory Commission on Intergovernmental Relations, *Information Bulletin No. 73-6* (July 13, 1973).

23 Ibid.

24 While the great majority of the empirical distributions of housing tax burdens show the property tax to be steeply regressive—see, for example, ACIR, *Financing Schools and Property Tax Relief,* pp. 36-37—there are several reasons for not regarding these findings as definitive. One is the typical omission from the income base of the very income on which the property tax is levied—namely, the imputed rental return to owner-occupants. Another is the use of current, rather than permanent or lifetime, income, a difficulty that is discussed in Netzer, *Economics of the Property Tax,* pp. 62-66. A third weakness is the failure to include either mobile homes, which are typically undertaxed compared to single-family dwellings and which are owned as principal residences mainly by the lower income groups, or second homes, which are more frequent at higher than at lower income levels. The effect of all these inadequacies is to bias existing empirical distributions of housing tax burdens in the regressive direction.

25 George E. Peterson and Arthur P. Solomon, "Property Taxes and Populist Reform," *The Public Interest,* no. 30 (Winter 1973), p. 73.

26 Further criticism of traditional views about property tax regressivity may be found in M. Mason Gaffney, "The Property Tax is a Progressive Tax," *Proceedings of the Sixty-Fourth (1971) Annual Conference on Taxation* (National Tax Association, 1972), pp. 408-26.

27 See, for example, Arthur P. Becker, "The Erosion of the Ad Valorem Real Estate Tax Base," *Tax Policy,* vol. 40 (National Tax Association—Tax Institute of America, 1973).

28 This was the second highest property tax rate in the forty-seven industry groups shown, being exceeded only by hotels and other lodging places, which showed a rate of 31.1 percent. See Leonard G. Rosenberg, "Taxation of Income from Capital, by Industrial Group," in Arnold C. Harberger and Martin J. Bailey, eds., *The Taxation of Income from Capital* (The Brookings Institution, 1969), pp. 174-77.

29 Peterson and Solomon, "Property Taxes," pp. 70-71.

30 Rosenberg, "Taxation of Income."

31 Henry J. Aaron, *Shelter and Subsidies: Who Benefits from Federal Housing Policies?* (The Brookings Institution, 1972), p. 55.

32 In his report to the Metropolitan Council of the Twin Cities Area, Julius Margolis, for example, assumed that 60 percent of business property taxes were needed to finance community services to business enterprises. See University of Pennslyvania, Fels Center of Government, *Metropolitan Fiscal Disparities: Problems and Policies* (1971), ch. 4.

Responses to *Rodriguez:*
More Reform or Less?

In San Antonio Independent School District v. Rodriguez,[1] a closely divided Supreme Court seemingly ended one of the briefest reform movements in American legal history, the effort to compel revision of public education finance through the courts. I propose to examine if any further reform litigation is possible, either by working on the loopholes in Justice Powell's *Rodriguez* opinion or by developing a broader attack on the whole system of local public finance.

A Summary of the Rodriquez Opinion

Rodriguez was brought in behalf of Texas children residing in school districts having a small property tax base and consequently low per pupil expenditures for education. These plaintiffs contended, on the basis of ambivalent earlier case law (and ignoring other arguments not essential here) that they were classified on the basis of wealth, that wealth-based classifications are inherently "suspect," and that the Texas finance system could prevail only if a "compelling state interest" in maintaining the discriminatory classification could be shown. The defendants successfully

A substantially longer version of this chapter, written for lawyers and with more detailed citation of legal authority, is available from the author.

countered that no "suspect classification" was involved, and that the state's scheme had a rational basis in that it fostered local control.

Justice Powell carefully identifies and tests out possibilities that the Texas school finance system discriminates against, first, those who fall below some absolute measure of poverty, second, those persons relatively poorer than others, without reference to any absolute measure, or third, all persons, rich or poor, who live in tax-poor districts.

Surveying the earlier case law, he discerns only a narrow test of suspectness, limited to persons who

because of their impecunity . . . were *completely unable to pay* for some desired benefit, and as a consequence, . . . sustained as *absolute deprivation* of a meaningful opportunity to enjoy that benefit [italics added].[2]

Since the plaintiffs in Rodriguez had neglected to introduce evidence linking low-taxing and low-spending districts to an incidence of absolute poverty, this should have ended the case right there, if the earlier cases were to be followed, since neither relative wealth or district wealth discriminations would fit those cases as Justice Powell reads them. Significantly, however, Justice Powell does not stop at this point, and by inference at least, he expands the potential scope of constitutionally suspect wealth-based classifications.

As to the theory that all, rich or poor, who live in tax-poor districts were being discriminated against, Justice Powell concluded that the class of plaintiffs thus described is too "large, diverse and amorphous," and as such,

is not saddled with such disabilities, or subjected to such a history of purposeful unequal treatment, *or relegated to such a postion of political powerlessness* as to command extraordinary protection from the majoritarian political process [italics added].[3]

There is some ambivalence here. While purporting to reject the district wealth theory in general terms his choice of language suggests that district wealth characteristics might, in some unspecified circumstances, not be so "large, diverse and amorphous" as to be nonactionable. The key is in Justice Powell's "political powerlessness" idea, to which I shall return.

As to the relative wealth theory also, Justice Powell seems to move beyond the earlier case law. While not explicitly accepting the proposition that it is unconstitutional to discriminate against those who are relatively less wealthy, he does not reject the idea, and he holds against the plaintiffs on this aspect of the case only because of failure of proof. The nub of plaintiff's evidence was a statistical study that plaintiff thought demonstrated a direct correlation between relative wealth and school expenditure but which, upon the court's reanalysis, mentioned further below, failed to hold up.

The ambivalence of Justice Powell's opinion can also be seen in his treatment of the second aspect of the suspect classification test: that (no matter how the classification be described) the effect of the discrimination be an absolute deprivation of the benefit claimed. It was of course true that the plaintiff's children did attend school. Defendants contended that all children got at least an "adequate" education, and the court noted that "[n]o proof was offered at trial persuasively discrediting the state's assertion."[4] Again, instead of relying flatly on the doctrine of absolute deprivation, the court emphasizes failure of proof, and thereby implies that absolute deprivation may be linked to the much more unmanageable, but productive, issue of educational quality.

Apart from the unsettled and disputed question whether the quality of education may be determined by the amount of money expended for it, a sufficient answer to [plaintiff's] argument is that at least where wealth is involved the Equal Protection Clause does not require *absolute* equality or *precisely* equal advantages [italics added].[5]

But plaintiffs need not demand "precisely equal advantages" and might be very happy to win on a theory of absolute deprivation of an "adequate" education. That Justice Powell seems to accept this very significant proposition is indicated by a further passage:

Whatever merit appellees' argument might have if a State's financing system occasioned an absolute denial of educational opportunities to any of its children, the argument provides no basis for finding an interference with fundamental rights where only relative differences in spending levels are involved *and where—as is true in the present case*—no charge fairly could be made that the system fails to provide each child with an opportunity *to acquire the basic minimal skills* necessary for the enjoyment of the rights of speech and of full participation in the political process [italics added].[6]

The court seems to be uncertain about what to do with the question of educational quality, implying at very least that some undefined degree of gross inequality should not go uncorrected. Especially when compared to Justice Stewart's brief concurring opinion, which goes out of its way to close the loopholes in the majority opinion (but which, of course, does not represent the majority's point of view), Justice Powell has to be seen as at least a little bit open to the possibility that a stronger case for public finance equality might convince the court.

I cannot in good conscience, however, describe him as anything more than "a little bit" open. At base, what bothers Justice Powell is what has bothered all of the judges who have decided school cases, even those who have decided in favor of reform—a judicial fear that unrestrainable consequences could be released by any constitutional foray into the finance equality realm. Inability to enforce a decree, "manageability" of judicial standards, the likelihood of creating "chaos," concern about ordering the legislature to increase appropriations, concern about the political reluctance to redress the situation, concern about whether money really is the answer to the nation's educational problems, concern about stifling innovation in constitutionally frozen doctrine, are the recurring phrases. These concerns are legitimate, and meeting them ought to be the task for those who favor reform. It is in this context that I suggest responses to Rodriguez.

Responses to Rodriguez: The Educational Context

In the foregoing analysis, I have identified what seem to me to be two significant loopholes for future litigation: better facts and emphasis on educational quality standards. In this section I will explore in general terms the size of these loopholes plus one other, not heretofore mentioned, which centers on state-created tax ceilings. For the moment, I wish to hold all three points within the educational context, reserving for the final section consideration of a broader approach to finance problems.

The "Fact" Loophole

Although the factual problem in *Rodriguez* cropped up in several contexts, at base it involved the question of whether poor people (either absolutely poor or relatively so) live in "poor" districts, that is, those with an inadequate tax base and commensurately low school spending.

The first problem is to define "absolute poverty." Lacking persuasive data from plaintiffs, the court relied heavily on a study of Connecticut school districts which concluded, "the popular belief that the 'poor' live in 'poor' districts is clearly mistaken."[7] The study was based on the Census Bureau's definition of poverty, keyed to a basic (or "economy") food plan suited to "emergency or temporary use where funds are low."[8] Justice Powell, on the other hand, speaks of "persons whose incomes fall below some identifiable level of poverty or who might be characterized as functionally indigent,"[9] a condition Powell implies to be a step back from "absolute" indigency. By leaving an ambiguity as to this critical premise, the Court's reliance on the Connecticut study seems faulty, and relitigation seems inevitable.

What is needed is data that persuasively identifies a level of "functional indigency" in the context of education. One approach might be to establish a minimum personal income needed to support a realistic tax burden; another might be to borrow the federal Title I approach, correlating low family income with unacceptably low test scores. (Achievement testing, in this sense, would not be used to measure educational "quality," which is an unresolved academic issue, but rather to identify a poverty level that is "absolute" in Justice Powell's "functional" terms.) Once a measure of functional indigency is established, the relationship between "absolute" poverty and school spending could then be reexamined.

There is also data available which suggests that a better case can be made for the relationship between relative poverty and low school spending. The difficulty with plaintiff's data in *Rodriguez* was that a statistical inversion appeared through the broad middle-range of school districts sampled. In these districts, school spending actually dropped as personal income rose, leaving a direct relationship between wealth and school spending only in the very richest and the very poorest districts. However, a study of North Carolina school finance, summarized in table 3.1, suggests the much smoother correlation that the court seemed to be looking for. While these data are pre-*Rodriguez,* they suggest either that the Texas data cannot be generalized, or that a careful restudy in Texas might make a better case for the plaintiffs. (It is also worth noting that

TABLE 3.1
Variation in Per Capita Personal Income and Comparison with Selected Variables, 142 School Units, Fiscal Year 1970-71

Per Capita personal income	Number of units	Mean appraised property value/ADA	Mean local current expenditures per ADA	Mean state current expenditures per ADA
Less than $1,500	6	$18,924	$ 53.97	$451.65
$1,550-$1,749	21	21,809	73.45	491.27
1,750- 1,949	16	22,875	73.24	484.76
1,950- 2,149	22	26,020	92.17	465.20
2,150- 2,349	20	25,634	92.19	446.37
2,350- 2,549	17	33,817	98.66	443.19
2,550- 2,749	21	33,320	128.89	448.56
2,750 and above	19	41,520	165.09	443.06
All Units	142	$29,036[1]	$101.62	$459.97

Source: Campbell et al., Report on North Carolina School Finance Institute of Government, University of North Carolina (1972), tables I-26, I-27.

[1]Based on 130 units.

North Carolina, which is unique among the states in providing state funding for upwards of 80 percent of the current expense budget, is able to accomplish a significant, albeit imperfect, leveling in the expenditure discrepancies between rich and poor districts.)

There is one additional factor in the wealth-classification fact loophole that is of significance. Justice Powell professes no surprise that the poor cluster in wealthy districts—poor people, he assumes, live in grimy but tax-rich industrial cities. But nowhere does he deal with the considerable body of urban fiscal crisis material, which concludes that our cities full of poor people are in a desperate condition of public poverty.[10] Before letting the finance cases fall into the gap between the Connecticut analysis and that of urbanologists, district wealth should be recast to include a measure of what is generally called "municipal overburden" to see if the gap can be closed. It is myopic to consider the relationship between personal and district wealth without considering the competing demands for tax dollars and uniquely heavier demands present in large urban centers. Indeed, it may be that one reason the North Carolina data show the personal-district wealth nexus more clearly, even omiting an explicit overburden factor, is that in North Carolina the degree of urbanization is somewhat more constant statewide than in many states, thus minimizing the usual skewing effects of the omission.

In correlating individual and district wealth, it would seem to make legal sense to reduce the gross wealth base of a jurisdiction, by the amount actually used for noneducation purposes and then to state the net base available to education in per-pupil terms. For instance, if a large city in fact can allocate only 50 percent of its budget to education, it might be argued that only half of its wealth base is an "educational wealth base," whereas a surburban jurisdiction that can spend 75 to 80 percent of its tax receipts on education has a larger proportion of its taxable wealth "available."

Viewed broadly, the overburden concept suggests a shift in litigational focus from school children as such to the whole community, or at least to the whole body of taxpayers. This shift would minimize the technical difficulties of the overburden calculation (as well as the difficulties of the money-quality nexus in education) and make the gist of the wealth discrimination complaint the much simpler one of direct correlation between personal income and per capita district wealth. Both are objective figures (assuming equalized assessment) and as such can provide an objective measure of the capacity (though not the willingness) of a jurisdiction to provide for itself. Although this shifts the substantive focus of the finance cases sharply, I will nevertheless argue in the final section that it is the more appropriate way in which to judge the adequacy of a state's compliance with equal protection mandates.

The "Quality of Education" Loophole

As I have noted, Justice Powell makes much of Texas' assertion that its aid program insures an "adequate" education for each of its pupils irrespective of district wealth. One would have thought that Justice Powell would have rigorously excluded any consideration of educational quality, in view of the very real problems of defining and measuring it. Indeed, he cites this conflicting literature and makes the argument in general terms but this only underscores the significance of the loopholes he then leaves open. There is pragmatic wisdom in the Justice's concern that some level of disparity remain actionable, but if his intention was to limit the loophole to the grossest situations, it seems to me that he has uncapped a considerable, and perhaps uncontrollable, genie. Even the grossly aberrant case requires that a standard of minimum quality be identified, and once a technique for doing so is accepted, there will be inevitable pressure (and why not?) to apply the same technique more broadly.

Nor does it seem to me that a reasonably objective measure of adequacy is as much beyond our grasp as the court would intimate. One judicially tenable way of giving meaning to Justice Powell's loophole would be to use actual expenditure data to indicate quality. The virtue of using actual expenditure data—the ultimate expression of a complex and interrelated bundle of political and educational value judgments—as a measure of quality statewide is, of course, in their relative objectivity. Broadly speaking, per-pupil expenditures could be arranged along a continuum from high to low. Using available statistical techniques, an appropriate point could then be selected that would indicate a presumptive tipping point between adequacy and inadequacy, which could be rebutted by evidence showing that either a higher or lower figure was more appropriate.

Such evidence would necessarily include factual proof on specific financial components of quality, but since such proof would be relevant only in relationship to the objectively derived starting point, the factfinding would be kept within manageable bounds. What would probably happen (and I would think it quite desirable) would be for proof to be offered on specific locational variables such as pupil transportation or heating costs, items which are susceptible of proof, or on the issue of teacher salaries. This latter item is somewhat less objective, but it is such an overwhelming component of any school budget that the return on the effort of fact-finding would be handsome.

I will concede that this approach raises all the difficulties of the cost-quality relationship in education that have bedeviled the school finance suits. I further realize that Justice Powell himself indicates considerable doubt of its validity. Suffice it to say here that Justice Powess's calculated ambiguity underscores the inevitability of dealing with the problem.

In approaching a definition of adequate quality, I have been purposefully vague about the specific statistical calculation necessary to define the adequate/inadequate break point. As a policy-maker, I would prefer that it be at some point in excess of median expenditure, but the court might find it difficult to justify its selection of any particular arbitrary high point. Certainly, the concept of equal protection would seem to speak to either mean or median as a financially and legislatively manageable minimum level of adequacy.

As this median idea is explored, it is ironic that what begins in Justice Powell's analysis as an equal protection problem begins to look more and more like due process. Use of something like median is attractive in either case, however. By tying the fate of the least to that of the majority, political self-interest begins to assure that both even-handedness and minimum fairness are satisfied—and without, it should be emphasized, any substantive intervention by a court.

Finally, let me reiterate my caveat that this entire approach depends on the uncertain nexus between cost and quality. As I have said, the problem is of Justice Powell's own making, serving to illustrate the doctrinal bind that a cautious but thoughtful jurist can get himself into. I think the solution proposed here, while not free of difficulty, would be workable and responsive to Justice Powell's dilemma yet within the tolerable limits of judicial activism. However, its difficulties may be the best argument in favor of my running counter-theme that the whole basis of the school finance litigation ought to be shifted to focus on municipal finance and municipal tax-payers generally. As I will try to argue in the final section, this kind of focus eliminates by definition the nexus problems that plague us here.

The Tax-Ceiling Loophole

Justice White argued in his dissent to Rodriguez that it was an affirmative denial of equal protection for Texas to impose a tax ceiling of $1.50 per $100 on local school levies. In poor districts, he argued, this ceiling is reached more rapidly than in a richer district where the same tax rate is applied to a broader base of wealth. Justice Powell could avoid the issue, since plaintiff's school district was not in any event taxing at the ceiling rate, but he noted other caselaw[11] which suggests that this argument has some validity. Further on, he also has this to say:

It is equally inevitable that some localities are going to be blessed with more taxable assets than others. Nor is local wealth a static quantity. Changes in the level of taxable wealth within any district may result from any number of events, some of which local residents can and do influence. For instance, commercial and industrial enterprises may be encouraged to locate within a district by various actions—public and private.[12]

Taken together, these passing comments suggest two potentially powerful lines of argument. If "municipal free enterprise" must be relied upon to correct tax base inequities, as the above quotation suggests, then it should follow that, first, the state must not even indirectly put roadblocks in the way of some jurisdictions by imposing tax ceilings, and second, it cannot ignore de facto roadblocks which have the same effect.

The de facto argument is the harder one, especially since hypothetical figures presented by Justice Marshall in dissent, which demonstrated the astronomical tax rates that representative poor districts would have to levy to equal the expenditure levels of wealthy districts, were ignored by the majority. Suppose, however, that Justice Marshall's figures were present reality, as is virtually the case in my home city, Newark. The concreteness of Newark's situation might give the majority more pause than Justice Marshall's abstractions.

In Newark, the nominal tax rate levied in 1972 was $9.63 per $100. (It dropped to $9.39 in 1973 because of a massive, one-time revenue sharing input, but is expected to rise again.) Even after equalization, the rate was $7.54. Furthermore, it has been estimated that three parcels of taxable property are abandoned every other day in Newark, and the city's overall taxable property wealth has declined by almost 10 percent ($310.2 million) over the last ten years.[13]

The Newark figures suggest the extreme case of an almost confiscatory tax rate amounting to a de facto tax ceiling. The figures also give the lie, again at least in an extreme case, to Justice Powell's implicit defense of the *Rodriguez* holding on the grounds that every jurisdiction, in classic free enterprise terms, can go out and get itself a tax base if it is willing to work at it. Too many years of the urban crisis, and too many millions of dollars of redevelopment money (much of it, ironically, spent to create tax-exempt properties) speak to the contrary.

Justice Powell's free-enterprise defense also suggests a second possibility, as yet mostly hypothetical but almost certain to become a major significance in the near future. An attack along a broad front has already begun on the problem of exclusionary suburban zoning ordinances which severely restrict the availability of low and moderate income housing. Courts in some states have acted to restrict particularly egregious zoning practices,[14] and attacks on a much broader scale are now in litigation.[15] Inevitably, these judicial pressures will force a political response, which will almost certainly involve creation of regional planning and zoning bodies with effective power to locate high- and low-wealth ratables in such a way as to indirectly deprive individual communities of the "free enterprise" rights Justice Powell intimates. In short, what may very well happen is that the state will impose an effective tax ceiling by withdrawing the opportunity to search for the new ratables that Justice Powell seems to have made a part of the tax ceiling concept.

If regional planning does eventuate, of course, the legislature may provide for tax sharing or compensatory state aid mechanisms without judicial compulsion. The political pressures to do so are obvious, and New Jersey already has an example of this in its Hackensack Meadowlands regional development law,[16] which has tax-sharing provisions. Where such enlightenment is not forthcoming, the *Rodriguez* opinion offers a basis for reaching a similar result under judicial mandate, and the Meadowlands experience offers both a model and some assurance that a judicially imposed plan could be workable.

Conclusion

I must approach my own arguments here with some diffidence. While each is tenable, in frankness it must be said that the spirit of Justice Powell's opinion, as well as considerable chunks of explicit language, narrow the likelihood of successful challenge considerably.

I suppose it might be argued that all of the loopholes should be tried any way, since there is nothing to lose. But there is a momentum to constitutional litigation that often overwhelms its technical fine points, and in this sense *Rodriguez* has already dealt the reform movement a body blow. Before another loss is risked—it might be the coup de grace—it would be well to stand off and consider whether a different approach to the underlying problem, calling on different lines of authority and doctrinal analysis, might not be preferable. It is to this ironic possibility of having greater success with more, rather than less, reform, that I now turn.

Responses to Rodriguez: The Broader Context

For a number of reasons, future litigation should focus on inequality in providing the broad range of locally financed goods and services, rather than education alone, and should emphasize the constitutional injustice done taxpayers rather than school children. This broader approach would be sufficiently different from *Rodriguez* to command the Court's reexamination. Taxpayers are a more ascertainable class than school children, and there is comfortable precedent for dealing with them in equal protection terms. Many of the problems of proof discussed above would be simplified, and the nagging question about measuring educational quality would disappear. But most important, this broader litigation would directly confront the beast lurking in the dark shadows of every *Rodriguez*-type opinion, apprehension that the logic of a school finance rule will have to be extended without limit to other areas of local finance. If education, why not public health? If public health, why not public swimming pools, and so forth. So long as the issue is thus posed in programmatic terms, I agree that the reformers' logic cannot be cabined. Paradoxically, however, if one restates the analysis in terms of the tax base that supports these individual programs, a manageable rule becomes much easier to see.

The premise of this section is that the courts should be asked to insure that each local jurisdiction have available to it, either in actual tax base or in compensating state aid, per capita equality of resources out of which to finance its entire bundle of goods and services. Doctrinally, this can be accomplished either by invocation of the equal protection clause and the voting reapportionment cases, or by revitalization of a substantive due process argument.

Equal Protection and Tax Base Reapportionment

It has been suggested that the system of school finance approved by *Rodriguez* violates the equal protection clause, as interpreted in the voting reapportionment cases.[17] This depends upon a presumption that the proponents of increased educational spending will have a harder time establishing their case in poor districts than in rich ones, which in turn means that the proponents of educational spending in a rich district are more powerful (or have a more effective vote) than persons of identical persuasion in a poor district. It is, therefore, concluded that a constitution violation exists, since a differential in voting power (expressed as a differential in the political effectiveness of one's ability to persuade the voters on the issue of educational expenditure) is based on the impermissible factor of geographic location.

That a differential in "persuasiveness" exists can hardly be denied. But to therefore invoke the voting cases is to wrongly assume that educational expenditure decisions are made in common by all of school districts of the state. I do not think the voting cases can be directly invoked, because they teach that locational differentials are constitutionally impermissible only when they result in different political effectiveness within the same legislative body. The various school districts of the state are, of course, "within" the state, but they are not making a single expenditure decision common to all of them.

A hypothetical situation illustrates this point. Suppose City A and City B, each with a population of one million voters. A has a city council consisting of five elected members; B, a council of ten members. If the state in which A and B are located provided that all members of city councils were to sit as state legislators, the hypothetical arrangement would obviously violate the one person, one vote doctrine, since B would have twice as many representatives for its size as A and consequently would have twice as much political power at the state level. But if we confine our attention to the internal affairs of A or B and assume further that decisions taken in A have no bearing on those in B, and vice versa, then it should matter not a whit whether A has five council members or thirty-three. Furthermore, and this is perhaps of even greater doctrinal importance, the lack of common decision-making eliminates the need for any representative structure to carry the political opinion of A's citizens into a common (usually a higher) forum with B's citizens.

Of course, if education is characterized as a responsibility of the state, it becomes an issue for decision making common to A and B. Even so, the common issue thus defined is not the level of educational expenditures (since each city will set its own level by political procedures in which all voters of the city presumptively share on an equal basis) but rather the prior issue of tax base allocation. Thus, what the voter-dilution proposition works down to, at least in my contemplation, is a wholly different cause of action concerned with the constitutional adequacy of permitting tax-base variations to exist at all, a cause of action that has little or nothing to do either with education or with the dilution of votes within local units of government. The voting reapportionment cases are still pertinent, but somewhat farther removed than is usually suggested.

The underlying concept of the reapportionment cases and the Equal Protection Clause is that the basic tools of political democracy should be distributed "equally," which is to say, in a manner that insures the equal opportunity of every citizen to participate in and to influence the decisions reached by the system of governments. The finance case that I conceive would present one aspect of this basic constitutional principle—the right to have the common financial resources of the state divided up equitably. I do not flirt here, of course, with any constitutional obligation to redistribute individual income, but rather with the purely public claim of access to such resources for public purposes.

The reapportionment cases recognize a parallel aspect of this constitutional responsibility, equality of representation in any common legislative body. And the reapportionment cases also stand as persuasive evidence of a pragmatic constitutional preference for the "big" structural solution which, by making the system more "just," obviates the necessity for judicial intrusion into a host of smaller substantive issues. This preference, I should think, would be appealing to those like Justice Powell who perceive the injustice of our present school finance system but shrink from judicial intrusion at too detailed a level.

The principal bar to this line of analysis is that, as an intrusion into the tax policy of the states, it runs afoul of a doctrine that tax statutes are presumptively valid. Justice Powell notes this doctrine in *Rodriguez:*

No scheme of taxation, whether the tax is imposed on property, income or purchase of goods and services, has yet been devised which is free of all discriminatory impact. In such a complex arena in which no perfect alternatives exist, the Court does well not to impose too rigorous a standard of scrutiny lest all local fiscal schemes become subjects of criticism under the Equal Protection Clause.[18]

From this, as I have noted, the Court reaffirms a

presumption of constitutionality that can be overcome only by the most explicit demonstration that a classification is a hostile and oppressive discrimination against particular persons and classes.[19]

However, when one examines the specific tax issues involved in the cases upon which the Court relies for its presumption doctrine, the appropriateness of that rule to the finance questions posed here becomes much more questionable. The cited cases fall into two broad categories: claimed discriminations caused by differential taxes burdening corporate taxpayers more heavily than individuals or partnerships; and claimed discriminations that turn on the geographical location of the person or thing being taxed.

As to the corporate cases, it is significant to note that the heavier tax burden which is "presumed" valid was uniformly (in the litigated cases cited by Justice Powell) placed on the corporate class. By way of comparison we may well ask what would result if a state instead exempted corporations from a form of tax that individuals had to pay, without imposing some compensating alternative. The supposed wealth and political power of corporations would naturally lead to a suspicion of improper or undue influence on the state legislature, and would most likely prompt a closely reasoned analysis by the Court, rather than an empty indulgence in "presumptions."

Similarly, in the cases involving a geographical tax discrimination, the "presumption" has been used either in cases where the tax discriminated *against* residents of the levying state, or where the tax affected only residents of the levying state but applied unequally to in-state and out-of-state property. In either case, the taxpayers burdened by the differential had, by definition, fair access to the political process by which the tax was levied, and in that context the "presumption" invoked by Justice Powell makes sense.

To be sure, in the cases cited by Justice Powell fair access to the political process meant nothing more than citizenship within the state. I think the concept can be pushed further, however, where, as here, we are dealing not with an individual tax but with a whole system which relies on local tax bases. Paradoxically, the reason for this is that in the tax base situation, the very size of the affected class permits a valid generalization about the likelihood of receiving even-handed treatment that is not possible in an individual taxpayer's case. The situation is the same in the voting re-apportionment cases, and both causes of action therefore satisfy Justice Powell's concern that the rights of a definite class be litigated.

Accepting this, it seems to me beyond argument that an inner political check inherent in the allocation of tax resources is nonexistent. Whatever the distribution between rich and poor districts, at some point the number of relatively rich ones will become sufficient to militate against any legisla-tion that will have the effect of shifting taxable bases from the wealthier majority to the poorer minority. The economic districting cases cry out for the invocation of the "political powerlessness" basis for overruling "the majoritarian political process" that Justice Powell recognizes in *Rodri-guez*. Isn't an intuitive confidence that this is so why we keep throwing ourselves at these finance questions, in spite of opinions like *Rodriguez?*

It must be conceded again, of course, that the "feel" of the *Rodriguez* opinion indicates little taste for this approach, but this is not to say that it cannot be coaxed along. The tax-base cause of action offers a gain in clarity and, in my opinion, might succeed with the Court if a workable remedy for tax-base distortion can be formulated. This in turn suggests moving to a "minimum welfare" argument, whose peculiar strength is in its amenability to a discrete and judicially workable decree.

Minimum Welfare

Professor Michelman has cogently criticized the whole doctrinal basis of the school finance cases, suggesting that a due process/minimum welfare approach would be preferable to the equal-protection-based litigation that has heretofore been undertaken.[20] In pragmatic terms, at least, the un-happy fate of the *Rodriguez* litigation seems to underscore the pertinence of his criticisms. Professor Michelman's argument is difficult to simplify, but if I understand it correctly his argument, based on substantive due process, is that the state has a constitutional obligation to provide a mini-mally acceptable amount of education, sufficient for every student to come into the adult world fairly equipped to do battle for whatever prosperity and satisfaction his abilities and inclinations are suited to. Having placed a floor under every student, Michelman would regard it immaterial that some students receive "more" or "better" education.

Substantive due process poses enormous difficulties of implementation, since it seemingly forces judicial resolution of policy questions that we have come to think judges ought not to be involved in. Asking a court to define what constitutes a constitutionally adequate education seemingly implies questions more appropriate to a school board. Michelman's theory does have considerable compensating attractiveness, however, in that it avoids to a considerable extent antagonizing the articulate and defensive wealthy school districts that see any reform scheme as a threat to their "right" to spend on lavish buildings, enriched curricula, and the like. Thus, however much his notion may offend a rigorous egalitarian perspective, it accords with the reality of political thought and therefore could be put into effect judicially without asking the Court to get too far out in front of prevailing sentiments. That Justice Powell seems to flirt with this concept is a further indication of its viability.

The critical problem then becomes that of finding a way to implement the minimum welfare concept in "judicially manageable" terms that do not require too much policy discretion on the part of the Court. I have argued already that it could be implemented in education by taking a statistical expression of actual expenditures as the measure of a minimum acceptable level for the state as a whole, and the same technique could be applied across the whole range of municipal expenditures.

Approached this way, some mean level of expenditure evidencing a political consensus about the amount of money required per capita to finance the minimally acceptable range of public services could be selected by analyzing the whole range of actual municipal expenditures. Although an approximation, such a computation would be judicially manageable and would leave to each local jurisdiction considerable (if not total) political discretion as to how the money was to be allocated to individual items. Thus, the virtue of local control, which the *Rodriguez* Court so loudly affirms, would be respected in a manner not unlike that now accomplished be federal revenue sharing.

The minimum welfare approach can also be presented in terms of tax base instead of expenditure level by computating the median tax base across the range of taxing jurisdictions and determining an appropriate yield for "each" percent of tax effort.[21] In this approach, the tax base represents the opportunity to provide adequate amounts of public welfare to all of the citizens of the jurisdiction, although at some point wealth again has its advantage.

Thus, the doctrine can be worked out either way, and its implementation really comes down to a question of alternate remedies—changes in state aid practices if the expenditure approach is used, support of district power equalizing if the tax base approach is used. A court might well prefer to give the state its option. Indeed, there is nothing in this approach that need foreclose the state from making any number of reforms on its own initiative. For instance, the state may wish to realign inapt political boundaries. It might shift local finance to regional bodies or, by way of compromise, devise a tax-sharing scheme for regional groups of jurisdictions somewhat on the model of the previously mentioned Hackensack Meadowlands plan. It might withdraw from local jurisdiction the power to tax broad classes of property so as to remove the distorting effect of, say, major industrial plants in a lightly developed area. Undoubtedly, the ingenuity of the public mind can devise any number of tenable approaches, once the initial hurdle is cleared.

When all is said and done, however, it cannot be gainsaid that what is being sought is judicial entry into a major field of litigation and reform, one from which it has previously shrunk, and not without some reason. What I have attempted to do here is to marshal a congeries of doctrinal arguments, none of them wholly satisfactory standing alone, which when taken as a group seem to point unavoidably to a conclusion that constitutional solutions are both inevitable and workable. Like the great questions of civil liberties and racial discrimination, equitable public financing is an underneath kind of issue which, once worked out, can add the luster of "rightness" to our legal system and at the same time provide the framework within which other public questions will take care of themselves without judicial intervention.

Notes

1   411 U.S. 1, 93 S.Ct. 1278 (1973)
2   *Rodriguez, supra* n. 1, at 20, 93 S.Ct. at 1290.
3   *Id.* at 28, 93 S.Ct. at 1294 (emphasis added).
4   *Id.* at 24, 93 S.Ct. at 1292.
5   *Id.* at 23-24, 93 S.Ct. at 1291 (footnotes omitted, emphasis added).
6   *Rodriquez, supra* n. 1 at 59, 62, 93 S.Ct. at 1310, 1311 (footnotes omitted).
7   Note, *A Statistical Analysis of the School Finance Decisions,* 81 Yale L.J. 1303, 1327 (1972).
8   *Id.* at 1324, n. 102.
9   *Rodriguez, supra* n. 1 at 19, 93 S.Ct. at 1289.
10 See, *e.g.,* Schultze et al., Setting National Priorities: The 1973 Budget 291-317 (1972).
11 See *Hargrave* v. *Kirk,* 313 F.Supp. 944 (M.D. Fla. 1970), *vacated* 401 U.S. 476, 91 S.Ct. 856 (1971).
12 *Rodriquez, Supra* n. 1 at 54, 93 S.Ct. at 1307.

13 City of Newark, Annual Budget 1973 (January 1973).

14 See *National Land & Inv. Co.* v. *Kohn,* 419 Pa. 504, 215 A.2d 597 (1965) (4 acre zoning).

15 As this material goes to press, the proponents of zoning reform have met a stunning success in New Jersey. In *So. Burlington Council, N.A.A.C.P.* v. *Twp. of Mt. Laurel,* 67 N.J. 151, 336 A.2d 713 (1975), the New Jersey Supreme Court mandated that all developing regions within the state make affirmative provision for their "fair share" of the region's low and moderate income housing needs.

16 See N.J.S.A. 13:17-1 et.seq.; See *Meadowlands Regional Dev. Agency* v. *State,* 63 N.J. 35,43, 304 A.2d 545, 549 (1973).

17 Schoettle, *The Equal Protection Clause in Public Education,* 71 *Colum.L.Rev.* 1355,1393-1412 (1971).

18 *Rodriquez, supra* n. 1 at 41, 93 S.Ct. at 1301.

19 *Id.,* quoting *Madden* v. *Kentucky,* 309 U.S. 83,87-88, 60 S.Ct. 406, 408 (1940).

20 Michelman, *Forward: On Protecting the Poor Through the Fourteenth Amendment,* 83 *Harv.L.Rev.* 7 (1969).

21 Coons, Clune & Sugarman, *Private Wealth & Public Education* (1970).

4 *Kenneth Back*

Property Tax Administration: Current Conditions and Future Possibilities

A review of public finance literature reveals that much space has been allocated to criticism of the property tax. The basis and intensity of this criticism has changed over time along with the public image of the tax. As property tax burdens have increased to meet the ever-increasing expenditures of local governments, the property tax—and especially its administration—has come under increasing fire from a number of directions. For the low- and fixed-income groups the burden squawk-point has been reached in many jurisdictions. For property owners generally, the property tax no longer seems to have any rational relation to many of the high cost social-type services rendered by local governments. The inequities of the tax are constantly being highlighted by all groups. Indeed, for the first time the property tax and especially its residential component has become a national issue.

The increased public concern with the property tax and its administration has many manifestations. Some of these are reflected by the recent presidential and congressional involvement in property tax matters and the unprecedented legislative activity which has recently taken place on the state-local front. Moreover, the court cases involving both the school finance issues in general and those which challenge the assessment and administrative aspects of the tax in particular indicate to me at least one type of reaction to this public concern which may become a major catalyst forcing the greatest change in the future of the tax and its administration. The underlying reasons for this increased public concern are numerous. In addition to those already cited, one could add the rapid socioeconomic changes in society that have directly influenced the property tax and its administration, such as: the rapid inflation in real estate values; the increasing fluctuation, both decreases and increases, in property values in many jurisdictions (especially urban jurisdictions); the land boom in general and increased speculation in land in particular and urban sprawl and leapfrogging.

Equalized Assessments—A Major Goal of Property Tax Administration

A primary objective of property tax administration is to distribute the tax burden equitably among properties in accordance with their market values. To distribute the burden equitably under this concept, market values for all kinds of taxable properties must be determined with a relatively high degree of accuracy. Yet, in contrast to the base of most other types of taxes, the base of the property tax—value—is a subjective determination and is not susceptible to precise measurement. It is for this reason that the assessor often finds himself in an adversary position with the property owner. While standardized valuation techniques and procedures have been developed which facilitate an orderly and consistent approach to value determination, the final value selected is in every instance an estimate, the accuracy of which will depend upon the value indicators available and the judgment and experience of the valuer.

In the final analysis, the assessor's primary concern is equalization both as to market value and as to the assessment of similar properties. By its very nature, however, the assessing process cannot reflect market value with complete accuracy and timeliness. Faced with the rapidly changing and generally rising value of property, the assessor must base his assessments on the behavior of such a market. As a result, he must always follow the market rather than attempt to anticipate it. Of necessity then, his assessments will tend to be somewhat lower than the desired level, since he can act only after the market has demonstrated its reaction to supply and demand.

Where real estate markets exhibit rapid changes, either increases or decreases, an acceptable degree of equalization can only be achieved by frequent reassessments. Ideally, this requires annual reassessments; however, few if any assessment jurisdictions are provided sufficient resources to revalue all properties annually, despite the fact that most state laws require that all property be assessed anew every year. Increasing pressure for actually carrying out the requirement for annual reassessment of all

properties is presently being evidenced in a number of assessment jurisdictions. The feasibility of accomplishing this has been substantially improved with the economies introduced by the use of electronic computers
and advanced statistical techniques. For example, in conjunction with
other data, sales data may be utilized to produce a multiple regression
equation with which to develop by computer tentative values that require
only minimal field reviews and can be updated annually or biennially at
relatively low cost. In my opinion, increased implementation and experimentation with existing computer technology and improved and developing statistical methodologies by the assessor in analyzing the various value
indicators which he makes use of presents one of the greatest potentials for
improving property tax administration. In addition, many assessment
jurisdictions make use of private appraisal firms for installing systems and
updating valuations. These firms for the most part offer competent professional services to the assessor, and many have made a substantial contribution to improved assessment administration.

The Role and Use of Sales-Assessment Ratio Studies

The degree of equalization achieved in the assessment product and the
average level of assessed values in relation to market values can be as-
certained by statistical sales-assessment ratio analyses. The percentage
relationships of market value indications, usually sales prices, to existing
assessed values of properties both individually and on the average, by
property use, property type, geographic area and other groupings represent the basic elements usually contained in a sales-assessment ratio analysis. Such an analysis may be used to derive not only the average ratio of
assessed values to sales price but also ratio dispersion measures to identify
the present degree of equalization and the areas and property types most
in need of reevaluation. In addition to revealing the level and quality of the
assessment product, published findings of assessment-sales ratio studies
are useful and essential for other purposes, such as guidance for the individual taxpayer in determining the equity of his assessment and disclosure of the full value of taxable property as one index of a community's
fiscal ability. Moreover, the assessor can obtain substantial guidance for
his program development and planning through making proper use of
sales-assessment ratio studies.

Approximately forty states currently make some type of sales-assessment ratio studies. Essential data needed for sales-assessment ratio
studies are improving and becoming more available, especially as a result
of the increasing number of states that make use of property transfer
taxes. There are presently three times as many states having property

transfer taxes (thirty-six) than only ten years ago. Increasing the availability and validity of sales data and greater use of these data by the assessor will better reflect the quality of the valuation product and assist in making further improvements in valuation procedures and programs.

Full Disclosure Policies

In an effort to remove some of the secrecy and mistrust which has long plagued the assessment process, a recent encouraging trend throughout the country has been to pursue what is commonly referred to as a full public disclosure policy. Typically, this involves providing information to property owners regarding the estimated full market value of their properties, the assessed value of the properties, and the average ratio of assessed values to market value by type of property for the total assessment district. With this information, the property owner is better able to audit his own assessment, and if he wishes, prepare a more rational appeal of the assessed value of his property.

Twelve states have adopted full disclosure programs over the last ten years. Further implementation of these policies by additional taxing jurisdictions would contribute to increasing the understanding of the assessment process by the general public, thereby providing a significant potential for improving property tax administration and the public image and acceptance of the property tax in general. However, most discussions and writings on the need for and trends in full disclosure policies and their components concern only one side of the street, namely, that the tax administrator (assessor) provide full information to the taxpayer regarding his assessment. I think full disclosure policies could make an even greater contribution to improving property tax administration if consideration were given to the establishment of disclosure policies that provided a two-way street, through which the owner (taxpayer) of certain types of properties would be required to provide the tax administrator with data regarding his property. For example, if owners of income-producing properties were to provide the tax administrator with the actual earnings from the property and perhaps other selected data for various property types, the entire assessment job might be improved and done more effectively, economically, and equitably.

One basic and important element of property tax administration is that of taxpayer appeals. Generally, the first step in the appeal process is to a local board of equalization. Most states provide that the property owner may also appeal to a state board of equalization and from there to the courts. Present boards of equalization are often criticized for being composed of members who may not be qualified in property valuation and as being cumbersome and expensive for the taxpayer.

With increasing property tax burdens and public demands for greater equity, the number of appeals have been increasing in most jurisdictions. Indeed, in some jurisdictions, groups protesting the property tax and especially assessment policies have begun to organize, encourage and advise taxpayers to appeal their assessments in mass. Moreover, more taxpayers seem to think of the appeals process not for its intended purpose but as a vehicle through which to obtain a reduction in the tax bill. Many taxpayers seek to use the appeal process as an opportunity to establish a one-to-one relationship with the property tax system (the only place where such an opportunity exists in the system) to reduce the tax burden. Richard R. Almy in his article "Rationalizing the Assessment Process" presents data on one jurisdiction indicating that in 40 percent of the cases an assessment appeal was motivated by an apparent desire to reduce the taxpayer's tax burden, since in these cases the complaints did not mention valuation factors. He further reports that many of these "high tax" appeals come from areas with low effective tax rates, while few appeals were received from areas with high effective tax rates. *Property Tax Reform* [The Urban Institute, 1973], p. 175.) Unfortunately, too many assessment appeal systems presently operate in an arbitrary fashion and do not protect the legitimate interest of the taxpayer or the taxing jurisdiction.

Given these conditions, it is not surprising that present property tax appeal systems are being reviewed, and in many jurisdictions these systems are being improved. For example, greater efforts are being made to advise the taxpayer of his appeal rights and methods to affect such appeals, efforts reflected in the actions of eight states which recently required that assessment notices include a statement regarding taxpayer appeal rights and the procedures for bringing an appeal. Appeal systems are being streamlined and recent reorganizations and trends are toward separating the appeals process and machinery from the assessment process. Twelve states have introduced separate appeals systems since 1962. Thus, these improved systems of appeal provide not only evidence of better property tax administration, but also provide additional potential for further improvement.

Jurisdictional Differences

Property tax administration is not uniform but varies from jurisdiction to jurisdiction. This is due to many factors, such as the differences in size of assessment jurisdictions, the manner in which competent assessment personnel are employed and retained, the types and numbers of properties to be valued, and the state-local governmental relationships and responsibilties for property tax administration.

A major present deterrent to effective administration is the geographical fragmentation of assessment districts and the existence of overlapping assessment districts in some states. For the most part, the property tax is administered by the political subdivision it finances. Many assessing offices are too small to realize the economies of optimal operation, and some jurisdictions may not even support a single full-time assessor. Further, regardless of the size of the assessment jurisdiction, the supervisory and control powers that the state exercises also vary greatly, ranging from very little control or complete autonomy of the local assessor to very strict state control. In a few states the entire valuation function is performed at the state level. The trend appears to be for the states to perform a more active role in supervisin and assisting in the assessment process. One-third of the states have strengthened their property tax supervisory agencies over the last ten years, while eight states have established such agencies.

Professional assessors and others interested in improving property tax administration have consistently recommended assessment districts of such size as to support an adequate and well-equipped professional staff to perform the valuation function. Efforts to achieve this objective in the past have largely failed because of local politics and the belief that in the interest of local home rule the assessing jurisdiction and the political jurisdiction must be the same. Yet there is a movement toward increasing the size of assessing jurisdictions and also of increased cooperation between assessment jurisdictions, in order to gain the maximum advantage of economy and efficiency in the use of modern computer technologies. For example, nine states recently have taken steps to consolidate local assessment jurisdictions and six states have authorized local governments to establish joint assessing agencies. If these trends continue, there is an enormous potential for improving property tax administration through reducing jurisdictional fragmentation and increasing state assistance.

Professionalizing the Assessor

In contrast to the relatively slow but recently increasing progress in consolidating small and medium size assessment jurisdictions, the education and professionalization of assessment personnel has increased at a rapid rate in recent years. In view of the complexities of the valuation process and the long history of the property tax, one might expect that a high level of professionalization would have existed in property tax administration from its beginning. This, however, has not been the case. In an earlier era of our history, the assessing function consisted of little more than the clerical process of recording the property owner's estimate of value and copying the assessed values from year to year. The assessor was most often elected to office, and his primary qualification was his ability to get elected by the voters.

Unlike his predecessors, today's assessor is confronted on the one hand with a rapidly changing real estate market and a wide range of property types to be valued, and on the other hand with taxpayer demands for equalization which grow more intense with each increase in property taxes. As tax burdens have increased, the taxpayer and the courts have demanded more equitable assessments. More and more assessors are realizing that to effectively respond to present day demands requires the full time attention and skills of a competent, well-trained staff.

The selection process, job qualifications, salary, and tenure of assessors vary among the states. At present about one-half of the states provide for elected assessors and one-half for appointed. The trend has been toward appointment, with some required qualifications as a prerequisite. Many assessors have absolutely no experience in valuing property prior to entering office. Unlike most other professions, individuals come to the assessing profession with a wide variety of backgrounds. No specific assessor curriculum or degrees exists at the college or university levels. Thus, a person entering the field of assessment administration receives most of his professional training after he comes to the job.

To be a professional assessor requires much training and education and a dedication to a standard of professional competence and code of ethics. The International Association of Assessing Officers is the assessor's professional organization, and it has provided the major impetus to professionalizing and upgrading those who perform the assessment function. Extensive training, education, and assistance programs are conducted in all aspects of the valuation process. Among its many programs, one of the more important is a professional designation program for those who meet the requirements and subscribe to a rigid code of ethics and standards of professional conduct. Those of us who serve as assessment administrators are firm in our belief that the one basic essential to quality property tax administration is the education and professionalization of assessment personnel. Indications are that the states are beginning to realize the importance of trained professional assessors, as reflected by the fact that fifteen states have strengthened assessors training over the past ten years and fourteen states provide for certification of assessors based on examination—a requirement virtually nonexistent a decade ago.

The Tools of Assessment

Even the best-educated and professionally competent personnel need certain basic tools with which to carry out the assessment function. These include tax maps for property identification, configuration and description; a manual which contains procedures for mass appraisal as well as construction costs and depreciation schedules; property record or inventory cards which can accommodate data resulting from the application of the three standard approaches to value; records of all valid sales; property income data; building permits for all new construction; and records of all property transfers. The availability and use of these basic tools varies from state to state, but the more progressive assessment offices make full use of all of them. The basic tools which have proved to be the most difficult to obtain—maps, valid sales records, and income data—are now more readily available to many assessors. Widespread use of aerial photography has greatly simplified and speeded up the mapping process, and the adoption by many states of property transfer taxes has made available to assessors more valid sales price information. Income data from business income tax returns are more and more being made available to many local assessment offices.

How best to record, analyze, and make the most effective use of information about properties and of valuation data has been one of the major problems facing assessment administrators. The sheer volume of data to be handled makes manual processing costly and time-consuming. The electronic computer to store, process, and print large volumes of data is a relatively new tool in the assessing field. Its uses vary, but generally they may be classified as follows: (1) clerical and accounting; (2) sales ratio analysis; and (3) value determination. While clerical, accounting, and computation adaptations to the computer are significant first steps, the more promising use of the computer is in the area of estimating property values.

The increasing demand which has been placed on the time and talents of assessors to value large numbers of varied types of properties in a short span of time necessitated a search for new and improved methodology. The use of the computer to estimate values offers much promise to the assessor in keeping abreast of a workload which is growing at geometric rates, particularly in large urban and suburban residential areas, and in currently reflecting the value increases resulting from rapid inflationary pressures. Significant new experimentation is taking place in the use of the computer to store and manipulate vast amounts of data concerning property characteristics and recent sales prices, in an effort to predict a probable selling price for similar types of property that have not sold. The statistical technique employed to develop predictive equations for value estimation is commonly referred to as multiple linear regression analysis. Much progress has been made in the use of these technologies to predict values, especially for residential properties that exhibit a high degree of homogeneity in their characteristics.

To effectively utilize existing computer and statistical technologies requires changes in traditional organizational structures and in assessment personnel who fit within it. The typical generalist assessor is still needed and will continue to play an important role, but he will require retraining in order to make the most effective use of his professional abilities. In addition, specialists in computer programming, systems design, market analysis, statistical methodology, and other functional specialties will play an important part in the production of estimated values by use of the computer.

Effects of Poor Administration

Effective administration is a crucial factor in the application of any tax, and this is especially so for the property tax. Its visibility as a local tax, the inequities resulting from the impreciseness of value determination, and the absence of any direct ability-to-pay test place the property tax squarely under the spotlight of public opinion. Recent public opinion polls imply that in the minds of many people the property tax is the most unpopular major tax in the United States. Poor administration, which is characterized by assessments that substantially lag behind market values and are inequitable as between properties, is one of the primary factors leading to the unpopularity and lack of general respect for the tax. Where weak assessment administration results in infrequent and inadequate reevaluations, you may be sure that assessment levels will vary as between classes of property, and will vary, often widely, as between individual assessments within property classes.

A persistent criticism of the property tax is that it fails to keep pace with economic growth because of the lag between assessments and market values. At a time when property values are increasing rapidly and often erratically, the all too common three-, six-, or even ten-year reassessment cycle reduces the revenue capability of the property tax and makes a mockery of any efforts to maintain equalization. Poor administration also contributes to the regressiveness of property tax burdens and to the lack of information as to who actually pays the property tax and its burden distribution. Even with good administration, the ad valorem property tax as it applies to housing is often criticized because of the burden placed on very low income groups. During the last decade, many states have introduced an ability-to-pay concept (known as the circuit-breaker) which generally provides that property tax burdens cannot exceed a given percent of annual income for selected low-income taxpayers.

Efforts to eliminate inequities which contribute to the regressiveness of the property tax have been a major impetus in the broader movement to improve the overall administration of the tax. Some of the more serious equity problems resulting in large part from poor administration and infrequent assessments are (1) inequities of assessments in relation to market value, and particularly as to low- vs. high-value properties, (2) discriminatory assessments as between classes of property, and (3) gross undervaluation of land, as opposed to improvements in most jurisdictions.

It would be fair to say, I think that some assessment officials intentionally or unintentionally classify properties for assessment purposes when the laws call for uniformity, and they seemed to do so with at least the passive consent of the electorate. This practice doesn't seem to benefit any one group, but rather appears to favor taxpayers in the whole range of possible categories. Owners of commerical, industrial, and public utility properties have asserted, for years, that homeowner-voters have been deliberately underassessed. Now come Ralph Nader and the tax protest groups to declare that the big influential guy is given the break and that small property owners are being overassessed. Regardless of who is right, I think it would be safe to say that for every property that has been misassessed intentionally, there are thousands that have been misassessed unintentionally.

Unfortunately, the property tax is still poorly administered in many jurisdictions; however, maladministration is not necessarily inherent in the tax. Indeed, much progress is being made, especially in assessor education and professionalization, in improved valuation procedures and techniques, and in the use of advanced computer technology as applied to the assessment process. Technically, an acceptable assessment product is attainable, but obtaining an adequate budget and public support for a quality assessment program is no easy undertaking. Legislative inertia and political timidity are major impediments to improving assessment administration. Although seldom mentioned in textbooks on the property tax, a major deterrent to periodic reassessments of real estate is political in nature. Fearing the wrath of those whose assessments will be increased, legislators try to keep reassessment years and election years from coinciding.

One of the important functions of the assessment administrator is to seek and obtain public support for good assessment administration. Indeed, if an assessor can make a significant contribution to establishing a public constituency for improved assessment administration, he will have tapped into one of the most significant vehicles through which reform in assessment administration can be made. Unfortunately, in the past, the constituency for improved assessment administration has been very small.

One aspect of assessment administration often underemphasized is that of program planning and direction. The assessment administrator, especially in the large and medium size jurisdictions, is primarily a program manager. It is his job to develop and manage large scale programs that will assure the maximum possible degree of equalization among property values. Such program plans must take into account the present average level of assessments in relation to market values, and the existing degree of equalization. Some other considerations include an analysis of the rapidity with which the market is changing by areas and types of properties, and the constraints imposed by time, resource limitations, and the availability of the basic tools, including computers, with which to carry out assessment programs. Thus, proper development of program plans and their effective execution offers an excellent potential for improved property tax administration.

Future Possibilities

As to the future possibilities, the following areas seem to hold the most promise for achieving better property tax administration:

1. a modern property tax law that lends itself to good administration;
2. assessment districts large enough to support a professional and well-organized staff;
3. competent assessment personnel with adequate pay and tenure of office;
4. financial support adequate for the task to be performed;
5. greater state involvement and assistance;
6. more effective use of electronic computers in the assessment process in general and their increased use for valuations in particular;
7. simplified and improved appeal procedures;
8. full-disclosure policies that provide more and better information to both the taxpayer and the assessor;
9. increased attention to the development of adequate public information programs that lead to the creation of a public constituency which believes in and lends support to improvements in assessment administration.

I need not elaborate further on these nine points, except to say that in spite of recent substantial progress, few assessing jurisdictions measure up to all these criteria. Since no tax is any better than its administration, it is of vital importance, it seems to me, not only to the future of the property tax, but especially to local governments whose major revenues come from the property tax, to travel the road toward improved property tax administration at top speed.

Moreover, there are technically no insurmountable barriers to achieving acceptable property tax administration. To achieve the necessary improvements in property tax administration through those steps identified and perhaps others would not require hugh sums of money. More, yes, but not more relatively than that which is presently allocated to the administration of other important tax and governmental programs. Despite what some critics say, the property tax is relatively easy to administer and administer well. The major cost relates to the valuation function, which requires highly skilled professional assessors. But income and sales taxes also require, and are provided in many jurisdictions, highly trained professionals such as lawyers, accountants, economists, and public administrators. However, unlike income and sales taxes, the real property tax does not require complex accounting, annual processing of returns, auditing of books and records, and expensive tax delinquent programs. The fact that delinquent taxpayers can forfeit their property in the tax sale process makes collection of the property tax virtually self-enforcing and precludes the need for the criminal prosecution for tax evasion used in other tax enforcement.

In summary, the trends which are evident in the recent history of property tax administration provide, in my opinion, the basis for substantial optimism. Significant possibilities remain for improving property tax administration, however. If we make as much progress over the next ten years in improving property tax administration as we did in the last ten years, we will be well along the road toward acceptable standards of excellence.

II. LAND-USE EFFECTS

Introduction

"Property Taxation and Land-Use Effects" was the title and concept originally conceived for this section. Given the not altogether unusual propensity of humankind, academic and otherwise, to wander afield, it may not surprise the reader that the chapters here included consider a variety of property tax and economic effect interrelationships. Nevertheless, the primary thrust is toward land-use effects.

The first chapter by Helen F. Ladd explores the relationship between local public nonschool expenditures and the composition of the local property tax base. The empirical analysis considers fifty communities in the Boston metropolitan area, relates the resultant findings to measurement of the relative fiscal capacity of the local units, and gives evidence on the quantitative aspects of expenditure effects associated with alternative local property tax base compositions. Next, Mason Gaffney in a rather unusual chapter considers the employment effects and capital utilization results of received tax patterns and presents his view of appropriate policy adjustments.

The third chapter in this set is by Douglas N. Jones. His provides an interesting and effective survey of the unique land-use problems of Alaska. Against this backdrop Jones discusses the use of property taxation as a land-use and environmental control device. He concludes that, on balance, direct regulation is a preferred policy alternative. A paper on the use of blighted land by William Vickrey contributed substantially to the conference program, but was an apparent casualty of time conflicts, and so is necessarily relegated to the oral tradition of the conference series.

Finally, in Part II, Frederick Stocker views property taxation, land use, and their possible relation to and undergirding of a rational urban growth policy. His piece suggests, at least to this reader, that (1) application of sophisticated mathematical treatment to property tax issues is of doubtful utility, and (2) that removal of tax-induced land use distortions will provide ample room indeed for exercising virtually all of the near-term potentials of the tax policy maker. This set of chapters could not be expected, of course, to cover completely the matter of property-tax-induced land-use effects; they do, however, provide a basis for consideration of policy alternatives that comes next in this particular sequence.

5 *Helen F. Ladd*

Municipal Expenditures and the Composition of the Local Property Tax Base

Very little is known about the relationship between local public expenditures and the composition of the local property tax base. Despite the heavy reliance of local governments on property tax revenue, few researchers have directly addressed the question of whether communities which have differing percentages of their property tax bases in the form of residential, commercial, or industrial property are likely to differ systematically in the size and composition of their expenditure packages.[1] The purpose of this study, therefore, is to focus directly on this relationship, although it should be noted that the empirical results presented below are limited to nonschool expenditures. Hence, this study represents only one part of a more extensive empirical investigation of this issue.

The conceptual framework is presented in the first part of the chapter, and the empirical results, which are based on a 1970 cross section regression analysis for a sample of fifty communities in the Boston metropolitan area, are discussed in the second. The third reviews and evaluates the major underlying assumptions and limitations of the empirical analysis. The chapter concludes with an attempt to relate the empirical findings to

This chapter is a revised version of the paper presented at the 1973 TRED Conference. The main difference is a modification of the estimated equations. The equations reported here are taken from the author's Ph.D. dissertation, "Local Public Expenditures and the Composition of the Property Tax Base" (Harvard University, 1974).

the policy issue of measuring the relative fiscal capacity of local communities.

Conceptual Framework

The goods and services provided by the local public sector are assumed to be characterized by rivalness in consumption.[2] In this sense, they resemble private goods rather than Samuelsonian public goods. Unlike private goods, however, they are provided through the budget mechanism rather than the market mechanism and require that the same level of services be provided to all residents. For a given tax structure, the utility maximizing public service level of residents within any one community will vary in line with each resident's income, tax price, and preferences for publicly provided goods. Since this variance prevents most residents from achieving their public service desires, the quantity of local public services actually provided will depend upon how the local political system reconciles these conflicting demands.

The assumption most often made about the political system in this context is that it is characterized by majority rule, which implies that the effective demand of the community is the quantity demanded by the voter who desires the median quantity of public services. Although this median voter concept is generally employed here, it is recognized that complete reliance on the median voter mechanism for translating individual demands into community demands may be misleading, because of its failure to capture some of the relevant political forces acting on the local decision-making process.[3] For example, interest groups are represented in such a formulation only to the extent that they affect the identity of the median voter, whereas, in fact, certain interest groups may have sufficient political power to influence directly community expenditure decisions. In addition, the possibility of logrolling may allow some measures to pass in practice that would not ordinarily command majority support. Hence, explicit recognition of the power of interest groups may be desirable.

In the context of this individualistic public choice model, it is necessary to be explicit about how the components of the property tax base affect expenditures when a proportional property tax is the sole source of public revenue. Consider first a strictly residential community. The value of property owned by each resident in relation to the average property holdings in the community determines each resident's tax price, or share of the cost, of per capita public services. It is through this tax price mechanism alone that the tax structure affects the desired level of public services.

Two additional potential effects of residential property that are unrelated to the use of the property tax as the revenue source can be identified. Both depend on each resident's absolute level of property holdings rather than on his relative holdings. First, residential property may act as a proxy for the total wealth of individuals, thereby exerting a wealth effect on the demand for public services. Second, it may reflect tastes or preferences for particular public services. For example, high-valued residential property (holding income constant) may strengthen preferences for certain public services, such as police services, that provide services directly to property.

Nonresidential property, the value of which is taxed at the same rate as residential property, also may affect the demand for public services in several ways. As a first approximation, the effects can be conceptually divided into two categories: (1) tax price or revenue effects, and (2) need or taste-determining effects.

Tax Price Effects of Nonresidential Property

Let us assume away all need and taste-determining effects of nonresidential property in order to focus on the tax price effect. The demand function of the community for resident-related services can be derived from a model in which all families maximize a utility function of the form

$$U = U(X, S, h),$$

subject to a budget constraint of the form

$$Y = P_x X + (t + d)P_H H,$$

where

X = private goods
S = publicly provided services received per family
h = housing services derived from housing stock
H = housing stock
Y = family annual income
P_x = price of private goods
t = annual effective tax rate of the community in which the family resides
P_H = price per unit of housing stock
d = fraction of the value of the housing stock expended yearly (e.g., for maintenance, mortgage interest, and return on equity)

Thus,

$d \cdot P_H \cdot H$ can be interpreted as the annual cost of housing services, and
$t \cdot P_H \cdot H$ is the annual cost of services received from the local public sector.

Implicit in this characterization of the budget constraint are the assumptions that all local public expenditures are financed entirely by the local property tax, and that residents perceive as part of their tax burden only that part which falls on them directly as homeowners.[4] It is also assumed that all residents are homeowners and that the housing and location decisions of all families have already been made, so that the quantity of H is fixed.

Recognizing that the tax rate in each community is the total expenditures per family of each community times the number of families (i.e., $S \cdot C \cdot n$, where C is the resource cost of public services and n is the number of families), divided by the total property tax base (B), the budget constraint can be rewritten in the form[5]

$$Y = P_x \cdot X + \frac{S \cdot C \cdot n}{B} P_H \cdot H + dP_H \cdot H$$

Maximization of utility subject to this constraint yields the equilibrium condition[6]

$$\frac{\partial U / \partial S}{\partial U / \partial X} = \frac{C(n \cdot P_H \cdot H_B)}{P_x}$$

In other words, rational residents of a given community will desire that level of public services which equates their marginal rate of substitution in consumption between public and private goods with the "price" ratio on the right hand side of the above equilibrium condition.

This "price" has three parts. The first is C, the cost in dollars of providing one unit of the given service. The remainder can be rewritten as $R \cdot H_M/H_A$ where R is the fraction of the property tax base that is residential ($R = n \cdot P_h \cdot H_A/B$ where H_A is average housing stock) and H_M/H_A in the ratio of the housing owned by the median voter (H_M) to the average housing stock in the community. The emphasis in the empirical investigation will be on R, which will be referred to as the tax price of public services.

Thus, the demand function for public services by any one community has the form

$$S = F(Y_m, C, R, H_M/H_A)$$

where

Y_m = the income of the median voter

C = the resource cost of public services

R = the fraction of the base that is residential

H_M/H_A = housing value of median voter divided by average housing value

The model predicts that the signs of the "price" variables will be negative. The obvious explanation for the negative effect of R is that the higher the percent residential, the larger the residents' share of the costs of public services, and hence the smaller the quantity of public services demanded. It should be emphasized that the tax base effects of nonresidential property on local expenditure decisions are postulated to operate exclusively through the variable R.

Taste- and Need-Determining Effects of Nonresidential Property

Three types of nonrevenue expenditure effects can be identified: (1) externalities which affect the derived demand for resident-related services (2) direct demands by business firms for business-related government services and (3) public service demand effects of community characteristics highly correlated with nonresidential property. It should be noted that the magnitude of the three nonrevenue effects associated with commercial property may differ significantly from those associated with industrial property.

Externalities Effect of Nonresidential Property.—Business property affects the demand for public services by altering the production relation between factor inputs and desired outputs. To give one example of this externalities effect, the demand for police service inputs will be derived from preferences for protection from crime and automobile accidents. The extent to which residents feel protected is defined to be inversely related to the probability of the resident being victimized by crime or traffic accidents. Assuming that voters in all communities have similar preferences for protection vis-à-vis consumption of private goods and services, it can then be shown that under reasonable assumptions the derived demand of the median voter for police services will vary positively with the relative amount of nonresidential property in the community, *ceteris paribus.*

Specifically, each resident voter chooses a level of police services that maximizes a utility function, which has as its arguments protection and private goods, subject to an income constraint and a protection production function constraint. Thus, each resident maximizes:

(1) $\quad U = U(P, X) \quad \partial U/_{\partial P} > 0, \quad \partial U/_{\partial X} > 0$

subject to:

(2) $\quad P = P(S, B) \quad \partial P/_{\partial S} > 0, \quad \partial P/_{\partial B} < 0, \quad \dfrac{\partial^2 P}{\partial S \partial B} \geq 0, \text{ and}$

(3) $\quad Y = P_x X + P_s S$

where

   P = protection from crime and automobile accidents per resident
   X = private goods per resident
   S = police services per resident
   Y = resident income
   P_s = price of police services
   P_x = price of private goods
   B = business property per resident

The utility function (equation 1) is the same by assumption for all residents in all communities. Implicit in the budget constraint (equation 3) is the assumption that the tax system requires all residents to pay an equal amount for public services and that nonresidential property is untaxed. Equation 2 is a protection production function in which the effect of business property is to lower the level of protection for any given level of police services. This is reasonable, since business property increases the daytime population in the form of workers and consumers in relation to the nighttime, resident population. This added congestion in the community is likely to increase the probability of crime and, therefore, reduce the level of protection for any given level of police services.

From the following standard first-order conditions

$$(1) \qquad \frac{\partial U/\partial P \cdot \partial P/\partial S}{\partial U/\partial X} = \frac{P_s}{P_x}$$

$$(2) \qquad Y - P_x X - P_s S = 0$$

the effect on desired police services of a change in the amount of business property can be found by solving for dS/dB from the system of total derivatives. The result is that dS/dB is unambiguously positive as long as the signs of the first and second order partial derivatives of the utility function and the protection production function are as specified.[7] Hence, business property is predicted to have a positive effect on the demand for public services through its adverse impact on the production of public services.

Direct Demand for Business-Related Services.—The second potential nonrevenue effect of nonresidential property is the direct demand effect for business-related services. Since the basic assumption of the local expenditure model under consideration is that resident voters make expenditure decisions that will maximize individual utility, it is not readily apparent how business demands for strictly business-related services fit into the expenditure decision-making process. How, in other words, do business firms make their demands effective in the context of a model in which only residents vote?

One mechanism involves fiscally induced migration of firms within a metropolitan area. For a given level of resident-related expenditures and tax rate, firms may threaten to leave or refuse to enter the community unless demands for particular services, such as rubbish collection, are met. Resident voters, in turn, would be willing to provide such services up to the point that the perceived net benefits from the marginal firm just equal the residents' share of expenditures for strictly business-related services. Perceived gross benefits would include tax base benefits, consumer shopping convenience, and jobs, the importance of the last depending on the nature of the resident work force and the availability of jobs in nearby communities. Costs include additional public expenditures on resident-related services induced by the externalities effect discussed above and nonfiscal costs in the form of smog and ugliness associated with some types of business property.[8] This type of argument suggests that communities would be willing to provide fewer services to firms that provide few jobs, yet create significant disamenities, than to other types of firms.

If firms are immobile with respect to public services provided, however, it appears at first that no compelling reason exists for residents to vote for strictly business-related services. As was mentioned above, however, the translation of individual preferences into a social decision-making process is more complicated than the straight median voter model implies, as a result of political considerations. Thus, the explanation may fall in part on lobbying action by individual business firms or by groups of firms working through such organizations as the local Chamber of Commerce. By voicing their complaints and requests to finance committees or larger voter groups through public meetings, newspaper advertisements, and other forms of communication, business groups may be able to convince voters of the desirability of increasing business specific public services. The effectiveness of such lobbying might depend on factors such as the percentage of local business owners who reside in the community, the size of the business establishments, the types of businesses involved, and the activity of such groups.

Correlation with Other Taste-Determining Characteristics.—The third nonrevenue fiscal effect of business property works indirectly through the correlation among types of property and other characteristics of the community that affect preferences for publicly provided amenities.

Specifically, the assumption made above in the externalities context, that residents in different communities have similar preferences for public services such as crime protection, may need to be modified. In fact, the preference structure of the typical resident of a highly industrialized community may differ substantially from the preference structure of the typical resident of a wealthy residential or commercial community, even controlling for income differences.

In summary, this discussion of the tax price and other effects of nonresidential property suggests that there is substantial leeway for the hypothesis that different types of property have different local expenditure implications. This is true even with respect to nonschool expenditures alone, which will be the focus of the empirical work presented in the next section.

Empirical Results

This section examines empirically the relationships discussed above, using cross section regression analysis for communities in the Boston metropolitan area for the year 1970. The uncomplicated governmental structure in Massachusetts, in which local municipalities have responsibility for most public functions including that of local public education and in which county government and special districts are relatively unimportant, means that cities and towns are the appropriate unit of observation for fiscal decisions. Moreover, the use of the local town meeting, in either its pure or representative form, in Massachusetts towns makes the underlying individualistic utility maximizing assumption of the model more acceptable than it might otherwise be. The analysis is limited to the fifty (out of a possible seventy-eight) towns and cities in the Boston SMSA for which comparable expenditure data is available for 1970.[9]

Form of the Equations

The expenditure equations were estimated in the following two forms:

(1) $MUN = AY^{\alpha_1}\bar{B}^{\alpha_2}\bar{T}^{\alpha_3}R^{\alpha_4}$

(2) $MUN = (\beta_0 + \beta_1 Y + \beta_2 \bar{B} + \beta_3 \bar{T})(1 + \beta_4 R)$

where

MUN = per-capita expenditures on municipal services (includes general government, health, sanitation, hospitals, public safety, highways, libraries, and recreation)

Y = median family income

$\bar{B}$ = vector of business-related variables that reflect nonrevenue effects of business property
$\bar{T}$ = vector of community characteristics affecting preferences for public services
R = fraction of the tax base that is residential

There is no factor cost variable in either equation, an omission justified by the assumption that the metropolitan area constitutes a single market for factor inputs used in the production of public services. The only price variable in the equation is R, which, as discussed above, represents the tax price to residents of publicly provided services.[10] Since R is a price, the coefficents, α_4 and β_4, are expected to be negative. Equation 1 imposes constant elasticity on all the variables and hence implies partial derivatives that vary with the expenditure level. Equation 2, on the other hand, which is a linear equation with a nonlinear tax price term, yields unit impacts for each of the nonprice variables that are independent of the expenditure level but are dependent on the tax price. The tax price expenditure elasticity in equation 2, i.e.

$$\left(\frac{\beta_4 R}{(1 + \beta_4 R)} \right),$$

remains independent of the expenditure level, however.

The function of the business-related variables in the vector $\bar{B}$ is to pick up the externalities and direct-demand expenditure effects of nonresidential property. Unfortunately, it has been impossible to separate the two effects in the current study. An attempt has been made, however, to separate the resident preference effect from the other two effects. This was achieved by including in many of the reported regressions the variable BLUE, defined as the number of manufacturing workers *residing* (as opposed to working) in each community expressed as a fraction of the resident population.

Various variables suggest themselves for inclusion in $\bar{B}$. These include employment, total sales, value added, and total property value of commercial and industrial property. Sales and value-added variables were ruled out on the basis of unavailability of current data, the latest year for such data being 1966. This leaves employment and property variables, both of which are available for 1970. In the reported regressions, various combinations of the variables commercial workers (CWOR), manufacturing workers (IWOR), market value of commercial property (CBASE), and market value of industrial property (IBASE), all expressed per resident population, are included. It should be emphasized that in the context of the model used here, the justification for including manufacturing and commercial property, in addition to, or instead of, manufacturing, and commerical workers rests solely on their appropriateness as proxies for the true variables creating the taste or need effects of business property. It is hoped that all revenue effects of such property are incorporated in the tax price variable. Whether or not this appears to be the case will be discussed below.

In all of the reported equations, the fraction of families with below poverty-line income (POV) and the fraction of total housing units that are occupied by renters (REN) are included in the taste vector $\bar{T}$. A positive coefficient on POV can be interpreted in a variety of ways, none of which can be distinguished here: (1) non-poor voters, including the median voter, receive consumption externalities from providing services to the very poor; (2) the presence of poor people alters the production relation between, say, police service inputs and protection from crime outputs, thereby affecting the derived demand of the median voter for police services; or (3) poor people in any one community have relatively strong demands for public services because of a low perceived tax price, and are able to make their demands effective through the political process. The coefficient of REN can also be interpreted in several ways. The argument is often made that renters have strong demands for public services because of their perception that they do not pay the property tax (implying a perceived tax price close to 0). For this to have a positive impact on expenditures, renters would either have to be numerous enough to affect the demand of the median voter or would have to have sufficient political power to impose their will on the majority. Other explanations of a positive coefficient of REN include the positive correlation of REN with other community characteristics, such as density, that might affect expenditures positively, or its negative correlation with public school children as a fraction of the total population. This latter variable is expected to have a negative impact on municipal expenditures to the extent that school expenditures compete funds away from noneducational expenditure categories.

One final variable used in many of the reported regressions is the residential property base per capita (RBASE). As discussed above, this variable may be interpreted as a proxy for the total wealth of individuals or as reflecting tastes or preference for those public services that yield services directly to property.

Estimated Equations

Tables 5.1 and 5.2 present the basic equations for both the multiplicative form (table 5.1) and the linear form (table 5.2). Before turning to the specific implications of the point estimates, a few general remarks should be made. The equations in table 5.1 were estimated using ordinary least squares with all variables in log form. Hence, the reported coefficients are expenditure elasticities. The numbers in parentheses are the absolute values of the t-statistics. The equations in table 2 were estimated using a one-dimensional search procedure over the parameter β_4. The reported coefficients are the parameter estimates associated with the value of β_4 that minimizes the sum of squared residuals. Elasticities, calculated at mean values, are in brackets below the t-statistics.

Definitions of the variables used follow (prefix L refers to the natural logarithm; see chapter appendix for sources):

MUN = Municipal nonschool expenditures per capita (includes general government, public safety, health, sanitation and hospitals, recreation, highways, and libraries)
$\overline{\text{MUN}}$ = 105.82

Y = Median family income
$\overline{Y}$ = 13,358

R = Fraction of total tax base that is residential
$\overline{R}$ = .75

RBASE = Market value of residential property per capita
$\overline{\text{RBASE}}$ = \$5466.00

CBASE = Market value of commercial property per capita
$\overline{\text{CBASE}}$ = \$724.63

IBASE = Market value of industrial property per capita
$\overline{\text{IBASE}}$ = \$492.33

CWOR = Commercial workers per capita
$\overline{\text{CWOR}}$ = .117

IWOR = Industrial workers per capita
$\overline{\text{IWOR}}$ = .109

POV = Fraction of families with income below poverty level
$\overline{\text{POV}}$ = .0375

REN = Fraction of housing units occupied by renters
$\overline{\text{REN}}$ = .2738

BLUE = Manufacturing workers residing in the community divided by the population of the community
$\overline{\text{BLUE}}$ = .0936

Looking first at table 5.1, all equations include LY, LR, LPOV, and LREN where the prefix L refers to the natural logarithm. The equations differ primarily in the particular commerical and industrial property variables included to capture the nonrevenue effects of such property (that is, they differ in the specification of the vector $\overline{\mathbf{B}}$). Equations 1, 2, 7, and 8

TABLE 5.1
Nonschool Expenditures: Log Form
(Dependent Variable LMUN)

	LY	LR	LRBASE	LCBASE	LIBASE	LCWOR	LIWOR	LPOV	LREN	LBLUE	$R^2/\bar{R}^2$
1)	1.132 (3.862)	−.4915 (2.771)	.1658 (1.771)	—	—	.1422 (2.916)	−.0818 (2.249)	.2870 (2.914)	.2390 (4.594)	—	.65/.60
2)	.7225 (2.334)	−.4396 (2.652)	.1674 (1.249)	—	—	.1512 (3.332)	−.0493 (1.380)	.2910 (3.182)	.1893 (3.675)	−.2868 (2.778)	.71/.65
3)	.9738 (3.383)	−.3508 (1.864)	.2504 (1.845)	.1200 (3.375)	−.0148 (1.233)	—	—	.3531 (3.736)	.2334 (4.655)	—	.67/.62
4)	.6529 (2.327)	−.3046 (1.776)	.2185 (1.767)	.1325 (4.067)	−.0071 (.6326)	—	—	.3673 (4.272)	.1895 (3.979)	−.2909 (3.149)	.74/.68
5)	1.065 (3.480)	−.3817 (2.022)	.1808 (1.255)	.0902 (2.080)	−.0087 (.5819)	.0752 (1.304)	−.0532 (1.259)	.3258 (3.346)	.2311 (4.548)	—	.69/.62
6)	.6196 (1.982)	−.3191 (1.851)	.1853 (1.418)	.0980 (2.487)	−.0101 (.7455)	.0792 (1.513)	−.0154 (.3817)	.3335 (3.775)	.1775 (3.605)	−.3045 (3.104)	.75/.69
7)	1.332 (5.616)	−.4025 (2.513)	—	—	—	.1587 (3.394)	−.0930 (2.645)	.2714 (2.771)	.2395 (4.587)	—	.64/.59
8)	.9247 (3.480)	−.3499 (2.327)	—	—	—	.1679 (3.845)	−.0607 (1.745)	.2752 (3.018)	.1899 (3.663)	−.2863 (2.755)	.70/.65

Absolute value of t-statistics in parentheses. Constant term not reported. For definition of variables, see text.

TABLE 5.2
Nonschool Expenditures: Linear Form with Nonlinear Tax Price
(Dependent Variable MUN)

1) MUN = .0070 Y + .0072 RBASE + 156.48 CWOR — 95.62 IWOR + 270.84 POV + 140.95 REN — 26.60 [1 — .398 R]
   (2.505)   (1.826)   (2.322)   (2.142)   (.8371)   (4.578)   (1.124)
   [.6185]   [.2582]   [.1218]   [—.0693]   [.0675]   [.2566]   [—.4241]

   R² = .61   S.E.E = 18.070

2) MUN = .0058 Y + .0070 RBASE + 164.82 CWOR — 69.59 IWOR + 386.58 POV + 144.67 REN — 402.69 BLUE + 14.10 [1 — .477 RL]
   (1.977)   (1.569)   (2.288)   (1.349)   (1.108)   (4.389)   (1.847)   (.4832)
   [.4670]   [.2272]   [.1170]   [—.0460]   [.0879]   [.2404]   [—.2336]   [—.5569]

   R² = .64   S.E.E. = 17.630

3) MUN = .0089 Y + 164.82 CWOR — 93.15 IWOR + 225.06 POV + 127.14 REN — 32.74 [1 — .260 RB]
   (4.811)   (2.775)   (2.467)   (.7811)   (4.690)   (1.300)
   [.8962]   [.1466]   [—.0772]   [.0642]   [.2648]   [—.2422]

   R² = .59   S.E.E. + 18.340

4) MUN = .0072 Y + 166.64 CWOR — 63.40 IWOR + 335.28 POV + 123.91 REN — 378.71 BLUE + 15.163 [1 — .3175 RL]
   (3.177)   (2.740)   (1.448)   (1.118)   (4.414)   (1.960)   (.4540)
   [.6816]   [.1403]   [—.0497]   [.0905]   [.2442]   [.2606]   [—.3125]

   R² = .63   S.E.E. = 17.795

5) MUN = .0043 Y + .0050 RBASE + .0214 CBASE + .0026 IBASE + 435.8 POV + 103.4 REN — 40.56
   (2.157)   (1.906)   (3.783)   (.5977)   (1.794)   (4.844)   (1.574)
   [.5428]   [.2582]   [.1465]   [.0120]   [.1544]   [.2675]

   R² = .63   S.E.E. = 17.51

6) MUN = .0027 Y + .0041 RBASE + .0209 CBASE + .0048 IBASE + 529.95 POV + 90.96 REN — 343.45 BLUE + 17.12
   (1.372)   (1.668)   (3.926)   (1.155)   (2.282)   (4.385)   (2.496)   (.5103)
   [.3408]   [.2117]   [.1431]   [.0223]   [.1878]   [.2353]   [—.3102]

   R² = .68   S.E.E. = 16.50

Absolute value of t statistics in parentheses. Elasticities in square brackets. Constant term not reported. For definition of variables, see text.

include only employment variables, 3 and 4 only property value variables, and 5 and 6 both employment and property value variables. Equations 7 and 8 differ from 1 and 2 in the exclusion of the residential property wealth variable, the wealth or taste effects of RBASE being picked up in part by the income variable. In addition, each basic equation is regressed with and without the resident taste variable LBLUE.

Table 5.2 presents the same basic array of equations for the linear form of the model. Equations 1-4 include only employment variables, while equations 5 and 6 include only property tax base variables. Again, all equations have been run with and without the taste variable BLUE. A note about equations 5 and 6 is in order. Both these equations were originally regressed with a nonlinear tax price term as in equations 1-4, but the value of β_4 that maximized the R^2 was in both cases essentially zero. Hence, the equations were rerun in the straight linear form reported here. Presumably, there is insufficient independent variation in the business property value variables to separate statistically the tax price effects from the other effects of business property when the equation is specified in linear form.

With the exception of some of the coefficients of industrial property or industrial workers, almost all of the parameter estimates are statistically significant. Moreover, the magnitudes of the coefficients are generally consistent across all fourteen equations.

The frequent negative sign on the industrial property and worker variables is somewhat surprising in light of the expected externalities and direct demand effects of business property which would predict an impact greater than or equal to zero. It should be noted, however, that the addition of the resident taste variable BLUE or LBLUE in all cases reduces (in absolute value) the negative coefficient of the industrial property variables and renders the coefficient statistically insignificant. BLUE or LBLUE comes in negatively as expected in all equations. The low magnitude and frequent statistical insignificance of the industrial coefficients suggests that the expenditure impact of such property is negligible.

Although the percent of the variation in the independent variable "explained" by the regressions is higher in the log formulation, such a comparison is meaningless because of the difference in the dependent variables. A more meaningful comparison of adjusted sum of squared residuals, however, provides statistical support for preferring the log form to the linear form of the model.[11]

Expenditure Elasticities by Property Type

Tables 5.3 and 5.4 present expenditure elasticities derived from the equations in tables 5.1 and 5.2. The total elasticity for each type of property (except for equations 5 and 6 of table 5.2) is composed of two parts,

TABLE 5.3
Expenditure Elasticities by Property Type
(equations 1-8, table 5.1)

	Direct	Indirect	Total
Equation 1*			
Commercial	.14	+.05	.19
Industrial	—.08	+.03	—.05
Residential	.17	—.12	.05
Equation 2*			
Commercial	.15	+.05	.20
Industrial	—.05	+.03	—.02
Residential	.17	—.11	.06
Equation 3			
Commercial	.12	+.04	.16
Industrial	—.01	+.02	.01
Residential	.25	—.09	.16
Equation 4			
Commercial	.13	+.03	.16
Industrial	—.01	+.02	.01
Residential	.22	—.08	.15
Equation 5*			
Commercial	.17	+.04	.21
Industrial	—.06	+.03	—.03
Residential	.18	—.10	.08
Equation 6*			
Commercial	.17	+.03	.20
Industrial	—.03	+.02	—.01
Residential	.19	—.08	.11
Equation 7*			
Commercial	.16	+.04	.20
Industrial	—.09	+.03	—.06
Residential	N.A.	N.A.	N.A.
Equation 8*			
Commercial	.17	.04	.21
Industrial	—.06	.03	—.03
Residential	N.A.	N.A.	N.A.

Source: Calculated from Table 5.1.
N.A. signifies not applicable.
*1% difference in CWOR assumed to equal 1% difference in CBASE.
 1% difference in IWOR assumed to equal 1% difference in IBASE.

TABLE 5.4
Expenditure Elasticities by Property Type
(equation 1-6, table 5.2)

	Direct	Indirect	Total
Equation 1*			
Commercial	.12	+.04	.16
Industrial	—.07	+.03	—.04
Residential	.26	—.11	.15
Equation 2*			
Commercial	.12	+.06	.18
Industrial	—.05	+.04	—.01
Residential	.23	—.14	.09
Equation 3*			
Commercial	.15	+.03	.18
Industrial	—.08	+.02	—.06
Residential	N.A.†	N.A.	N.A.
Equation 4*			
Commercial	.14	+.03	.17
Industrial	—.05	+.02	—.03
Residential	N.A.	N.A.	N.A.
Equation 5			
Commercial	.15	0	.15
Industrial	.01	0	.01
Residential	.26	0	.26
Equation 6			
Commercial	.14	0	.14
Industrial	.02	0	.02
Residential	.21	0	.21

Source: Calculated from table 5.2.
N.A. Not applicable.
*1% difference in CWOR assumed to equal 1% difference in CBASE.
 1% difference in IWOR assumed to equal 1% difference in IBASE.

referred to in the table as direct and indirect. The first refers to the impact of each type of property holding the tax price variable (R) constant, and the second to the expenditure impact through the variable R. Using mean values for the relevant variables, 1 percent increases in commercial and industrial property lower R by .105 percent and .071 percent, respectively (thereby raising expenditures), while a 1 percent increase in residential property raises R by .25 percent (thereby reducing expenditures). For simplicity, it is assumed that workers per capita and property values per capita are perfectly correlated for each type of property, so that a 1 percent increase in, say, commercial workers per capita can be translated into a 1 percent increase in commercial property. This facilitates the addition of the components of the expenditure elasticity when the business variables are in employment form.

As can be seen in tables 5.3 and 5.4, the total expenditure elasticity with respect to commercial property ranges across equations from .14 to .21, with the lowest elasticities appearing in equations with no employment variables. For industrial property, the total elasticities are much lower, the range of the point estimates being —.06 to +.02. As noted above, the equations with BLUE or LBLUE yield less negative expenditure elasticities for industrial property and in many equations the point estimates are insignificantly different from zero. Hence, it appears that industrial property has little or no impact on municipal expenditures in contrast to a significant and consistent positive impact for commercial property.

At first glance, the residential property elasticities appear much less consistent across equations. The range is from .05 to .26, with the low estimates being the result of the large negative indirect effects of residential property in the log equations. It should be noted, however, that in calculating the residential property elasticities, family income is assumed to be constant. Since family income and residential property per capita are strongly correlated, allowing income to vary with the residential base will raise the total residential property base expenditure elasticities. Moreover, it will raise them differentially across equations because of the differing estimated income elasticities of demand. Making this income adjustment, the residential property elasticity range for the equations without BLUE or LBLUE is reduced to the range .38 to .47.

Although tables 5.3 and 5.4 are interesting in that they point out the relative insensitivity to the specification of the equation of the expenditure elasticities associated with each type of property, they do not permit meaningful comparisons of expenditure effects across property types. This is because equal percentage differences in the various types of property do not correspond to equal differences in the market value of the total property tax base. Table 5.5 shows the range (across equations) in the municipal expenditure impact (expressed as a percent) associated with differences in each type of property equivalent to a 1 percent difference in the total property tax base. Hence, the figures in the table are expenditure elasticities with respect to the total tax base when the difference in the tax base takes the form of the specified type of property.

The conclusion is clearcut. The nonschool expenditure implications of differences in the per capita property tax base depend heavily on the composition of the base. Not only does the total expenditure elasticity of residential property (especially when adjusted for associated income differ-

TABLE 5.5
Comparable Expenditure Elasticities

Type of property	%difference in expenditures for 1% difference in total tax base[1]
Commercial	1.33 to 2.00
Industrial	—.84 to .28
Residential	.06 to .35
Residential with associated income difference	.51 to .63

Source: Calculated from tables 5.3 and 5.4.

[1] Percent differences for each type of property equivalent to a 1% difference in the total tax base are 1.33% for residential property, 9.52% for commercial property, and 14.08% for industrial property.

ences) differ from the elasticities for both types of nonresidential property, but even more striking is the large difference in the expenditure effects of commercial and industrial property. While the expenditure elasticity associated with commerical property is greater than one, implying that differences in nonschool tax rates are positively associated with differences in commercial property, *ceteris paribus,* the expenditure elasticity with respect to industrial property is negligible or perhaps even negative.

The differing magnitudes of the commercial and industrial property elasticities are reasonable in light of the nonrevenue effects of business property. Since industrial property is likely to be located in industrial parks separated from the rest of the community, while commercial property is located in the center of the community, the externalities effects on resident-related public services caused by congestion are likely to be stronger for commercial property. Moreover, the disamenities associated with industrial property, such as pollution and truck traffic, will reduce the net benefits from business property and hence may make residents less willing to provide services directly to industrial property than to provide them to commercial property.

Assumptions and Limitations

In this section, the underlying assumptions and methodological limitations of the analysis are discussed and evaluated. These include the use of median family income to represent the income of the median voter, two objections to the appropriateness of the tax price variable *R,* and specific data limitations.

Median Family Income and Median Voter

The concept of the median voter requires elaboration.[12] By definition, the public service quantity desired by the median voter is such that one-half the voters prefer a smaller quantity and one-half a larger quantity.

Without knowledge of the individual demand functions for public services, however, the income level of the median voter cannot be determined.

The following justification may be given for the assumption used in the empirical work that the median voter has median family income. Let us assume that all residents in a given community have similar preferences, but that their demand for public services depends positively on their own income and negatively on the tax price they face. If income and property ownership are perfectly correlated, then the use of a proportional property tax implies that the income elasticity of the tax price equals one. This means that high-income families will always demand more public services than low-income families if the following reasonable condition is met: the simple income elasticity of demand exceeds the absolute value of the tax price elasticity of demand for public services.[13] Hence, if this condition is met, the quantity of public services demanded will be a monotone function of income, implying that the median quantity demanded will be that of the voter with median income.

With a more complicated actual or perceived tax structure caused, for example, by uncertainty about who bears the tax on rental property, or with differing tastes among subgroups of the population, the argument that quantity demanded within each community is a monotone function of income is less likely to hold. Fortunately, however, recent theoretical work has shown that use of median family income is still legitimate provided that income distributions across communities meet certain regularity assumptions.[14]

Use of R to Represent Tax Price of Public Services

Two objections may be raised about the appropriateness of using R, the fraction of the tax base that is residential, to represent the tax price of public services.

First, it may be argued that the percent of the tax base that is residential is an underestimate of the true long-run price as perceived by resident voters, since residents take the perceived supply elasticity of firms into consideration when making current period expenditure decisions. Specifically, the fear that firms will leave the community in response to higher tax liabilities uncompensated by higher business-related services may temper the demand of residents for resident-related services relative to the situation in which residents believe firms to be immobile. Although factors such as availability of sites, quality of labor, material costs, and proximity to market probably outweigh fiscal considerations in interstate or interregional location decisions, the importance of fiscal considerations as a significant determinant of intrametropolitan location decisions should not be ignored.

Unfortunately, little is known about the responsiveness of firms to intra-metropolitan fiscal differentials, and even less is known about residents' perceptions of this responsiveness.[15] The model as estimated, however, still yields valid results, provided that there is a constant relationship across communities between the true long-run tax price as perceived by residents and the fraction of the tax base that is residential. Further research investigating the validity of this assumption would be desirable but is beyond the scope of this chapter.[16]

The implications of one departure from this assumption should be noted. Suppose that it is generally believed that expenditure and tax rate differentials across communities affect industrial location decisions but not commercial decisions. Then R is an unbiased measure of the tax price if commerical property is the only type of nonresidential property, but is an underestimate of the true perceived tax price if industrial property is involved. Hence, the estimated tax price elasticity would overstate the tax revenue impact of industrial property.

A second difficulty with the tax price interpretation of R is that it ignores the possible interaction between services provided strictly for business and the tax price faced by residents for resident-related services. If the level of services provided to business depends only on the characteristics of the business property and, hence, is independent of the level of services provided to residents, then the tax price interpretation of R as discussed above on p. 76 is still valid when the model is extended to include services to business.

If, on the other hand, the level of services provided per dollar of business property depends exclusively on the desired level of resident-related services per dollar of residential property, then the relevant tax price faced by resident decision-makers no longer depends on the composition of the property tax base.[17] The variable R will still affect total expenditures per capita, however, since the model becomes

$$E_T = \frac{1}{R} S_R C$$

where

E_T = expenditures on resident-related and business services per capita
S_R = quantity demanded of resident-related services per capita
C = resource cost of public goods
R = fraction of the tax base that is residential

Thus, R should still appear in the expenditure regression but with a different interpretation. In the log form of the equation, this assumption about business services implies that the coefficient of log R should be —1. As can be seen from table 5.1, the data does not support this interpretation, since the coefficient of log R is significantly different from —1 in all equations.

Use of State Tax Commission Ratios

A potentially significant limitation of this study is the use of State Tax Commission official assessment sales ratios to adjust assessed property values to market values. This implicitly assumes that all types of property within each community are assessed on the average at the same ratio to market value and that the State Tax Commission estimates are reliable.[18] Independent estimates of assessment sales ratios on single-family homes for a small sample of Boston communities suggest that the official figures may involve substantial error.[19] It should be noted, however, that it is the correlation of the equalized market values with the true market values that is relevant here rather than the absolute error of the official estimates. Moreover, the expenditure elasticities in tables 5.1 and 5.2 for different types of property are quite insensitive to the use of worker or property value variables, thereby giving tentative support to the hypothesis that the errors in the official estimates are random.

Implications for Local Fiscal Capacity

The purpose of this section is to relate the empirical findings of the second section to the policy issue of defining and measuring the fiscal capacity of local areas. The simplest view is that the total property tax base is the appropriate measure of the fiscal capacity of those local government jurisdictions that rely exclusively on property tax revenue. Some researchers have argued, however, that in the calculation of local fiscal capacity, different types of property should be weighted according to how, on the average, they affect a community's spending on local public services.[20] If this view is accepted, then, using the average of the expenditure elasticity ranges presented in table 5.5, this study suggests that industrial property should be given a zero weight and commercial property a weight of from three to six times that of residential property, the variation depending on whether one includes in the residential elasticity the expenditure effects caused by associated income differences. A major difficulty with this type of an approach to fiscal capacity measurement is that it fails to separate fiscal needs from fiscal capacity.

An alternative position is that the weights for the components of the tax base should reflect average spending differences associated with ability to pay or revenue effects alone rather than with total effects which include taste or need considerations. If no services are provided directly to business, then it is conceptually easy to separate the fiscal capacity effects defined in this way from the other effects of nonresidential property. Specifically, if the individualistic decision-making approach used here is valid, all capacity effects of nonresidential property would operate through the tax price term.

The separability of effects necessary to implement this concept of fiscal capacity becomes clouded when services to business are introduced. For example, provision of services to business may have a negative income impact on the demand for resident-related services. Moreover, if additional services must be provided to keep business from leaving the community, then the separation of tax base effects from other expenditure effects becomes fuzzy.

Putting aside these conceptual issues by assuming as a first approximation that ability to pay or revenue capacity effects of business property operate exclusively through the tax price term, what do the empirical results imply about the appropriate weights for the components of the tax base if this alternative approach to fiscal capacity measurement is accepted? To use this approach, a good estimate of the tax price elasticity of demand is necessary. As can be seen in table 5.1, the tax price elasticity in the log form of the equations ranges from —.30 to —.49. The variation is even greater in the linear form (in which the tax price term appears non-linearly). Since the estimated elasticity varies with both the form of the equation and with the included variables, the tentative nature of the following results should be emphasized.

Given the statistical superiority of the log equations, the ability-to-pay effects of the different types of property have been calculated on the basis of equations 2 and 6 of table 5.1. Equation 2 includes no commercial and industrial property value variables directly and consequently may result in an upward-biased estimate of the tax price effects of business property. Equation 6, on the other hand, includes both property value and worker variables and consequently may understate the tax price effects of business property.

The calculated ability-to-pay expenditure effects of a 1 percent difference in the tax base for the three major types of property are presented in table 5.6. It should be noted that the estimate for the effect of residential property includes the effect of associated income differences across communities. The results in table 5.6 suggest that business property on the average adds less to a community's ability to finance nonschool public expenditures than does residential property and hence should receive a lower weight in the measurement of fiscal capacity available for public services than does residential property. This result, in connection with the large

TABLE 5.6
Ability-to-Pay Effects of a 1% Difference in the Total Tax Base

Type of property	% difference in expenditures
Equation 2, table 5.1	
Commercial	.44
Industrial	.44
Residential (including associated income differences)	.50
Equation 6, table 5.1	
Commercial	.32
Industrial	.32
Residential (including associated income differences)	.56

total expenditure impact of commercial property which reflects need as well as fiscal capacity effects, suggests that communities with large amounts of commercial property have a fiscal disadvantage compared to other communities.[21]

Data Sources

Expenditure data were derived from Schedule A forms sent to the Massachusetts Bureau of Local Accounts by towns and cities for the year 1970. Although nominally required by law, completed forms were available for only fifty out of a total of seventy-eight communities in the Boston SMSA.

Tax base variables were calculated from data provided by the Massachusetts State Tax Commission, Department of Local Assessing. The percent breakdown of the assessed base is derived from estimates made by that office in consultation with local assessors. The original estimates treated rental property with four or more units as commercial property. The estimates were adjusted for this study to include all rental property as residential property. Official Massachusetts State Tax Commission estimates of assessment sales ratios were used to convert assessed values to market values.

Employment data by place of work are from 1970 computer printouts, Division of Employment Security, Commonwealth of Massachusetts.

Socio-economic variables are from either *1970 Census of Population* or *1970 Census of Housing.*

Notes

1   One major exception is found in Harvey E. Brazer et al., *Fiscal Needs and Resources: A Report to the New York State Commission on the Quality, Cost, and Financing of Elementary and Secondary Education.* Draft, November 1971.

2   The justification for this assumption is that it simplifies the exposition. It is not necessary to the basic argument, however. See footnote 6 below.

3   A good example of the political approach to local public expenditures can be found in Otto A. Davis and George H. Haines, Jr., "A Political Approach to a Theory of Public Expenditure: The Case of Municipalities," *National Tax Journal*, 19 (no. 3, September, 1966), 259-75.

4   Moreover, it realistically assumes that assessment/sales ratios for business will not be altered in response to expenditure changes. If they were, then, in the absence of direct expenditure demands of business, there would be a maximum amount of revenue that could be derived from nonresidential property that would depend on the elasticity of the business tax base with respect to the assessment/sales ratio. For a discussion and rejection of this alternative model, see Noel M. Edelson, "Efficiency Aspects of Local School Finance," *Journal of Political Economy*, January/February 1973.

5   This statement is correct, provided that no services are provided directly to business. See p. 92 for the tax price implications of business related services.

6   The model can be generalized to include the public good aspect of publicly provided services. Let the services received per family (S) be expressed as G/N^α where G is the total quantity of resident-related public services provided, N is the population, and α is a congestion coefficient that ranges from 0 (pure public good case) to 1 (private good case). Then total expenditures $E = G \cdot C = SN^\alpha C$ where C is the resource cost per unit of G. Rewriting $SN^\alpha C$ as $S \cdot N \cdot C \, 1/N^{1-\alpha}$ it is readily seen that the price of services received per family includes the additional term $1/N^{1-\alpha}$. Hence, in the pure public good case, the larger the population the lower the tax price. In two recent empirical studies using this type of a model, the hypothesis that $\alpha = 1$ could not be rejected for most expenditure categories. See T. E. Borcherding and R. T. Deacon, "The Demand for the Services of Non-Federal Governments," *American Economic Review*, 62 (no. 5, December 1972), 891-902, and T. C. Bergstrom and R. P. Goodman, "Private Demands for Public Goods," *American Economic Review*, 63 (no. 3, June 1973), 280-97.

7   The expression is

$$
\frac{dS}{dB} = \frac{-\dfrac{\partial^2 U}{\partial P^2}\dfrac{\partial P}{\partial B}\dfrac{\partial P}{\partial S} - \dfrac{\partial U}{\partial P}\dfrac{\partial^2 P}{\partial S \partial B} + P_s\dfrac{\partial^2 U}{\partial X \partial P}\dfrac{\partial P}{\partial B}}{\dfrac{\partial^2 U}{\partial P^2}\left(\dfrac{\partial P}{\partial S}\right)^2 + \dfrac{\partial U}{\partial P}\dfrac{\partial^2 P}{\partial S^2} - 2P_s\dfrac{\partial^2 U}{\partial X \partial P}\dfrac{\partial P}{\partial S} + P_s^2\dfrac{\partial^2 U}{\partial X^2}}
$$

8   The logical extension of this argument is that if the perceived net benefits from certain types of business property are less than zero then those types of property will be zoned out of the community.

9   For data sources, see the appendix to this chapter.

10 The absence of a variable representing the tax price effects of the distribution of residential property is justified if the distribution of housing ownership is constant across communities. A variable of this sort was constructed and found to have very little variation across communities. See Helen F. Ladd, "Local Public Expenditures and the Composition of the Property Tax Base," Appendix (Ph.D. dissertation, Harvard University, 1974).

11 This test involves adjusting the sum of squares of residuals from the linear equation by multiplying by the square of the inverse of the geometric mean of the dependent variable. See Potluri Rao and Roger LeRoy Miller, *Applied Econometrics* (Belmont, California: Wadsworth Publishing Company, 1971), pp. 107-11.

12 It can be shown that as long as preferences are single-peaked, the budget preferred by the median voter is the only budget that will get at least a majority of the votes when paired against any other budget. See Duncan Black, "On the Rationale of Group Decision-Making," *Journal of Political Economy*, 56 (February 1948), 23-34.

13 Specifically, the total income elasticity of demand for services across individuals within any one community is $\eta_S \cdot Y + \eta_S \cdot R \cdot \eta_R \cdot Y$ where $\eta_S \cdot Y$ is the partial income elasticity of the demand for services, $\eta_S \cdot R$ is the tax price elasticity of demand and $\eta_R \cdot Y$ is the elasticity of the tax price with respect to income differences. If $\eta_R \cdot Y = 1$, this yields the statement in the text.

14 See Bergstrom and Goodman, "Private Demands for Public Goods."

15 For an excellent review of the literature through 1961, see John F. Due, "Studies of State-Local Tax Influences on Location of Industry," *National Tax Journal*, 14 (June 1961), 163-73. Although there is not much direct evidence of the influence of tax factors on intrametropolitan location decisions, the finding of a recent NBER study that there was substantial movement of industry within the New York metropolitan region during a short period of time leaves substantial leeway for the hypothesis that some of the new location or expansion decisions were affected by fiscal factors. See Robert A. Leone, "Location of Manufacturing Activity in the New York Metropolitan Area," NBER, 1973.

16 For an empirical investigation of this assumption in the context of local education expenditures, see Helen F. Ladd, "Local Public Expenditures and the Composition of the Property Tax Base" (Ph.D. dissertation, Harvard University, 1974).

17 The business expenditure assumption, in this case, is: $S_B = S_R \cdot NR/R$ where S_B is services to business expressed per family, S_R is services to residents per family, NR is the nonresidential fraction of the base and R is the residential fraction. Hence, total expenditures are $S_R \cdot N \cdot C + S_R \cdot N \cdot C \cdot NR/R$ where N is number of families and C is the resource cost of public goods. Substituting this expression for the numerator of the tax rate in the maximization model on p. 75 yields the conclusion that the tax price is independent of the composition of the tax base.

18 Although data on assessment sales ratios by type of property are now in my possession, the adjustments necessary to make it usable have not yet been performed. In the meantime use of the official estimates must suffice.

19 See Daniel L. Rubenfeld, "Property Taxation, Full Valuation and the Reform of Education Finance in Massachusetts," Richard W. Lindholm, ed., *Property Taxation and the Finance of Education* (Madison, Wis.: University of Wisconsin Press, 1974).

20   In its 1971 study of state fiscal capacity available for state and local govern-
     ment expenditures, the ACIR takes the composition of the property tax base
     into consideration by using national average effective tax rates for each type
     of property as the appropriate weights. See Advisory Commission on Inter-
     governmental Relations, *Measuring the Fiscal Capacity of State and Local
     Areas* (Washington, D.C.: USGPO, March 1971). In a recent New York
     fiscal capacity study oriented specifically toward local fiscal capacity, a
     weighting scheme based on the coefficients of a regression of total local ex-
     penditures on income and the components of the tax base is employed. See
     H. Brazer et al., *Fiscal Needs and Resources.*
21   This conclusion should be interpreted with care. It does not necessarily mean
     that residents in communities with large amounts of commerical property are
     worse off than those in other communities. It is conceivable that local nonfiscal
     benefits from such property might outweigh the fiscal costs.

6 *Mason Gaffney*

Toward Full Employment with Limited Land and Capital

Capital is kept in existence from age to age not by preservation,
but by perpetual reproduction.—J. S. Mill

The Paradox of Surplus Labor, Shortages, and Inflation

"Though custom has dulled us to it, it *is* a strange and unnatural thing
that men who wish to labor, in order to satisfy their wants, cannot find the
opportunity." "There can be no real scarcity of work . . . until human
wants are all satisfied." Today, nearly a century after Henry George wrote
that, and with nearly 40 years of the New Economics, we are right back at
square one. Federal fiscal and monetary policies prove powerless to soak
up surplus labor, even while creating two-digit inflation. Prominent economists seem confused and helpless faced with the most basic malfunction
of the system, that is, shortness of work along with short supplies and
soaring prices, and we are at once overwhelmed and diverted by the spawn
of derivative evils. Why cannot these idle persons find work to fill those
shortages? If economics cannot solve this elementary but stubborn riddle,
it is not good for much.

Nor is a job what it used to be. United States wage rates have lost
ground since 1960 compared to many countries,[1] even as we who used to
soak up displaced world labor have reached out to control and exploit raw
materials of others.

At the same time, the other sinews of production, capital and land, are
growing short, and very dear. Materials prices are high, even though the
social cost of primary products is higher than the price because of massive

Research support from Resources for the Future is gratefully acknowledged.

tax benefits and other subsidies. The required complement or duty of land and capital per worker and consumer has risen sharply for many years, much faster than the work force. So now we are bumping into the ineluctable logic that if we require a vast complement of resources per worker, and require jobs for all, we will chew up lots of resources, and push on the limits of Earth. We will push up materials prices; we will pollute the environment; and we will provoke our neighbors by coveting their raw materials. We will push on the limits of our capital supply, too, unless it grows faster than it has been.

If we look to science and innovation to help us, these are mainly harnessed to the goals of saving labor, and using more land and capital to do it. Some, indeed, have revived the themes of Ned Ludd, John Henry, and Karel Kapek, and blamed unemployment fatalistically on science and innovation out of human control. While this vogue has happily abated for the nonce, it is true enough that Science has been in the saddle for a long time without meeting the present problem.

Along with short work we face a swelling array of derivative evils: crime, alienation and counter-culture, protracted apprenticeship periods, soaring welfare and dependency, frustration of idle housewives, forced early retirement, geriatric ghettos, imperialism to make jobs and acquire raw materials, weapons constituencies, other pork-barreling, glorification of waste, slowdowns, featherbedding, fear of change, stunting of creativity through grasping for tenure, seniority, and security, suppression of competition, exclusionary local codes and zoning, loss of flexibility and mobility, and rejection of the free market. All these evils have their independent roots, but are inflated by unemployment and the fear of it.

Some unemployment is iatrogenic; that is, caused by the doctor. Critics of welfare point out how welfare payments have boomed into a cause of unemployment. Since work shortage also serves to rationalize welfare, we have a vicious circle. But there is little doubt which came first, nor is there much doubt that we can solve the problem humanely only by opening more jobs, regardless of the direction of welfare reform.

Each of the derivative evils, like welfare, could be a study in itself. Yet until we face the elemental riddle at the fountainhead of all this trouble, each such study only diverts us from meeting the ultimate challenge for economists that George defined in 1879.

The failure of fiscal and monetary policy, in which we once had such faith that we talked of "fine-tuning," is by now so notorious we can merely postulate it as a premise. The New Economics foundered as it steered between the shoals of inflation and the rocks of unemployment and ran onto both at once. The New Economics taught that that would not happen. "Fiscal Policy and Full Employment Without Inflation" was Samuelson's promise[2] in 1955, and the world believed it. He wrote of the new "mastery of the modern analysis of income determination," and of the "momentous Employment Act of 1946 . . . to fight mass unemployment and inflation." Inflation could result mainly only from "overful employment."[3] All that has turned to ashes in the crucible of 15 percent inflation.

And yet the New Economics is what taught the generation now in command, and economists of influence seem capable of little but following Pavlovian responses learned in school twenty years ago: in a word, that the way to make jobs is to recycle money faster. Most of what we call macroeconomics today is an embroidery on that one simple theme, the simplicity hidden beneath elegant variations and elaborate circumlocutions that dazzle and boggle and addle without adding much substance.

The New Economics, when new, was positive and optimistic, and promised a lot. There were free lunches in those days—when you put the idle to work, there *is* such a thing. The Puritan ethic was the goat, obsolete and absurd, dour and dismal. But now the New Economics has become a New Dismal Science, a science of choice where all the choices are bad. "One must face up to the bitter truth that only so long as the economy is depressed are we likely to be free of inflation" (Samuelson, 1970).[4] "No one in the world has a recipe for correcting our price performance without some unfortunate increase in unemployment. . . . [the public] should be told the facts of life" (Arthur Okun, 1970).[5] This is not bread, but a stone.

Conservatives are not offering more. ". . . there is no other way to stop inflation. There has to be some unemployment. . . . It is a fact of life" (Milton Friedman, 1970).[6] "The election will show whether the American people are mature enough to accept a sustainable (low) level of activity" (Henry Wallich, 1970).[7] ". . . this economy can no longer stand a real boom with low levels of unemployment without kicking off a rampant inflationary spiral" (Alan Greenspan, 1972).[8] Thus it seems that conservatives unite with liberals in seeing the choice as a trade-off on a Phillips Curve, and differ mainly in preferring to disemploy more and inflate less. There is little challenge to the conceptual framework. Controlling spending is where it's all at.

Monetarists debate Keynesians over the most effective way to regulate spending, and are more disposed to favor less of it, and recognize other constrains. Yet neither side much deviates from the premise that spending money is the governor of the economy, the autonomous force which other activity obeys, the key of control. "The collective intelligence of the economics profession is unable to fundamentally restructure the intellectual substance of the field. . . . We have a theoretical apparatus that can be used for a wide variety of things. There is no other way, and I do not think we know how to find one (Otto Eckstein, 1974).[9]

Yet, along with the policy failures, there are intellectual substances and theoretical apparati one can identify which are clearly wrong, and must interfere with any effort to make jobs. Modern macroeconomics evolved under a different set of problems than we face today, and its founders built into its vitals a number of special premises and limitations. It is geared to assume no or few resource constraints, and has little response for the new challenges of environment, scarce raw materials, and anti-growthmanship. "Growth," indeed, is one of its ideals, and simply to make jobs in a stable equilibrium independent of growth is outside its purview. Geared to approve waste, it has nothing for emerging needs to conserve scarce resources. Geared to define the economic problem as how to dispose of surpluses, it ill becomes a world of excess demand and short supplies. Geared to treat capital as a glut, and the central economic problem as how to dispose of excess saving, it is at a loss with high interest rates and capital shortage.

The falling rate of profit is built into the apparatus, and Samuelson is still disputing that capital is really short.[10] Geared to treat both resources and capital as cheap, it all too easily lets labor be treated as the only cost of production worth mentioning—a new labor theory of value—ignores distribution, and plays into the hands of antilabor interests by picturing the economic scene as a continuous "wage-price spiral." It ignores the possibilities of substituting labor for land and capital. Geared to idealize federal spending, it drifts easily into mercantilism and imperialism, especially in the more idealistic, missionary faces of AID and "economic development." Geared to accept and live with concentration of wealth and economic power, it has little to say about the effects of industrial mergers in substituting capital for labor by putting plants on standby and laying off workers. It has no basis for not condoning the monumental waste of capital in urban sprawl, or the global sprawl of imperialism, because each inflated need is an investment outlet. On the contrary, continuous territorial expansion and development are its answers to the limited land supply.

In the apparatus of modern macroeconomics, it is built in that the best way to recycle stagnant money is to find investment outlets. Since the rate of profit is always threatening to push zero, such outlets are to be cherished, and we should subsidize and force-feed investment if needed, as by loans at low interest, to keep money recycling. If we stack up layers of capital at low productivity, that is no problem. Seminal investments like roads and water supplies that open new lands are best of all, for they induce ancillary investments which recycle yet more stagnant money. Boondoggling is all right because it makes jobs, and if it soaks up a disproportionate quota of capital per job, that helps dispose of excess saving.

The result of this attitude has been to let a thousand policies bloom which foster substituting capital for labor. This finds support from some other errors or half-truths left over from the old economics which die very hard.

One of these is to define "efficiency" as output per worker. Only very recently, with the birth of the concept of total factor productivity, and the new emphasis on energy-efficiency, are most economists beginning to escape this perverse concept with its built-in bias against use of labor.

Substituting capital and land for labor raises "efficiency," so conceived, only by wasting capital and land, and is only efficient in unrealistic models in which land and capital are underpriced or ignored. High labor-efficiency then means low land-efficiency and low capital-efficiency, either directly or at one remove in the form of low energy-efficiency, low water-efficiency, low feed-grain efficiency, etc.

Misled by this concept, we have exulted in high output per man as a symbol and measure of national and company "productivity," and accepted an extreme substitution of capital and resources for labor. The well-known displacement of farm labor is not an exception but more like the rule. John Kendrick calculated that the ratio of capital to labor for a large group of industries in the United States rose at an average annual rate of 1.3 percent from 1899 to 1953.[11] That means a 100 percent increase over that fifty-four-year period. More recently, the United States Department of Commerce studied nonfinancial corporations, 1948-1971. It found capital inputs growing at 4 percent yearly compounded and labor at 1.2 percent.[12] That means there was 2.5 times as much capital in 1971 with 1.3 times as much labor, which is 1.9 times as much capital per worker in 1971. Thus the rate of substitution seems to be increasing.

And that's not really the half of it. These studies omitted the public sector, the infrastructure into which we have poured so much public treasure at low interest rates. They omitted housing, which soaks up so much capital per job created. They omitted the recreation boom, which requires so much more land and equipment per consumer hour, and per measure of personal joy, than the quiet pleasures of yesteryear. And they omit the swing of consumers toward goods and services like electric power and natural gas, whose production is capital-intensive and whose prices fall relative to labor-intensive products when the capital input is subsidized.

Producers also use much more of these as inputs. A primary metal like aluminum will consume 135 kwh per dollar of value-added, compared to 10-20 in a normal manufacturing operation. It is energy-inefficient and thrives only on underpriced energy, thanks to which it is cheap relative to competing materials. For years we have been substituting energy for labor and calling it progress and efficiency, only to find that energy is scarce and labor surplus. A comprehensive accounting of our lavish input of capital and land per worker would reverse the common stereotype that labor invented featherbedding.

The second supporting ancient half-truth is that capital cannot really displace labor, in a vertically integrated whole economy, because labor produces capital anyway. This is the counterpart of the modern macro-economist's concept that investment employs labor. Either way you perceive it, the meaning is that benefits to capital are passed through to labor.

That is a half-truth, and the untrue half has helped lead us into our present crisis. The problem is that capital can substitute for labor. It is a problem that neo-Georgists, in their zeal to untax capital, have overlooked as well.

Keynesians and Georgists have this in common. Keynesians say investment creates jobs and Georgists say labor produces capital. Keynesians would subsidize investment and Georgists would untax capital. Many Keynesians would untax or downtax the income from capital, too, Keynesians focusing on the income tax and Georgists on the property tax. The investment tax credit, expensing of capital investments, accelerated depreciation and exempting imputed income of homeowners are the income tax counterparts of exempting buildings from the property tax. Jack Stockfisch had the insight to point out years ago that these Keynesian inducements to invest were Georgist ideals applied to the income tax.[13] Both schools share the idea that benefits to capital are benefits to labor.

But a great deal of the cash and service flow from capital imputes to capital as such, as interest. The longer the life of the capital item, generally, the larger share that is. A great deal of interest is internalized and invisible, hence too easily overlooked and forgotten. But a couple of simple examples should make the point.

When one buys a durable good on the installment plan, if the payments stretch out beyond fifteen or so years more than half the total is interest. Just how many years depends on the interest rate and the term, but at say 10 percent over a twenty-year term the yearly payment required is 11.7 percent of the principal. Twenty times 11.7 percent is 2.34. Since the principal is one, the interest is 1.34. So, 1.34/2.34 or 57 percent of the payments are interest.

Thus the cost of a mortgaged house, or a debt-financed highway, or a debt-financed war can be mainly interest. But even if these are not debt-financed, they cost interest—the interest foregone on the equity capital.[14] A house thus "financed" over sixty years at 10 percent requires yearly level payments of 10.03 percent of the principal. Sixty times 10.03 percent is 6.02, so 5.02/6.02 or 83 percent of the payments are interest. Accordingly, it is understandable that housing starts are more sensitive to financing than to any other cost.

But note now how little of the salable service flow is produced by labor. It would only be (100 — 83) percent or 17 percent even if the entire construction bill were for payroll. In fact, of course, onsite labor is only 20 percent or so of construction cost. Materials like lumber take another big chunk. But lumber comes from trees which take decades to grow. One dollar invested in forest regeneration must double every 7.2 years to yield 10 percent, so if lumber comes from second-growth cut at age 9 x 7.2 or 65, stumpage of 2^9 of $512 embodies $1 of planting labor and $511 of compound interest. Of course harvesting, hauling, milling, and selling apply more labor to add value, so lumber value embodies a higher share of labor value than timber alone. Still, timber is a splendid second example of capital-intensity where it is largely capital, and not labor, that produces capital.

Timber growth is a good example of "passive investment." It is internally financed in the most literal way. Each year's growth is a product, an income to the owner, which he automatically invests in growing stock, adding to capital. But this investment employs no labor. It only employs capital and land, that is, growing stock and site. Mature timber, finally, has not been produced by labor so much as by capital—the young growing stock—and land.

Preferential tax treatment for timber, then, is a good way to make work for capital but a bad way for labor. Capital-gains treatment of timber sales, expensing of interest and property taxes, and preferential low property-tax rates and assessments for timber tie up capital in the slowest of cycles and fence off land from labor, except once a century or so when the crop is cut. The job-creating efficiency of capital frozen this way is very low.

A third ancient error is that it takes a fixed quota of capital to "create" a job, visualized as a kind of niche made of capital in which we place one worker. The weekly ads of Warren and Swasey pound this theme recurrently, and Norman Ture, writing for the National Association of Manufacturers, has dignified it with an economist's formality.[15] If the premise were true, of course, then the way to make jobs is to create capital, case closed. But in fact, factor mix varies over a wide range, and policies which are more certain to raise capital needs than capital formation are not a way to make jobs. Capital is capable of complementing labor, but the extent to which it actually does so depends entirely on how it is invested and used, and cannot be assumed. The value of capital to labor depends on how active the capital is. Looking ahead, we will see that each time capital is recovered and reinvested it can recombine with and reactivate labor. But torpid capital, like that in trees, and many public works, and premature exploration, and so on is withdrawn from abetting labor. It may preempt land as well, just as the landlords' sheep did in sixteenth-century England.

In the growth models of and following Harrod and Domar, New Economists have been quite comfortable with assumed constant ratios of capital to output. Growth was linked closely with capital formation. This harmonized nicely with the Warner and Swasey assumption. It all served to reconcile the Marxist streak in the New Economists with the puritanism of capitalists. The New Economists viewed growth as an escape from the doom of oversaving; the capitalists saw it as their social duty, which rationalized and helped aggrandize their functions, prerogatives, incomes, wealth, and status. It has been a curious but powerful partnership, hardly challenged until it brought us double-digit inflation.

It has had to exclude, however, from its intellectual substance and theoretical apparatus the good news buried in a few obscure pages of Wicksell,[16] that capital can increase its "valence" (to borrow a chemical term) for labor easily, and combine with more or less, in response to relative prices. We may not need to find a new theory, but resurrect one.

Like any entrenched system, the New Economics was unassailable when things went tolerably well, regardless of its merits. Now that its single-minded preoccupation with purchasing power as the job-maker is inflicting us with intolerable inflation, and failing to make jobs, it is time to review and reconstruct. The New Economics has grown old, and become a terminal case. It had to break down because it was superficially based. The suffering is not welcome, but the opportunity for review is.

Faced with a surplus of labor and a shortage of land and capital, an obvious way to adapt is to substitute labor for land and capital, at the margins of course, making all processes more labor-using. Thus we would increase the use of labor without pushing on the limits of Earth, without invading others' land, and without needing more capital.

It is not a question of stopping growth. There is no need to divide into factions for and against growth. We can grow by combining more labor with the same land and capital. It is simply a matter of modifying processes and products and consumption.[17] Each time the capital recycles it can embody new techniques as well. Growth of capital is not needed for progress; turnover is. And since one way to substitute labor for capital is to turn over capital faster, this also accelerates embodiment of new knowledge in real capital.

This study develops a thesis that we can employ ourselves as fully as we wish without any of the unpleasantness we now suffer in the name of jobs: without inflating, without borrowing, without fighting, without polluting, without any compulsion to "grow," "develop" and expand, without wasting, without price and wage controls, without invading more wilderness, without impoverishing posterity, without socializing labor or capital, without *dirigisme,* without giving up freedom, and without overspilling our national boundaries. Economic policy can offer better than dismal choices.

The problem is too much displacement of labor. It is "too much" because it results from biased institutions, a large set of them, operating over many years, which artificially induce substituting land and capital for labor. The way to solve the problem is to identify and remove the biases. This will increase demand for labor without requiring any more resources or capital.

No special rate of growth is required. We simply need to grow (or even not grow) in such a way as to combine each worker with less land and capital than now; to run with a leaner mixture of wealth, richer of labor.

There is no need to go any further and reverse the bias in favor of labor. The operation of a free market with flexible prices to serve as equilibrators should do the job. The idea is to make jobs not by waste but in the process of mixing inputs more efficiently. This is the very sort of thing that a flexible economy can do. Just as the United States could retool for war quickly in 1942, given the will, now we can retool for new jobs quickly given the will, the freedom, and a certain know-how in framing public policy.

We will also see that substituting labor for capital, "structural" change in another world from macroeconomics, refuses to stay in that pigeonhole. It entails faster recovering of capital, and faster ripening of capital into final goods. The first increases the rate of reinvestment; the second the flow of consumer goods. Thus the "structural" substitution is a macroeconomic effect of the most central kind.

Let us ask how those matters fit into the concerns of the Committee on Taxation, Resources and Economic Development and of those of other neo-Georgists. One set of institutional biases against labor is in tax policy—and I am limiting this paper to that set. These taxes affect the way we develop resources. In its founding articles the committee expresses a concern for how land taxation affects employment. It has focused on other aspects of its work, which was desirable to build a base of expertise, but is all the more reason for compensating now and building on that base to achieve the original, more ambitious goals.

The original high interest in land taxation as expounded by Henry George has never been matched since. George did not write primarily on municipal finance, important as that is. The problem he posed was more cosmic and gripping, the association of poverty with progress; of "industrial depression; of labor condemned to involuntary idleness; . . ." That is, George addressed the same problems as Keynes and the New Economists.

He said these resulted from an artificial scarcity of land. Like Keynes, he thought positively. He did not hand us another dismal iron law of inevitable suffering. He pointed to a solution—we could thaw the frozen land, the passive factor, by taxing it, and employ labor, the active factor, by untaxing activity and labor and its products, that is, capital. He said there was no limit in a truly free economy on jobs, other than human desires for the fruits of work. This theme commanded attention because that was *the* problem needing solving, even as today. In the more evolved lexicon of modern economics we would say he favored "changing factor proportions" or "substituting labor for land," but that would not change the substance or the importance.

Again like the New Economists, George was weak on capital theory. He ran labor and capital together, seeing their interest as one and set off against landowners'. He overlooked the substitutability of capital for labor, that which looms so large in Austrian School economics. Keynes and George alike treated the Austrians as their natural enemies, an unfortunate and needless impoverishment of their respective philosophies.

The oversight in George was not so serious, because he wanted to untax labor, not just capital. The oversight by neo-Georgists is serious, because their emphasis has been largely on untaxing capital. But if we untax capital and continue to tax payrolls, we stack the cards against labor, we bias the system to substitute capital for labor.

It *is* important, as George said, to use more workers per unit of land and primary products. It is also important, as he did not say and we are in danger of overlooking, to use more workers per unit of capital. To support that thesis, I have four points in what follows:

A. Factor mixes vary over a wide range and are by inference sensitive to relative costs and other stimuli like tax bias.
B. Tax bias force-feeds land and capital into the production mix but militates against labor.
C. Demand for capital is not a sufficient or even necessary condition to make jobs. It often helps, but there is a trade-off in the factor mix between labor and capital. We must distinguish among investment outlets and find policies to guide investment into more labor-using ones.
D. Using labor for capital means recovering and replacing capital oftener, which increases aggregate demand for labor, as well as the flow of consumable goods and services so long as there is surplus labor to employ. It increases the *flow* of gross investment associated with any given *fund* of capital.

Based on that analysis we can then see how to invest so as to put capital where the jobs are, to invest so that the "job-creating efficiency," if you will, of capital and land is higher—not a maximum, but an optimum where idleness is only voluntary and the amount of capital suffices that people save voluntarily. And we can finally mention wnat tax policies would serve to remove the present bias.

A. Factor Mix Is Sensitive to Factor Prices

We can make more jobs by using more workers (W) per unit of land (L) and capital (K). That this is feasible is suggested by showing that the mix of factors already ranges widely, that some employers already mix enough workers with their land and capital to employ everyone if only most other employers were moved to act a little more like them. That which needs doing is already being done, it just needs to be done more. We will identify some of the kinds of firms and employments that use more labor in the mix, i.e., a high $W/(L + K)$. Then we can see how to stop penalizing them, and get more like them.

The goal is not to make work for its own sake. Where the "job-creating efficiency" of wealth is higher, the goods-creating efficiency is higher, too. We will show that one can produce many times more from the same land by applying more labor, and without wasting labor.

The most ancient, basic and self-evident of economic relationships is that between land and opportunity. Tribes and nations have warred over control of rich and strategic land, and we are still at it. But more perceptive observers, of whom few could match Adam Smith, have noted that the value of the resources to labor depends on how actively the owners use it. "In plenty of good land the English colonies of North America . . . are . . . inferior to those of the Spaniards and Portuguese. . . . But the political institutions of the English colonies have been more favorable to the improvement and cultivation of this land. . . . First, the engrossing of uncultivated land . . . has been more restrained in the English colonies than in any other. . . . The plenty and cheapness of good land . . . are the principal causes of the rapid prosperity of new colonies. The engrossing of land, in effect, destroys this plenty and cheapness. The engrossing of uncultivated land, besides, is the greatest obstruction to its improvement."[18]

Henry George gave this theme center stage in his philosophy, attributing unemployment to speculative withholding of some land from use. Labor needed access to land. It had access to some lands, but these were oases in the speculative desert. Today we call this "urban sprawl" or "scatteration," essentially a condition of extremely different intensities of use on neighboring lands, and a common one as we know. Smith and George wrote in black and white contrasts. More generally, land is fallow, "engrossed," or "held in speculation" by degrees, and in this sense sprawl and scatter are the universal condition.

Economists seem well aware that factors blend and mix in a range of ratios. The principle of variable proportions is well preserved by text writers, if only in formaldehyde. It lives when economists criticize engineers for taking a fixed "requirements" approach to the alleged "need" for some input like water or power by firms or consumers. Economists speak of tradeoffs, choices, and substitution in response to prices and incentives. They publish data on changes over time, as that cited above, (although regrettably one reads twenty times of declining capital to output ratios for once of rising capital to worker ratios). They note the contrast among nations and regions resulting from different relative prices: more labor per log in European than Canadian sawmills; more labor per acre on Japanese than Argentine farms; more capital per acre-foot of water in the citrus groves of arid Tulare County, California, than the rice fields of the Sacramento Valley. They have noted that larger companies and governments tend to favor more capital-using techniques.

They have been less good about attributing some of these contrasts to institutional bias. There is a strong positive relationship between belief in tradeoffs and devotion to the price system, and too often these contrasts of factor mix are adduced to rationalize the price system when in fact they display the bias of institutions like taxation.

They have been no good at all about working all this into macro-economics, which is supposed to help us make jobs. Labor is treated almost as the only cost, so wage cuts might only lead to "vicious downward spirals," and wage boosts can only be shifted forward in "vicious inflationary spirals." Since factor price flexibility up or down is vicious, the only way to make jobs is by "growth," with a fixed requirement of capital per job (as in Harrod-Domar models). There is no thought of making jobs simply by enriching the mix with more labor—that would be retrogressive, lowering "productivity," or reactionary and unmentionable. There is if anything a sense of predestination that forces us to use ever more capital per worker.

We are left with a theory of compulsive growth.

Worse, when it comes to intensifying the use of land, it often turns out to be other peoples'. We were ready to believe that jobs depended on taking land from the aborigines, and Alvin Hansen integrated Keynesian fatalism with traditional Americana by attributing stagnation in part to the closing of the frontier. Today, many economists sieze on our loss of cheap foreign oil and other primary products as the killer of jobs. In fact, the frontier was a great sink of capital, and the energy industry is, too, both in production and consumption.

Frontier expansionism neglects the inner frontier, the intensive use of labor on the land we already have. The old cowboy and sodbuster heroes left conservationist agriculture as an afterthought to immigrants and outgroups outside the mainstream. Current United States mercantilism, which has it that United States labor depends on foreign resources, overlooks the fact that cheap energy powers the farm machinery that drives labor off the farms—it combines with capital and land, not labor. Berndt and Wood are finding that energy use is highly related to capital use, not labor,[19] in a comprehensive study of American industry. Note that the "inner frontier" of energy refers not merely or mainly to producing more primary energy domestically, but to combining energy with more labor as we use the energy—otherwise perceived as economizing on energy.

To be sure we have urbanized, which looks like intensifying the use of land. Yet instead of really urbanizing the people we have suburbanized the cities. In forty years past we have halved the density of cities. "Intensification" has meant invading farm land, sinking enormous capital into new roads and pipes and lines. Providing urban water unleashes municipal hydro-imperialism, as cities range far away to capture remote waters rather than clean and develop near sources. Thus American urbanization replicates the continental frontier and global expansion. We intensify the other fellow's land, and use up our capital prodigally as we do.

It would be a mistake, then, to think that making jobs by applying more labor to land, the policy advanced here, would entail more conversion of farm to city land, more new towns, "development," shopping centers, industrial parks, and the like, or more territorial expansion or mercantilism. Those generally are aspects of raising, not lowering, the required complement of land per worker.

Here follow some data to illustrate how widely factor mixes range. The data refer to neighboring lands, generally, of comparable quality and in the same markets. The differences therefore display that factor mix is sensitive to shadings of input prices so slight that they are not equalized by the market—differences internal to families and firms such as result from credit ratings, tax positions, political connections, and other institutional biases. For example, an immigrant with many children goes heavier on labor, a speculator with friends in the banks and the Capitol favors lands, while a doctor with income to shelter might invest heavily in depreciable capital.

The first data are from California farming. In the San Joaquin Valley, east side, land is versatile among many competing uses. These range from dryland grazing up to citrus, fresh tomatoes, and berries. Grazing might gross $15 from the animal units; tomatoes might gross $1,500 a year, 100 times as much. The specific prices are subject to secular and cyclical and inflationary change, but the basic principles are not: the same land yields

TABLE 6.1
Crop Production, Friant-Kern Canal Service Area

Crop	Acres	Value per acre ($)
Barley	15,696	51.09
Corn	10,490	96.68
Rice	907	167.66
Sorghums	17,279	74.77
Wheat	3,176	87.85
Alfalfa hay	63,460	144.11
Irrigated pasture	17,388	77.66
Beans, dry and edible	4,293	107.14
Cotton, lint (upland)	108,928	352.80
Asparagus	1,383	418.70
Beans (processing)	27	900.00
Beans (fresh market)	75	975.33
Corn, sweet (fresh market)	254	205.91
Lettuce	423	336.51
Cantaloupes, etc.	507	547.02
Onions, dry	686	495.70
Potatoes, early	12,711	366.04
Tomatoes (fresh market)	1,343	881.16
Alfalfa	1,279	151.79
Berries (all kinds)	80	1,215.60
Oranges and tangerines	24,952	915.51
Grapes, table	43,795	545.24
Olives	7,172	327.45
Peaches	6,371	644.38
Prunes and plums	3,288	674.00
Walnuts	1,374	338.14

Source: Sacramento Office, U.S. Bureau of Reclamation, 1958. Minor crops omitted.

a little or a lot, depending on what you mix with it. Table 6.1 is a crop report gathered by the United States Bureau of Reclamation from its Friant-Kern Canal Service Area. Not all the land is versatile among all the options, but a close study of the area has shown that the margins between the uses are ragged.[20] Almost every area has several options, and many of them are choices between the highest and the lowest gross. Labor's share of gross rises with intensity, defined here simply as nonland inputs ÷ output.[21] For grazing, this is on the order of $6/$15 = 40%. For tomatoes it is more like $1,400/$1,500 = 93%.

Of course the return to land from tomatoes is highly leveraged and volatile, as a short-run gamble, but that is not our concern here. Averaging out the good years and the bad, the return to land from tomatoes is very sensitive to wage rates and other costs of hiring like payroll taxes. A slight rise of 7 percent nearly wipes out the rent; a drop of 7 percent nearly doubles it. But the same wage changes would only imperceptibly change the returns to land from grazing. Thus a slight drop of labor costs applies great pressure to shift land to tomatoes and other high-yield, labor-intensive crops, making a very elastic demand for labor.

The scope for this kind of change is manifest in the fact that most of California's farm output comes from a tiny fraction of her good farm land, that which is used intensively.

Of the several million acres of irrigable land in California, there were in 1960 21,000 acres in plums, 36,000 in freestones, and 65,000 in navels.[22] Most of the other land was and is used at lower intensities, using less labor to yield fewer dollars worth of barley, alfalfa, forage pasture, hay, sorghum, safflower, rice, or cotton.

In irrigated farming, water is an indirect land input, since a water right is the right to the water yield of a vast watershed. One might then think the tomatoes really use a lot of land in the form of irrigation water. But in fact the high-grossing crops such as tomatoes, citrus, peaches, and berries are modest users of water. Pasture, alfalfa, and rice are thirsty crops, and they yield only $50-$200 per acre, not one-tenth of the high yielders.

The high-grossing crops use more labor per acre not just in the fields but in the packing houses, the railroads, the stores, and the kitchens. A $900 tomato crop will use more labor at every step to the consumer than a $15 weight gain on a calf, do it sooner, and much more often. Thus a higher use of labor in the field increases demand for labor beyond the field. Reciprocally, lower costs between consumer and farmer, raising field prices by say 7 percent, would (in our example) double land returns from tomatoes and increase demand for labor on the farm.

In Iowa, a more uniform state, Shrader and Landgren have calculated that if all farmers followed the standards already practiced by the most advanced farmers, Iowa alone could supply the nation's output of feed grain.[23]

Farm land use in general varies so much from farm to farm that "farm sprawl" and "horticultural sprawl" are as common as urban sprawl. But this reminds us that all our cities are dominated by sprawl, which is essentially a condition of extremely different intensities on adjacent lands. Different mixes of land with nonland inputs are not the exception but the rule.

It does not surprise tax economists, of course, to learn about differences of factor proportions, for that is at the heart of the problem of tax enclaves. As everyone knows, localities compete to attract capital-using plants and to repel labor-using ones, and they find large differences among them.

Factor mix also tends to change with size of business and wealth of individuals. As a broad statistical truth, the application of labor to property tends to be regressive. The larger holdings use less labor per unit of property value.

The United States *Census of Agriculture* ranks farms by value of gross sales. In 1950, "Class I" farms, those grossing $25,000 or more, had 22 percent of the land in farms but 7 percent of the farm labor. The small

TABLE 6.2
Land, Buildings, and Implements and Machinery; Average Values per Acre, by Size of Farm, 1940

Size group (acres)	Land $/acre	Buildings $/acre	I & M $/acre	As percentages of land value	
				Bldgs	I & M
Under 3	728.00	1,618.00	192.00	222.2	26.4
3-9	156.00	225.00	22.00	144.2	14.1
10-19	79.00	69.00	8.85	87.3	11.2
20-49	41.00	28.00	5.00	68.3	12.2
50-99	30.00	19.00	4.59	63.3	15.3
100-174	29.00	15.00	4.54	51.7	15.7
175-259	30.00	13.00	4.36	43.3	14.5
260-499	26.66	8.34	3.44	31.3	12.9
500-999	18.50	4.50	2.28	24.3	12.3
1,000 & over	8.29	1.13	0.64	13.6	7.7
Total, U.S.	21.90	9.81	2.88	44.8	13.1

Source: United States Department of Agriculture, *1940 Census of Agriculture*, vol. 3, p. 80. Percentages calculated by writer.

TABLE 6.3
Profits per Employee, Large and Small Industrial Firms, Ranked by Net Worth

Group	Net Worth ($000,000)	Profit after taxes ($000,000)	Employees (000)	Profits/employee ($)
Top 10	40,090.	5,470.	1,662.	3,291.
All 500	133,660.	14,839.	9,966.	1,489.
Lowest 10	116.	8.826	29.687	297.

Source: Calculated from data in the *Fortune Directory*, 1964.

Note: Like any data, these might be massaged a good deal more. In particular I surmise that adding unrealized appreciation to profits would raise the profits per employee more for the top ten than for the others, since six of the top ten are oil companies, and all ten are major mineral owners. But this information is not available.

The lowest ten include one net loser, without which the profits per employee would be $690 instead of $297. However, negative profits are also relevant, and there are twelve firms in the 500 with net losses. Most of these are in the lowest 100, so it is representative to find one loser among any group of ten. Therefore $297 seems more accurate than $690.

Net worth was used for ranking in order to reduce the bias of regression fallacy. (Had I ranked by profits, the top ten would not have changed much, but the lowest ten would all have been firms with negative profits.) Although it is only partly successful in that, the trends shown are strong enough to survive further purification.

producers of course made the figures balance by applying more labor per acre.

The use of labor on land by and large increases with the improvements there—not so much in building them, for they are infrequently replaced, but in using them. Farm machines tend to displace labor. Farm buildings shelter and store outputs and inputs and labor itself, complementing labor. From 1900 to 1940 the United States *Census of Agriculture* reported separately on land and buildings. Table 6.2 supports the thesis of regressive use of land. (1940 is the latest year available, because unfortunately the United States Census then discontinued the series.)

Note that implements and machinery, which displace labor, decline much less with acreage than buildings do.

John Riew presented similar data from Wisconsin farm counties, at last year's meeting of this committee.[24] Other studies finding this pattern are by Morton Paglin[25] and Albert Berry.[26] Don Kanel, Peter Dorner, John Strasma, Philip Raup, and several other farm economists have piled up data showing the point.

Turning to "industrial" corporations, the regressive use of labor on property may be inferred from data in *Fortune* Magazine's yearly report on the largest 500. I tested the thesis by ranking them by "net worth" or invested capital, and calculating profits (after taxes) per employee. Table 6.3 shows the broad results.

The choice of profits/employee to test the case premises that profits in general are the realized earnings of and some index to the real assets of a firm. In fact, if the larger firms use their property less intensively (as this and other evidence suggests), then their realized profits as an index understate the assets of larger firms compared to smaller ones.

If there is something about size of business that discourages labor use, it would follow that mergers tend to result in reduced jobs on given assets. Jon Udell has found just that in his study of mergers in Wisconsin.[27] A wealth of fragmentary evidence suggests that this finding would be duplicated elsewhere.

The largest organization is government. The public sector is the most property-using of all. It has a reputation for wasting labor, and in some cases conspicuously does. But it pays the market for labor, while it borrows below the market. As to land, it still holds much more than anyone, tax free and unmortgaged, with little internal pressure or shadow price to reflect the foregone gains.

The military, for example, holds 20 percent of San Francisco and Washington, D.C., virtually idle. The annual value of this kind of lavish land input does not appear in the budget. The National Forests use much more capital (as timber) per man employed than do private ones, espe-

cially small private ones, a fact of which Forest Service doctrine makes a
virtue. Richard Muth has concluded that the outstanding distinguishing
trait of public housing is its higher capital-intensity.[28] Civil engineers,
generally working for governments, have become notorious for producing
white elephants by treating capital—not labor—as a free good, and for
overstating future benefits next to present costs by using low interest
rates.[29] One can justify any project using a low enough interest rate and
ignoring land costs, and many agencies have, because at zero interest the
present value of future rents in perpetuity equals infinity.

Private utilities are capital-using, of course. But governments supply
the most capital-using utilities, like water and sewer, which are increasingly costly because of urban sprawl. Governments are always called on to
put up social front money, to push back and invade frontiers, territorial
and otherwise, where the payoff is too slow for private capital. Public
buildings (other than schools) are often monumental, baroque, cavernous,
marbled, and better sited than their function warrants.

Few city governments have analyzed the costs and benefits of peripheral
expansion carefully before plunging outwards. The taxpayers of older
areas characteristically finance the development of new areas for years and
decades before the newly serviced lands return enough taxes to pull their
weight. It is another long span of years before they return the advance of
capital, by generating fiscal surpluses above their share of public costs.
Such is the lag of private building behind public works that the public
capital is sunk for years before payout.

A perfectly analogous case that has received detailed study is the lag of
private behind public capital in irrigation projects. The classic is Weeks
and West.[30] Public capital flowed into irrigation ten to thirty years ahead
of complementary private capital, leaving the public to finance dead
capital in the meantime. But that was before the great explosion of state
and federal financing, and later problems have grown larger.

Factor mix also changes over time. We often read of declining capital/
output ratios, but these do not show declining capital intensiveness because labor/output ratios are declining faster. The data from John Kendrick and the United States Department of Commerce were cited above.
As noted, they only cover part of the private sector and omit the public.
The public has been freezing up capital in public works, much of it at low
productivity at a disproportionately high rate. Ironically, much of this was
done in the name of making jobs.

If labor had been scarce, and capital surplus during the period of these
changes, the changes would have made sense. But labor has suffered
chronic and at times acute unemployment, while the world cried out for
capital, and nations have warred over lands and minerals. It would seem

to show a set of factor prices and/or institutional biases that do not reflect the facts. Marxists and other technological determinists have averred that changing techniques are inevitably more capital using, but most economists today would recognize that the course of inventions and their application depend on relative costs. Technology evolves in response to costs, rather than being an autonomous mover of history. We are left with institutional bias as the likely cause of the failure of the economy to soak up surplus labor.

The source of this bias is not far to seek. To enrich the mix with labor we would need to encourage the things that humble folk do, and take the fun out of many things that the rich and mighty do. It is not impossible, but it does call for a more effective philosophy than the poor and needy have embraced in the New Economics.

Let us underscore what the facts just cited imply about the elasticity of demand for labor. On some lands and in some firms labor is 90 percent of costs. Property gets 10 percent. The return to property is here highly leveraged by changes in the price of workers. An 11 percent drop to labor doubles the return to land and capital; an 11 percent rise wipes them out. At the other extreme, where labor is 10 percent of costs, one could cut the wage rate in half and only raise the property income by 5.5 percent.

All of the above may seem only marginally relevant to some readers because of their beliefs (1) that land is a minor input relative to capital and (2) that labor produces capital anyway. In (2), industry employs labor to produce the capital, and such investment is the motor of the economic machine.[31] As to the first belief, I believe it is wrong for reasons I have marshalled elsewhere.[32] As to the second, let us treat it now, anticipating point C. What is the labor-content of capital?

Let us say farm machines displace farm labor. Looking upstream, we see labor helping produce the machines. Is capital displacing labor, or is it merely labor stored in machines displacing onsite labor? We know the machine needs fuel, and fuel is capital-intensive to produce, but that doesn't tell us much until we know what "capital-intensive" means, for refineries too are produced by labor. So let us just focus on the farm machine. Keeping it simple, we ignore marketing costs between factory and farm.

To answer, let us follow one machine through its life. It lasts n years and yields a service flow worth \$1/year. I is the warranted investment to produce the machine, and equals the present value of the future service flow:

$$(1) \qquad I = \frac{1 - e^{-ni}}{i}$$

In equilibrium, as a result of competition, machine costs settle into this relationship to service flows. The cumulated value of the service flow over n years is $\$n$. The share of investment cost (I) in the total flow is:

(2) $\dfrac{I}{n} = \dfrac{1 - e^{-ni}}{ni}$

(2) is a decreasing function of n (table 6.4 and figure 6.1).

TABLE 6.4
Investment Cost (I) as a Share of Cumulative Service Flow (n) when $i = 8\%$

n	I	I/n
5	3.99	.80
10	6.71	.67
20	9.82	.49
40	11.92	.30
80	12.47	.16

Figure 6.1 shows the same information graphically.[33]

Now what is labor's share in the service flow? It is no more than I/n—the rest is interest. I/n is the share when I is 100 percent payroll. More generally, labor's share is wI/n (w 1), where w is the share of I that is payroll, plus the share of other costs that trace back to labor in the same manner.

If machines are produced at a constant rate, say one a year, there must be n machines out bearing interest for every work crew making them, so again the share of labor in the income is a decreasing function of n. It is not only *a* decreasing function, it is exactly the same function. This is shown in appendix 1.

This simple relation lets us detour all those involved Clark-Böhm-Bawerk and Knight-Hayek debates and generalize that in a going concern, with replacements balancing retirements, the share of labor in the flow of service from capital decreases as the life of capital lengthens. A total economy is a going concern of this kind, better balanced than in-

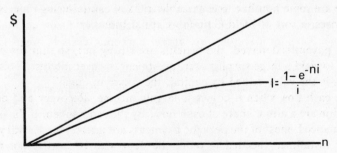

Figure 6.1.—Investment cost (I) and cumulated service flow (n).

dividual concerns, and there is negligible error in saying that labor's share is a decreasing function of the average life of capital.

Appendix 1 also shows that the share of land rises relative to labor with life of capital. Labor is applied less frequently to land where labor is embodied in capital of long life.

There are two kinds of capital: that which is storing up value, and that which is releasing it in the form of service. The one is appreciating, the other depreciating, and for short I refer to the one as "growing" and the other as "flowing" capital.

The above all refers to flowing capital. The same relationship between long life and labor's share also obtains with growing capital, only more so. We follow \$1 through the life of a tree it is invested to plant. The tree is cut after n years and sold for $\$e^{ni}$. I is \$1. So labor's share is we^{-ni}, another decreasing function of n. I omit any table or graph, because growth at compound interest is so familiar. The share of labor in growing capital is less than for flowing capital of the same carcass-life. The labor in flowing capital starts to flow out early on, but that in growing capital is locked in until the product is ripe, and joined by yet more capital which is not produced by labor at all but by land and other capital, the invisible inputs.

With growing as with flowing capital, the basic principle is unaffected by having a going concern. If we have a normalized forest of n cells or patches, and cut and regenerate one patch each year, then we must keep n patches in inventory drawing interest for every one that we put workers on. As before, the function relating labor's share to life is the same, whether we look at one patch of trees over life or at one normalized forest over one year of its life—which is not surprising, considering that the normalized forest is a cross section of the whole life of one patch of trees, there being one patch of every age. Knut Wicksell demonstrated this long ago in his *Lectures*. The mathematics is in appendix 1, and again there I introduce a land input. As before, there is less labor per acre when labor is used less frequently.

Here are some familiar, recognizable traits of capital-using objects and enterprises, a sort of Field Guide to Capital Intensity:

1. The payout is deferred, the benefits are strung out, so that the object has to yield a large surplus over investment to cover interest. This surplus is the value-added by capital, the Austrian "agio".
2. The cash flow when it comes is largely income. Recovery and depreciation are a minor share of cash flow. By the same token, if the object is financed, most of the periodic payments are interest for several years. The installment needed to retire the debt with interest is not much higher than simple interest on the original principal.

3. Demand is very sensitive to changes in interest rates, as with housing and all durable capital. Demand is also sensitive to property taxes.
4. Only a small share of the objects are normally replaced each year.
5. A large share of the objects suffer obsolescence at any given time.
6. If the objects are attached to a site, as the most durable ones are, labor is applied onsite in a bulge, a one-shot payroll. There is no fund quickly recovered to reinvest to sustain the payroll.
7. The services stored up do not flow through to consumers for a long time, so production creates incomes without yielding up the goods to match them.
8. The fund-to-flow ratio is high: a large stock per unit volume.
9. Finally, it is fair to say that the owners and other beneficiaries of these objects often demand relief from the test of competitive interest rates, a test they cannot pass. They also demand special relief from property taxes.

It would be interesting to display examples of the wide range of lives of familiar assets and goods, from a few minutes for a restaurant meal to hundreds of years for road cuts and fills. There is a full range of technical options in most fields. The choice depends on relative input costs, that is, the cost of labor vs. the rate of interest.

Just as with the labor/land mix, there is a leverage effect that makes demand for labor elastic. Where labor is 90 percent of costs, a drop in unit labor cost to employers raises property income with a nine to one multiplier on the percentage change: 1 percent off labor cost adds 9 percent to property income, drawing new investment into labor-using enterprise in the most compelling way. Symmetrically, dear labor screens out labor-using investments, and high interest rates screen out capital-using investments. This means that dear labor screens out shorter ones, and high interest longer ones.

In Figure 6.2 R is ripe value, the value of an object of growing capital when ripe. The solid curve $R = e^{ni}$ is the locus of all values of R which yield i over n years (a straight line on the semilog scale). In equilibrium the value of all growing capital will rise to touch this locus, at which time it is ripe. If we discount any value on the curve at i, its present value is unity.

The two dash lines below the solid one show the effect of discounting at a higher rate than i. The present value of shorter maturities like n_1 falls less than that of longer ones like n_2. At the higher rate, the shorter maturity gains a premium over the longer. Thus the market responds to scarcity of capital by raising discount rates, which screen out long maturities in favor of shorter ones.

This makes sense in the simplest terms when we observe that the cost of producing the long maturities is mostly interest, that is, value added by

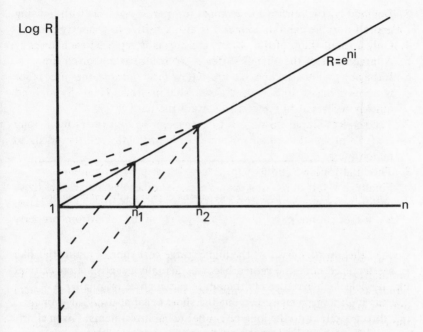

Figure 6.2.—Effect of discount rate on present value, different maturities.

capital. They are prodigal of capital, so naturally a high price of capital screens them out.

Leverage may be observed on the graph. The decline in wages needed to absorb the higher interest rate is slight for short maturities and great for long ones.

The two dash lines above the solid one show the reverse effect when we discount at a lower rate than i. Now n_2 is preferred to n_1. At the lower rate, the longer maturity gains a premium over the shorter. Thus the market solves a glut of capital by letting it be sequestered in long maturities.

The second adjustment was always the ready answer to the Keynesian "impasse" over which so many people fretted not long ago, how to find outlets for surplus capital. Martin Bailey has pointed this out.[34] The first adjustment is the ready answer to our current crisis of capital shortage. *Invest in shorter maturities, deliver the final goods faster to consumers, recover and reinvest the capital faster in payrolls to use the whole labor force.* That is my thesis in a nutshell.

Figure 6.3 shows how high labor cost, conversely, screens out shorter cycles. In the figure, the wage cost of investing in growing capital assets of different maturities is originally unity in equilibrium. Then it rises by 10 percent to 1.1. On the semilog scale, the investor's rate of return is the

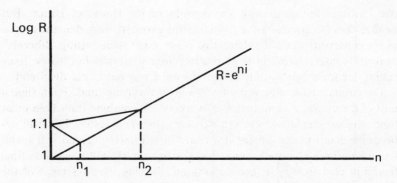

Figure 6.3.—Effect of higher wage cost on rates of return, different maturities.

slope of the growth curve. At the higher wage cost shorter maturities like n_1 are screened out—the return becomes actually negative. Longer ones like n_2 yield higher returns (although not as high as originally).

Thus high wage costs screen out the short or labor-using investments, and direct capital into the long or capital-using investments. Given shortness of labor, this adjustment would combine capital with less labor and cure the shortage.

The models above refer only to growing capital. I omit analogous models for flowing capital redundant here. The same principles apply. Mathematically, a unit of growing capital is the building block from which formulae for flowing capital (like those used for table 6.4) are derived by summation. So principles that hold for growing capital generally carry over to flowing capital as well, with a few minor *mutatis mutandis.* [35]

The key to full employment then is raising the labor-combining valence of capital by turning it over faster. Active capital moves labor, while torpid capital merely occupies land and often displaces more labor than it employs.

The key to activating capital in this way is to let labor costs fall and the cost of capital rise. Conservative economists have long advocated something like that, of course. Those of more analytical bent have stressed "Richardo Effect," the substitution of cheaper labor for capital. Labor of course has resisted that message. They have all, however, failed to observe that we can lower wage *costs* without lowering wage *rates,* or take-home pay, by abating institutional biases like payroll taxes and withholding taxes. Likewise, we can raise capital costs without raising interest rates, by removing income tax loopholes for capital and taxing property more heavily. Thus one can advocate lowering wage costs and raising capital costs without lining up with the demons in the House of Labor. But neither does this preclude one from faulting excessive wage demands, even as the conservatives do. In short, this is not a gut issue pitting "liberals" against "conservatives" in tired routine combat rituals, but a new issue calling for some celebration and promising a way out of old dead ends.

The capital stock of an economy is a great revolving fund. Each time a unit of it recycles, it combines with workers. To combine the whole great fund with surplus labor, we need only turn the whole faster. This will deliver ripe goods to consumers at a faster rate: growing capital will spend less time growing before harvest, and flowing capital will spend less time frozen in cold storage before thawing and flowing. Reinvestment of the recovered capital will increase incomes with which to buy the augmented flow of goods and services.

Here we collide with one of the firmest biases in our cultural impedimenta, the bias against rapid replacement. To many people that connotes waste, shoddiness, flimsiness, the fast buck, speculation, suede shoes, cultural degradation, demolition of treasured antiquities and cherished memories, tinsel, planned obsolescence, fly-by-night, throwaways, litter, and ticky-tacky. That those are indeed only connotations and perversions of the principle, not the essence, does not placate some people. Long life to them connotes reliability, stability, soundness, trustworthiness, economy, character, respect, and old-fashioned goodness. These values lie deep in the cultural subconscious and will not yield easily. They are indeed part of what sustains the institutional bias that causes unemployment and inflation.

An economist cannot plead against them so well as point to the high price of indulging them: inflation and unemployment, as well as neglecting the positive values of flexibility, adaptability, early embodiment of technological advance, reduced capital requirements and easier entry, replacement of obsolete equipment, stimulus to creativity, mobility, and evolution. To be sure there are those who oppose change and attribute modern malaise to future shock, but fifty years ago we lived with cars, telephones, radios, electric lights, sewers, water works, and elevators, even as today, and Al Capone too, and it makes more sense to trace the malaise back to the fear of unemployment and its derivative evils listed earlier.

It may help some to note that the "life" of flowing capital, as the term applies here, is not carcass life but service life. The idea is not to shorten carcass life, but to speed the delivery of value to consumers, and with it the recovery of capital invested. If the carcass survives that, well and good, it is a bonus.

The purpose in demolishing an old carcass of, say, a house, is to recycle the site it preempts. This offends the preservationist in many people, but two observations are in order.

Demolishing old buildings and replacing them with new is a way of preserving more old capital than is demolished, just like replacing a car's dead battery, or pulling a sick tooth. Surgical demolition is preservation, in the larger sense. Replace the sick house and preserve the neighborhood; preserve the neighborhood and preserve the city, with all its capital infrastructure and all its valuable land.

Second, the best way to renew many sites is not to demolish but to rehabilitate. "Rehab" is labor-using, compared to new construction. So is operating the older buildings: maintenance and operation of buildings eats up an ever larger share of rent as they age. Shelter from old buildings is a product of labor more than of capital. Thus, our present tax biases that favor capital over labor tend towards premature abandonment of old buildings. The policies advanced herein are in tune with Jane Jacobs' image of the good city life. It may seem paradoxical, but reducing wage costs, which favors investment in capital of shorter service life, at the same time and by the same token favors extending the carcass life of old capital. It is quite consistent though, because one recycles the old carcass by patching it up with investments of shorter life than a wholly new structure would have, and by using more labor to operate it.

We have shown now that the value of land to labor depends on how actively the owner combines it with labor. The value of capital to labor again depends on the same thing. Combining capital with labor turns out among other things to mean recycling capital faster. We have shown that the elasticity of demand for labor is high for combining with both land and capital, owing to the leverage that labor costs exert over returns to land and capital when the factor mixture is rich on labor. We have shown that there is a great reserve of land and capital ready to combine with more labor, in response to small additional incentives. We have hinted at what such incentives might be. Next we look closer at tax bias against labor.

B. Tax Inducements to Displace Labor by Land and Capital

The tax system affords few shelters for the wage or salary earner as such, directly to him or indirectly to his employer. His income tax is withheld, beginning fifteen and a half months before the tax is otherwise due. All his income is "ordinary" and taxed at the full rate. If one has any question that the income tax is largely a payroll tax he need only try to remember when he last heard of an oil man taking salaried work as a tax shelter. Harry Kahn found that labor income rose from 66 percent to 81 percent of the base of the personal income tax, 1939-63.[36]

There was a time when income tax enthusiasts argued that it did not "disincent"[37] work because it was a percentage, and your best choice before tax was the same as that after tax. This neglected the considerable undeductible costs of working, including loss of welfare, and the rocketing rise of welfare from 1960 on shows that there is an alternative which, if not desirable, is preferable to paying taxes on low wages. And in wondering at the growth of crime, we should recall that tariffs always did beget smugglers, and ponder the music-hall wisdom of Fagin: "Better get some untaxed income. You've got to pick a pocket or two."

Those factors, fortified by minimum wage laws, shift some withholding taxes forward to employers. They in turn, naturally look for substitutes for labor.

Besides, of course, employer and employee both pay the O.A.S.I. payroll tax, making labor cost the employer another 10 percent or so more than the employee gets as incentive to work. The employee's tax is not deductible, as property taxes are, from taxable income.

Pension payments are also taken from payroll. If any worker includes them in his motivational income he has not been watching the C.P.I. lately. Employer costs are proportional to payroll. Interest earned by pension funds is tax-deferrable, but that helps the pensioner as a capitalist, not as a worker.[38] Some pension plan deductions (like those of the State of Wisconsin) are not tax-deferrable—the worker pays tax on unrealized income, even though property does not.

Then there are union dues and other little nicks in the paycheck. Some are small, but the sum is large, so that it now costs an employer much more to hire a man than the man ever sees.

The employee finally gets his take-home residual in cash. To convert cash to goods, he is taxed once again on retail sales. But many kinds of property income, like the service flow of one's house, avoid sales taxes.

Thus the tax system says to employers, hire labor, and government will charge you in many ways so that your labor cost is much higher than the worker's real wage. On the other hand, when it comes to holding land, the tax system is geared to make the burdens light and the rewards great. We next examine the tax treatment of land.

The only tax that adds to holding costs is the property tax, the part that is levied on land value. Even this is relieved by assessment practice. Most assessors give a good deal of weight, in valuing land, to its improvements and the gross business conducted there[39]—that is, the "land" tax becomes a tax on using land, not holding it. Preferential assessment laws now require this in many states. A good deal of land is exempt (although hardly any wage or salary is exempt from income tax). Government land is the largest exempt class. Much of it is let to private people for inadequate fees. Their possessory interests are seldom assessed adequately or at all, and the low fee structure tells them to waste government land to substitute for highly taxed labor. Low grazing fees, for example, let stockmen hold cattle on grass too long, just as low parking rates in cities let parkers hold scarce street space too long.

Turning to the income tax, it bears very lightly on land. The basic abatements for land may be classified and summarized as follows:

1. covert write-off of undepreciated and appreciated land value (as by allocating part of it to an old building or orchard on the land)
2. exemption: imputed income (homes, resorts, hobby farms) coupled with deduction of interest and property taxes: unrealized appreciation (as of advance purchases held until needed); capital gains at death; bequests; capital gains of exempt "non-profit" owners
3. deferral of tax on appreciation until realized by sale; expensing of carrying costs (interest and property taxes)
4. capital gains rate on realized appreciation; ordinary offset for carrying costs and (some) losses
5. deferral of tax beyond date of sale, by several devices
6. deferral of land-use income where there is intertemporal interdependence of income (as by planting orchards)

I have treated some details of these devices elsewhere.[40] Some of these abatements are so gross as to amount to 100 percent exemption from tax, and some of these, like covert write-off, are repeatable, resulting in actual subsidies in lieu of taxes for holding land. This is "double-dipping," triple- and quadruple-dipping much more serious than what currently goes by that name.

While keeping taxes low, government arranges high rewards for landowners by building public works, as well as by the whole complex of allied policies to support and sustain land values. Local works may be charged in part to local property taxpayers, but there are large federal tax favors here, too. Local bonds are exempt from federal income tax,[41] and are repaid from local taxes that are expensible (debt amortization in advance of economic depreciation should really be capitalized).

As to sales and excise taxes, they too bear lightly on land. There are taxes on the *transfer* of land, but these discourage selling as much as buying. They have a net impact on the motive to hold land, by gumming up the market, which adds to the incentive to buy in advance of need (by destroying the confidence one can buy at time of need). The bulk of sales taxes, however, fall on the turnover and exchange of goods and services; on activity, rather than possession. Incomes peculiar to land like ground rents are not taxed as sales. Capital gains and imputed income also escape.

The result of all that is a highly inflated incentive to buy more land than needed, sooner than needed, and to hang onto it longer than needed. This in turn results in spreading people and capital out thin over much more land than needed. And the last, finally, necessitates pumping billions of dollars of capital into stretched-out roads, pipes, lines, wires, and other linkages that tie the fragile web of society and economy together. Localities attract large capital resources to sink into extensions of low productivity, high risk, and deferred or imagined benefits by mortgaging the tax power to general obligation bonds. State and federal governments pour in additional capital, as by the highway trust fund. None of this public capital is subject to any property tax, and he would be an eccentric public accountant who added a shadow tax to the capital to show its real social cost.

But Aha! one might say (had he skipped too fast over the previous section), these inflated infrastructure needs are all investment opportunities, exactly what Dr. Keynes ordered. We can always open up more new land, too, by extending lines out into the great open spaces and urbanizing them, and reclaiming the deserts if needed to replace the farms. So much for your limits of the Earth!

In fact, capital in marginal line extensions creates fewer sustainable jobs per million sunk than it would if invested in almost any other way—as it would have been if not taken for this use. There is a one-shot payroll only. After that, the value added by the facilities is added mainly by the unrecovered capital and land, as has been shown in section A, and the factor input is mainly capital measured by interest, the hire of unrecovered capital. The capital per job is uncommonly, inordinately high above the mean.

The money spent recycles, to be sure, but that is no blessing in these inflationary times The fund of *real* capital stops revolving; active capital is converted to torpid. Ripe goods are not delivered to consumers, and the investor does not recover his capital to reinvest. The real capital advanced to workers now lies buried in the ground, unavailable to meet money demand in the next round of consumption. The policy only makes sense on the premise built into modern macroeconomics that there is a bottomless cornucopia of latent capital formation waiting for demand, and inflation is a remote danger. That premise has proven contrary to fact. These macroeconomics are pursued below in section C.

In addition to tax-induced waste of "land" in the narrow sense, there is the same for minerals. The set of tax subsidies to hype up minerals exploration and production are by now well known, and I merely remind you of the depletion allowance based on a value whose accrual was never taxed as income, use of wellhead value rather than *in situ* value as the base of the allowance, expensing of dry holes and intangibles, and capital gains treatment. When it comes to extracting foreign resources there are the foreign tax credit, tax exemption of ocean shipping, transfer of profit to lowest tax jurisdiction, tax deferral on unrepatriated profits, and the like.

As to the property tax, assessment is at its lowest when it comes to minerals.[42] There is negligible property tax pressure to utilize domestic minerals, nothing at all comparable to the income tax incentives to go after foreign minerals.

The results of the complex of tax measures are of course complex, and as Alfred Kahn has shown, they must be interpreted in terms of the cartelized industries,[43] and to this we should add other institutional biases, like the establishment of tenure through exploration[44] and military pressure.[45] But the broad results are analogous to those for other land. We spread ourselves too thin by overstimulating foreign production relative to domestic, and overstimulating exploration and capture relative to production and conservation. We thus involve enormous extra outlays for pipelines and infrastructure, and the foreign investments involve even greater outlays for military support. Military outlays may be regarded much like the extension of a municipal service such as police protection to new suburbs. The mercantilist metropolis makes the world its suburb. Like other outlays, these tie down capital until the flow of benefits returns the costs. It is symptomatic of the capital intensity of military outlays, if not definitive, that interest on the national debt about equals the armed forces payroll (about $25 billion each). As the debt is rolled over its cost can only go up.

There is a Georgist impulse to think of "production" as always good. But extracting more primary products with a high natural resource content, like oil or aluminum, is the substitution of land for labor, just as much as is spreading labor thin over farm land. In addition, lavish use of materials and energy for labor is the prime source of pollution and generation of residuals, both of which in turn require space and drive away people.

Thus in respect to minerals, as with other land, the tax system induces the use of too much, and requires large capital outlays to do it.[46]

Next we look at the tax treatment of capital. The property tax hits some kinds of capital, and rather hard. But public capital, as noted already, is exempt, and affords a wide avenue of escape.

Much other capital is also exempt, or given preferential low assessment. Timber makes a good example. Timber is almost everywhere underassessed by custom or law. The argument is that the investment would not pay if taxed, because of its long life—that is, its heavy use of capital. Yet when is the payroll tax or income tax abated because a labor-using business cannot survive it?

Preferential treatment of timber is granted in almost as many ways as there are states. Ellis Williams has summarized these as exemption or rebate, modified assessment, modified rate, deferred payment, yield tax, and severance tax.[47] These preferences are granted on top of rural tax rates, which are low anyway: around 1 percent of market value. Sylvan rates are even lower, because of the low complement of workers, and hence population, relative to inventories of timber. In some areas—northern Maine is an extreme case—voters are systematically excluded, preventing incorporation of local government and holding down the tax rates near zero by separating the people from the tax base. We hear a lot about tax enclaves for industrial plants, but most of the nation's timber capital is in tax enclaves too.

The "modified assessment" listed by Williams is often customary even where not formalized by law. Saplings are overlooked routinely until they approach merchantable age, even though they have a market value for investment. Assessments habitually lag behind the times, a built-in advantage for growing capital over flowing (depreciating) capital. Williams has published a collection of state assessment manuals that show unmistakeable special standards of solicitude for timber.[48] The Washington State manual, for example, specifies that sale prices of land with timber do not measure fair value because they do not take account of carrying costs to harvest. "Assess it low" is the message.

De facto exemption of premerchantable timber is of greater value on slower-growing timber, because it goes through a longer premerchantable life.

A good deal of other capital is exempt too. Anything on legs or wheels or water is hard to catch on assessment day, as are consumer durables, and most jurisdictions have stopped trying. But business inventories, which are short lived, are hit hard.

Buildings, which are durable and capital-using, are hit hard too. This would seem to constitute a bias against use of capital, and it certainly is a bias against improving land. But the effect on the individual building is reversed because the property tax is levied locally, and local governments use zoning and other controls to protect and fortify their tax bases. The thrust of local zoning, building codes, subdivision controls, occupancy limits, condemnation power, and "sewer power" is to raise the capital requirements of residing in a town. The net result is doubly bad. We get more sprawl, raising infrastructure capital needs, and more capital per dwelling unit on the land that is used.

Turning to the income tax, it contains many loopholes and abatements for capital, and these generally are geared to favor capital of longer life. I will itemize basic classes of preferences for flowing and growing capital, beginning with flowing.

1. Fast write-off and expensing. Whenever one writes off an asset faster than it actually depreciates he lowers the effective tax rate below the nominal rate.[49] Expensing is best of all, of course, being the fastest, and it lowers the effective rate to zero. It means the treasury puts up in year one a share of the capital investment equal to the tax rate, and thereafter gets only a return on its own investment.

Some important capital outlays which the Congress lets be expensed are costs of minerals exploration, intangible drilling costs, R & D, advertising, rearing breeding livestock, starting orchards, soil and water conservation,[50] many costs of land development,[51] interest and property taxes incurred to carry growing capital, losses incurred to create goodwill or appropriate resources allocated by user rights (like air routes or water rights), *any* investment of unrepatriated profits abroad, price war losses incurred to capture markets, movie-making,[52] and so on. One can see from the list that expensing is granted more freely to growing than flowing capital. Growing capital is the kind that ties up capital longer before any is recovered.

It is a constant theme of interest groups both private and public that profits are not profits but costs if reinvested in the same business in which earned, and strange as it seems to an economist there is a ready audience for this fallacy.

Almost all income-yielding capital is fully tax-depreciable well before its service life is over. About the only kind depreciated slowly is that of regulated utilities, to maintain the rate base and pass through the higher taxes to consumers.

2. There is double-dipping allowed when capital is sold and redepreciated. The excess of sale price over book value is taxed as capital gains, to "recapture" the excess depreciation, but recapture is several years after write-off and at the lower capital-gain rate. The longer capital lasts, the more dips are possible. Buildings are the main beneficiary. Besides their long life they have the advantage of being confusable with land, and a good deal of land value is written off normally with each dip, even though the land value is rising.

"Recapture" of excess write-off is based on a sliding scale, the lower rates applying the longer the capital is held. This helps limit the number of dips, but adds to the favoritism shown to longer-lived capital.

3. Consumer capital in houses and hobbies yields a tax-free imputed income, just as land does, coupled with deduction of interest and property taxes and indefinite deferral of capital gains taxes. If I am solvent and never move to a cheaper house I can defer the gains until fiscal extreme unction, forgiveness at death. The capital gain may derive mainly from the land, but to claim the land as residential I must have a house.

If I hire workers to build or improve my house, that is not deductible. If I pay out for repairs and upkeep, that is not deductible. The exemption is to the return on capital, the service flow in excess of cost. The more durable and capital-using the house, the greater share of the service flow that is. A cheap house or trailer, a shelter of low capital requirements, benefits little from this exemption. The benefit is to capital.

Here we meet an exception to the rule of no loopholes for labor. Labor on one's own house is tax free. There is even some inverse relationship between the capital in shelter and the labor input required to keep it going. On the other hand, the opportunity for tax free labor requires that one own a house, and the more land around a house the more the opportunity. The greatest outlet for home labor is when combined with land and capital.[53] A material share of the value of country estates and farms doubtless derives from their outlet for tax-free labor. The farther one gets from the exchange economy of cities and the nearer to self-sufficiency, the more labor is tax free.

In addition, it is the relatively wealthy who can afford to keep wives at home who do not work for cash. The tax-free labor of housewives is a bonus for the leisure class, of much less value to the waitress, seamstress, scrubwoman, and maid, who labor in the houses of others.

The income tax is a tax on sale and exchange of labor rather than on home labor—a critic might say on social behavior rather than narcissism. But on larger landholdings there is room to reap the benefits of specialization, cooperation, exchange, and society and still avoid taxes, by internal barter. In the later days of the Roman Empire *patrocinium* became common, evolving into the early feudal system. The overtaxed citizen commended himself to be a "client" of the large landowner "patron" to escape the heavy hand of the publican.[54] Today on large paternalistic ranches we see the same forces in a less-aggravated stage, and in tax-free religious brotherhoods of Hutterites and Mennonites the modern counterparts of old ecclesiastical benefices. There are many reasons why Houthakker found the farms of Texas to report no net taxable income whatever, but one reason is the outlet they offer for tax-free exchange of labor.

Thus the tax loophole for labor is open mainly to those owning land and capital. This narrows the loophole so that it hardly compares in scope with the exemption of imputed income of owned land and captial. The landless proletarian seeking tax relief has to resort to welfare and crime.

For sentimental reasons, tax benefits to homeowners are popular, along with many other subsidies, like cheap credit pumped in via the Federal Home Loan Bank Board and the host of predecessor and ancillary agencies. In result, capital is diverted from commerce and industry (the taxpaying branches at least) to homes. Yet capital in homes complements labor less than capital in offices, stores, factories, inventories, and so on. It makes no work places, it needs no processing, and it lasts much longer.

4. Deduction of interest and property tax. These costs of carrying capital are fully deductible from ordinary income, even though the income from capital is wholly or partly exempt from tax.

5. Investment tax credit. This on-again off-again device lets investors in many kinds of capital reduce their taxes by 7 percent of the investment. After that, one may depreciate the whole amount as well. This device has the potential of favoring shorter over longer investments. In form it is a premium on replacement, and thus labor-intensiveness. It could be a powerful device for quickly causing capital to combine with more labor. But Congress has forestalled this by permitting the credit only on a sliding scale favoring longer investments. The credit is not fully allowable for investments whose estimated economic life falls short of eight years. The net result is a lower overall tax rate on capital than on labor.

Those five abatements of course move investors to prefer capital-using over labor-using techniques, and combine more capital per worker in all processes.

In addition, the abatements are biased among forms of capital, consistently favoring those lasting longer. Capital cycling in less than a year is treated very harshly. It hardly achieves the status of "capital," indeed, in the eyes of the law. Economists have strung along, letting "investment" refer to buying capital to last longer than a year and appearing quite unconcerned over the logical, definitional, and modeling problem in drawing so arbitrary a line between "investment" and consumption spending.

The investor who recovers capital inside the year reports his costs and revenues on the same tax return, even though they may be nearly a year apart. He might gain by straddling the year ends, but the I.R.S., so careless with intertemporal advantages gained by owners of durables, is vigilant to this and forbids him to deduct the cost of goods not sold.[55] The effect is the same as requiring that increased inventories be reported as income. The Treasury will not help anyone finance working capital as it does durable capital. Eisner v. Macomber, the 1920 case which protects land, timber, mineral reserves, stocks, etc. from taxes on unrealized gains, does not apply to accumulation of inventory. The rules are bent against goods of higher labor content.

There is a concession to phantom inflationary inventory profits in LIFO accounting, but "very complex rules are involved and . . . LIFO is not ordinarily used by small business. . . ."[56] It is tailored for larger business—the ones that need more capital per worker.

As noted before, recapture of excess depreciation is taxed on a sliding scale, the rate declining with years held—another favor to long life. Improvements to land that add to sale value receive capital gains treatment, with all the many favors that implies. Unlike the cost of inventories, which is not deductible until sale of goods, these costs are often expensible and nearly always depreciable long before sale. Land improvements of course are more durable than inventories.

Depreciable lives are generally based on arbitrary class of asset, regardless of actual service life. The more the service life exceeds the write-off life the lower is the effective tax rate, a clear tax incentive to build in more durability. Depreciation paths are also important. Straight-line tax depreciation is most common, but shorter lived assets like, say, a delivery truck, depreciate like the Blue Book value of cars, faster than straight line. They get the tougher break. Buildings, on the other hand, depreciate slowly at first, along a path like the declining balance of an installment debt. But the I.R.S. allows them accelerated depreciation (double-declining balance and sum-of-the-years'-digits.)

Thus there is a consistent and pervasive tax bias in favor of capital, and among capital assets in favor of the longer-lived. That this is so consistent, and often explicit,[57] points to some sort of conscious intent, or systematic bias.

The above referred to flowing capital. Growing capital, which on the whole ties up capital longer, and admixes more interest input with the original labor input than does flowing capital, is treated even better.

The basic tax subsidy to growing capital is deferral of tax to date of sale. Income, in the meaningful definition of Haig and Simons, occurs when value accrues, that is, each year as the value grows. Thus growing capital is taxed after the income accrues, and the longer the wait, the greater the benefit. A mathematical proof is in appendix 2. In effect, by deferring taxes, the Treasury helps finance growing capital (except ordinary inventories of short life).

Associated with that is a higher propensity of Congress to allow expensing of the capital cost of growing than flowing capital. Agriculture makes a good example.[58] Under the cash-accounting privilege allowed to farm business, a "farmer" can deduct expenses of materials and services that "actually go into or are a part of a final salable product—such as feed, seed, stud fees, and management services." Machinery and building improvements have to be capitalized—they are flowing capital. Capital that falls in a twilight zone between the classes includes costs of raising livestock held for draft, breeding, or dairy purposes, and costs of starting up orchards and vineyards. These too are expensible, even though some orchards may bear for eighty years. Breeding stock may be depreciated as well—another case of double-dipping—and their sale not be taxed until the "herd" is liquidated, an incredible package of special privilege[59] for the kind of livestock that requires the most land and capital per dollar of value added, to say nothing of per unit of nutritive value.

Some large classes of growing capital are timber, livestock, minerals (the portion of their value added by discovery and development), some kinds of knowledge, orchards and vineyards (for part of their lives), and liquors. Most inventories are growing capital, but the bulk of them turn over within a year and enjoy no tax subsidy. Most of those listed are greatly favored, however.[60]

As Dangerfield points out, the investor will "maximize his tax shelter assets . . . while minimizing his nonshelter assets, such as machinery or buildings." That is, he substitutes growing capital like cattle for flowing capital.

Again we take timber as an example. Although the tax is deferred until sale, the capital costs of timber, interest and property taxes, are expensable as you go. On the other hand, the cost of labor used to reforest bare land is not an expense; it must be capitalized and not deducted until sale.

In addition, timber sales get capital gains treatment, although the interest and property taxes are expensed from ordinary income. The labor cost which had to be carried forward to sale is now deducted only from the capital gain.

Ordinary profit from vertically integrated downstream mills may be shifted to timber and get capital gains rates by the firm's nudging up shadow transfer prices. The I.R.S. watches these prices with some diligence, and it is not certain that fictional internal prices get by. But there is every incentive to raise nonfictional transfer prices by letting timber add more value on the stump at capital gains rates before becoming a log, processed by labor at ordinary rates. In the mills, value added by labor is taxed at ordinary rates, and so is the value added by profit.

Some of the gains subject to tax are illusory results of inflation, and on this basis one might think tax preferences are needed merely to prevent higher effective rates on growth of capital. The undeducted cost basis of ripe timber is however negligible, in any case, next to its merchantable value, so this doesn't amount to much. Carrying costs have been expensed right along. And in general, inflation adds to motives to hold real assets, for these reasons:

1. Inflation of property values has outpaced wage rates. The illusion would be to overlook that wealth holders as a class have gained on tenants, young people, pensioners, and depositors.

2. Inflation is an annual tax on holding money. Taxing the rise of equity values merely redresses the balance, and fails in that by a wide margin, because the inflationary loss is immediate, while the gains tax is deferred. Inflation hurts the most those whose need for liquidity is high relative to their real assets. These are those whose volume is high relative to their capital, because liquidity needs vary with volume. That is, these are those whose capital turns over fast. Lampman's study of the concentration of wealth found that money and near-money as a share of wealth declines with total wealth, so that inflation as a tax has a regressive quality compared to taxes on real wealth.
3. Inflation lowers the real cost of borrowing. Since small savers have few alternatives, and the Fed prevents competition from raising rates and some of this benefit is passed through to borrowers, and owners of real wealth are the major borrowers, and leverage is the name of the game, inflation has advanced them capital at very low real rates of interest, another subsidy to holding capital.
4. In terms of bias between long and short (lived) capital, gains on short-lived capital are equally the product of money illusion but are taxed sooner, and at ordinary rates.

A major compaign is underway to abate the taxation of "phantom profits," articulated by Joel Barlow, Norman Ture, Henry Wallich, George Terborgh, and others. Their proposals are to index cost bases, resulting in larger depreciation write-offs over time. This strikes me as a one-sided and unbalanced view, which overlooks points 1-4 made here. Appendix 4 shows how inflation on balance favors the longer-lived assets. Indexing would only worsen this bias.[61]

Turning to the corporate income tax, it is biased against income from corporate property by double-taxing it, or so it would seem. Yet the corporate form is so useful a device for sheltering property income, regardless, that some wealthy people set up personal corporations for tax avoidance. This calls for a second look.

The point is to avoid the double tax by not taking cash out for a long time, converting ordinary income into capital gains, forgivable at death. Public corporations, too, are moved to plow back profits. This puts more capital each year back in the control of corporate managers to reinvest, whether or not they have any good ideas. The capital does not have to meet the test of the market; it is free of all cost but the range of opportunities of the particular management. Thus the net impact of the tax system is to make internal capital artificially cheap to corporations, and push them into ventures of deferred payoffs.

In addition, of course, they avoid double taxation by financing with debt, and their collateral security rises in step with their retention of earnings. They also finance internally from pension funds, now totalling $170 billion, the income free of income tax.[62] Borrowing requires collateral, and law and custom favor solid, durable capital as the thing to pledge.

As to excise taxes, their impact is like that of income taxes, only more so, because costs are not deductible. Excise taxes in effect tax capital each time it turns over. The busy merchant who turns his capital several times a year is taxed on it as many times. But the same capital in a tree is taxed only once at the end of eighty years or so.

If tax bias were the only institution to favor wealth over labor, we could say it may offset other biases, but in fact there are reinforcing biases, which I will merely list: subsidized low-interest loans; regulatory bias and Averch-Johnson effect; licensing laws which dispose of resources, franchises, monopolies, etc. subject to heavy capital requirements; use of low interest rates in planning public works; ignoring opportunity costs of public land; logrolling, overcommitment, and resulting stretchout of public works; the Highway Trust Fund; the failure to provide any police or administrator-enforced abatement of pollution, leaving the citizen no recourse but the larger lot, farther out; and the price-umbrella effect that builds excess capacity into cartels. There are more, and I know of no comparable set of biases favoring inputs of labor.

C. Demand for Capital Is Not Enough to Make Jobs, because Capital Can Substitute for Labor

We have already laid the basis of the present argument and recapitulate briefly before moving into the macroeconomics.

If there were no capital, the way to make jobs would be clear and simple. We would tax land value as the property tax does, as a regular fixed payment based on value, not varying with use. This would put pressure on owners to intensify. We would not tax them for hiring labor and selling products. They would use more labor on less land and solve our problem. And this is still a big part of any solution, regardless of capital. We must use more workers per acre.

Since there is capital, the problem has a third dimension. We need to use more workers per acre, and also do it more often. The form of capital we create affects both relations—that is, how many and how often.

Just now, with capital short and land dear, we not only need to use less land per worker, we also need to use less capital per worker. It is not that more capital would not be good if we had it. Voluntary saving is splendid, and taxing land will doubtless encourage it by lowering the value of that asset and prompting people to fill the void with real capital formation. But at any time, we want to make do with what there is, and just now we need to make a short supply go around much further. The market will do it for us if we let it.

Investments differ widely in "valence" for labor, how much labor they mix with capital. So investments which take capital from job-creating uses of high labor valence to sink it into other uses of low labor valence are not helping make jobs. Unrepatriated capital overseas is not making jobs in America, except as Americans emigrate with it. Some capital like cattle has a high valence for land and deprives labor of land, as well as of capital in other forms. Some capital, like that in a giant strip-mine excavator, combines one operator with millions in capital and land, and hardly compares with one sewing machine, which also requires one operator and a few square feet of floor space.

But our ideologies tell us we should subsidize investment to employ labor, and untax capital, and finance tax-exempt public works, and so on. They tell us that labor produces capital anyway, so how can capital displace labor? In effect they tell us that if capital does not always combine well with labor in parallel, it still combines in series, and so the key to jobs is investment. And here they lead us into folly.

We see investment in, let us say, a large storage dam as using workers, but not as freezing up scarce capital. We see the dam produced by workers, but we overlook the service flow from the dam produced by the invisible capital input, that is, interest on the unrecovered principal over life, which accounts for and soaks up most of the cash flow. We see the demand for construction labor and think it is a net increase, but forget that the financing takes funds and thus real capital from alternative uses. We know that construction payrolls don't last, but we think that this is merely a local problem balanced out in aggregate social accounting: but in fact it shows exactly what heavy construction does to the aggregate economy. Each dollar frozen in concrete contributes to shortage of capital reinvestment and reemployment. We pay bread today for stones tomorrow.

It might be thought that I am overemphasizing the life of capital and should consider that capital combines not just with labor that produces it, but also with labor that works with it. Thus a factory "makes jobs." However, the factory produces goods too, which are capital of some life. If we think of an economic matrix in which we match all capital with the labor that produces it, then we have a comprehensive tableau. Further matching would be redundant and might double-count. That is, we can measure factor proportions by vertical integration, as I am doing; or alternatively by horizontal integration, as in a normalized model; but not by both at once.

We think that "intensive land use" must be good for labor, but forget that trees and livestock and farm machines and fully automated plants and the blank sterile walls of many modern city buildings drive labor off the land and last too long to hire reconstruction labor very often. Appendix 3 shows a mathemetical formula for the exact relation of labor-intensity and capital-intensity of land use. Long life of capital can mean high intensity of land use without much labor.

The problem is that to encourage investment we lower the cost of capital, and move investors to use it lavishly in place of taxable labor. We forget that the job-creating efficiency of capital varies from one use to another, and our measures to promote investing lead capital into the least job-creating uses, where capital substitutes for labor, because we make capital look cheap and labor look dear.

D. Factor Substitution and Replacement Demand:
The Microeconomic Basis for a Correct Macroeconomics

The great, the overriding fault of modern macroeconomics is its homogenized treatment of investments. One is as good as another; only the aggregate matters in the New Economics.

We must distinguish among investments. Adam Smith, as so often, gave us a morning star of light on the subject. Smith said, "The quantity of that labor, which equal capitals are capable of putting in motion, varies extremely according to . . . their employment . . . A capital . . . employed in the home trade will sometimes make 12 operations, or be sent out and returned 12 times, before a capital employed in the foreign trade of consumption has made one . . . the one will give four and twenty times more encouragement and support to the industry of the country than the other."[63]

Mill was like-minded. He and Smith saw "circulating" capital as "setting labor in motion," and "fixed" capital as not.

Mill said, "capital may be temporarily unemployed, as in the case of unsold goods . . . during this interval it does not set in motion any industry . . . capital may be so employed as not to support laborers, being fixed in machinery, buildings, improvement of the land and the like. . . . Capital is kept in existence from age to age not by preservation, but by perpetual reproduction. . . . To set free a capital which would otherwise be locked up in a form useless for the support of labor, is, no doubt, the same thing to the interests of laborers as the creation of a new capital . . . all increase of fixed capital, then taking place at the expense of circulating, must be, at least temporarily, prejudicial to the interests of laborers. . . . Suppose . . . a capital of 2,000 . . . half . . . effects a permanent improvement. . . . He (the capitalist) will employ, in the next and each following year, only half the number of laborers."[64]

Unfortunately Smith and Mill never got the bugs out of their wages-fund theory, which never became fully coherent and operative. In spite of the above quotations, it seemed to some that the "fund" could not increase except by slow increments of capital formation. Knut Wicksell corrected this: ". . . a true view of the famous wage-fund theory. . . . Capital in its free form is employed to advance both wages and rent. . . . If . . . a given capital . . . is employed year after year . . . then each year about an equal part of that capital will be set free. That part . . . constitutes the whole production of finished commodities and services (of capital) of the year. When the capitalist class has taken the surplus . . . it must, in order to maintain its capital, reinvest the remainder—which it does by hiring labor and land for new production. This part, therefore, is . . . the annual wage-fund. . . . The wage-fund may undergo considerable changes, in so far as the average *period of turnover* of capital is lengthened or shortened . . . it is only the part (of capital) annually set free which can purchase labor (or land)."[65]

"It is only the part of capital annually set free which can purchase labor (or land)." Here I think we have the basis for a correct macroeconomics, one that can exorcise the fallacy that investment of any kind adds to real demand for labor merely by recycling money. The only kind of investing that purchases labor truly, without the fraud of inflation, is investing which corresponds to delivery of real goods to consumers at the end of the pipeline. These real goods are the "capital set free which can purchase labor." This is what turns paper money into real money.

This device suddenly ties together micro- and macro-economics nicely. The way to use more workers with capital is to turn and recover the capital faster. And this is also the way to increase aggregate demand for labor. By far the bulk of the gross investment that generates payrolls has its source in the recovery of capital by sale of ripe goods and the services of flowing capital to consumers. Recovery and reinvestment of capital are the prime movers of the economic machine.

Wicksell saw capital soaking up any surplus labor. "If . . . more labor is available than can be employed . . . a *shorter* period of production . . . is adopted, and the capital which was before insufficient is now able to give employment to all workers. . . ."[66] He saw social capital as a wage fund, but a fund which can sustain any rate of flow because it revolves. This Great Revolving Fund does not limit wages. By recycling faster it employs more workers up to any needed number, and it speeds up when stimulated by lower wage rates and higher interest. In the idiom of modern macroeconomics, this increases replacement demand. Aggregate demand can fall short of full employment if capital turns slowly, but quicker replacement corrects things and fills the gap. Thus, ". . . the existing capital must just suffice to employ the existing number of workers. . . ."[67] The greater replacement demand is financed by greater capital recovery, and matched by a greater flow of finished goods, so it is not diluted by inflation.

Let us look at Wicksell's device[68] as a way of meeting the national payroll with a small capital. He was telling us in effect that the economy can do what the small businessman has to do all the time. He has to recover his capital quickly each time he sinks it, if he is to meet the next payroll without dropping workers.

Consider a baker on a busy corner open 365 days a year, with working capital of $200. To keep it simple, assume payments are made daily, and they spend the first day setting up, making no sales, but sinking the $200. Half goes for payroll, half for feed-stock, and we'll ignore overhead for simplicity. Thereafter they sell out each night. The $100 turning daily finances annual payroll of $36,500, and an equal flow of net production above cost. To this he need add only $10 for 10 percent interest on $100 of his working capital.

If it took two days instead of one to sell out, he would have to find another $200 of working capital, or drop half his bakers.

As a rough rule, the flow (F) you can handle equals your capital (K) times turnover (T). The average payout period (P) is the reciprocal of turnover:

$$(3) \qquad \frac{K}{F} = P$$

You must hold down that payout period by scheduling your sales so that your cash flow balances your outgo before you run out of capital. If $K = 6F$ (still assuming daily payments) you must sell the first cohort of goods out in six days, or fail to meet payroll no. 7.

As you get into financing slower inventories, compound interest adds to your capital required and $K > FP$. If your period is seven years,[69] then compound interest at 10 percent doubles the value of each item by the time it is sold. At this time your capital will be ten times your flow, rather than seven times, because the cumulative value of an annuity of one equals ten. 10 percent interest on ten equals one. The memorable thing about this period is that your annual interest bill now equals all your other costs, and takes half your cash flow.[70]

Meantime, your capital has virtually stopped sustaining any payroll. Instead of being 1/365 of volume, capital is now 10 times volume, or 3,650 times as much per job.

The demand for labor does not depend primarily on the amount of capital, then, but on how fast it turns over—how active it is. Each time capital cycles, it combines with and activates labor. Every investment in payroll creates labor income equal to capital on the first round. But for sustained impact it must keep recycling. Paybacks deferred are payrolls denied.

If you recover capital slowly, you constantly need more money, until you reach an equilibrium with cash flow balancing outflow—which by this time includes very large interest payments on all the unrecovered capital.

Some firms and agencies have gone on for decades without reaching that balance. The Bell Telephone Company is notable. In 1971 it went to the market for $4.5 billion in outside capital, about 20 percent of all the new capital raised from stocks and bonds by American industry.[71] "But it will take another 30 years, according to Bell's plans, for electronics switching systems to displace the older (electro-mechanical) equipment in the telephone network."[72]

The United States Bureau of Reclamation makes another case. In 1902 Congress endowed the new bureau with the Revolving Fund, to be recouped and reused every ten years. By now it was to have completed eight cycles, and might have, except for one problem: it has yet to complete the first. Each new project has drained capital from elsewhere—and frozen much of it tight. Instead of activating much labor, the bureau has deactivated much capital. In the process it has also frozen scarce waters in farm uses in areas where that use is seriously obsolete, so the capital is a public nuisance.

Many companies invest in excess of depreciation. A company can do that—by tapping others. An economy cannot, except by new saving. It is a closed system with a zero sum of capital transfers. To meet the *national* payroll the economy must deliver the goods, or cut the payroll. The national capital is indeed a Great Revolving Fund. The fund receives inputs from labor and delivers to consumers. Labor and consumption set limits on the throughput, as we know. But so does turnover of the fund—and that has been neglected.

Meeting the national payroll has two sides: spending money for work, and delivering real goods to back up the money. Turnover generally balances the two sides nicely. Replacement anticipates liquidation. The keepers of the fund—capitalists—anticipate the maturity and sale of their goods, and pay workers to replace them. This gives workers the income to buy the ripe goods. (Along with turnover there are net saving and investment, but these are small next to turnover—too small a tail to wag so big a dog, as the New Economics would have it.)

The New Economics takes care only of the spending side, the money payroll. Its fault is to assume that delivering the goods then takes care of itself. Turnover is assumed mutable, totally accommodating in response to the touch of spending. The fact is that turnover itself determines spending, since replacement anticipates liquidation. And turnover has become a bottleneck. The flow of income cannot exceed $K \cdot T$, capital times turnover (plus direct services).

The New Economics cannot address this problem any better than the guns of Singapore, facing out to sea, could turn around to meet the Japanese attacking by land. "Think Spending" is its motif, and discourage deliveries. This is to meet the fundamental macroeconomic problems of underconsumption, oversaving, underinvesting, and liquidity preference. If the problem is perceived as how to remove surplus goods from the market, the doctrines and policies that result will welcome investments with only deferred benefits. These create money incomes and no consumer goods. The result has to be inflation, and has been for many years.

New Economists have mocked Say's Law and taught two generations that supply does *not* create its own demand. Today's problem seems to be that demand does not create the answering supply. Merely spending money is cheap, and easy to arrange when you have your hands on the levers that control money supply and government debt. Delivering real goods is harder.

Smith and Mill sound quaint today when they say the office of capital is to advance subsistence to labor. We should have more such quaintness, rather than doctrines which would advance money to labor without subsistence to back it up, so that it shrinks in your hand. We have traded on the symbol and denied the substance until the symbol has lost its power to command.

The New Economics does not omit turnover from its equations. Rather it buries and obscures it by keeping it implicit. This occurs when one treats "consumption" as an income-creating expenditure. Now really, consumer spending as such does not create much income; it takes off the shelf goods already produced. Replacement is the spending that creates income. There is disinvestment and reinvestment. In macroeconomic logic these two transactions are netted out, so consumption creates income, and only the uncleared balance shows up as net investment—which is what "investment" means in modern macroeconomic logic.[73] The great mass of gross investment is called consumption. The turnover of capital required is assumed to occur passively, automatically, accommodatingly.

Only it doesn't. Turnover has its own set of determinants, including the tax biases we have surveyed. Furthermore, since replacement anticipates liquidation, and the time for liquidation depends largely on the physical character of the capital in question, turnover plays a strong role in determining income and consumer spending, rather than the other way around. It is the pacer, not the paced. Consumer spending is the result, not just the cause of the ripeness and sale of goods. It is this that keeps balance between aggregate demand and supply.

This is the missing link in the New Economics, enmeshed in its doctrine of consumer determinism. It is replacement, mainly, that determines gross investment which generates most income. Replacement in turn is determined by the schedule of maturity of capital in being.

This analysis would seem to explain better than orthodox New Economics our current predicament. Here, replacement spending falls short because of a *shortage* of ripe goods, not a surplus. If there are not enough jobs to go around it results from too few goods flowing out the pipeline, not too many. A shortage of ripe goods requires that they be rationed, and unemployment is the rationing agent. If there is not enough consumption to employ all workers, it is because there is too little to consume. It sounds very much like Stagflation.

What's happening is that turnover is too slow. A lot of good capital is simply wasted and lost forever too, which is worse in the long run but not very different in the short from freezing it up for twenty years. This means slow delivery of final goods, and slow recovery of capital to reinvest.

Reinvestment demand is not inflationary, because it anticipates or accompanies delivery of real goods. Lacking adequate reinvestment, modern macroeconomic policy seeks to simulate real demand by creating and recycling money faster. But the policy-makers have omitted the second half of meeting the national payroll. They are feeding out paper but not delivering the goods.

How can capital be short when there is so much, and you can buy it so cheap on Wall Street now? Easy. There is plenty of capital stuck in the ground. The shortness is of readily recoverable capital for reinvestment. The shortness raises discount rates and devalues common stock, but cannot transmute concrete into peaches or recycle 'phone poles into sugar. The moving finger has written. We have gone astray by thinking that what is good for capital is good for labor. It is a half truth, and we are now having to face up to the other half.

The microeconomic solution to unemployment also contains a macroeconomic solution. An important aspect of substituting labor for capital and land is to apply labor to land more often and recover and reinvest capital more often. This increases replacement demand, which is almost all of aggregate demand, and does it without any inflation. The key to good macroeconomic policy is not net new investment and growth of capital, but turnover, recovery and reinvestment of capital. Favors to capital are not favors to labor unless they come in such form as to accelerate the cycling of capital, as the investment tax credit could.

Conclusion

What can we now say about how to allocate capital so that its job-creating efficiency will be greater? A number of general rules follow from our analysis.

We need to stop regarding high output per worker as an adequate index to efficiency, when this index mainly reflects overapplication of land, primary products, and capital. Labor's interest is in having high marginal productivity, not necessarily average.

We need to foster things that humble folk do, directing capital where its valence for labor is high, and for land low. This does not call for subsidies, but for neutrality in taxation. There is some truth in the old slogan that the rich can best help the poor by getting off their backs. This calls for a considerable shift in values and attitudes, even on the part of the poor, who often think as their own worst enemies (and so remain poor).

We need to extract less from the earth, and to process and recycle, maintain and service more that we do extract. There is no rigid fixed multiplier, as spokesmen for primary industries allege, by which downstream jobs depend on upstream mining or logging. Cheap logs are butchered; dear ones are cherished laboriously. Cheap wood chips and natural gas are burned off as waste; dear chips and gas are handled with labor and love as feedstock and fuel.

We need to use and improve land more, especially land already within the perimeter of existing streets and roads and utilities. We need to expand less into, and even contract away from, submarginal peripheral hinterlands which soak up so much capital, and return so little, so slowly.

We need to invest capital nearer the consumer, on the whole, and farther from the bowels of the earth, for the labor content of value-added and service flows generally rises downstream, in processing, manufacturing ("making with hands"), services, trade, and so on. Even housing, much of which is lavish of land and capital, complements labor by sheltering it.

Yet I would not legislate on any of the above generalizations, for they are too vague, too exceptionable. That is why we have a price system, to pinpoint more exactly our goals, and help achieve them.

Thus there are sharp differences among extractive industries. Oil is capital intensive, to be sure, and cartelized as well, which makes it more so. But market-gardening is labor intensive, as shown in table 1. Strip-mining is land-using and capital-using, but pit-mining uses labor. We need something more subtle and accurate than a spasm of outrage against primary products. We need pressures that will encourage those primary producers who use more labor, and discourage those who waste capital and land, and will apply the same pressures in the same measure right down the line to the consumer. Again, that is what the market and the price system are for. We can achieve our goals best by working with them, not by throwing them out. The abstract generalizations of price theory (as in figures 1 and 2) often seem sterile and irrelevant because not clothed in material examples, yet they are more relevant to our actual policy needs than anything else because they deal with universal qualities of specific examples.

A general rule is that we should invest so as to recover capital faster. This means that more of cash flow will be recovery of principal, and less will be net income to the investor. This will cause a faster flow of reinvestment to employ labor, and a faster flow of goods to feed us all. As an example, most investment in drilling oil and gas wells is financed from the cash flow of extant wells on stream; that is, it is internally financed by recycling capital already in the industry. Each time capital goes into the ground it makes jobs. Then we must wait until it comes out again to make another round. The longer the wait, the fewer jobs created per decade by each million of capital. Oil and gas owners happen to carry an inventory of proven reserves whose minimum estimated Life Index is twelve years (and probably ranges much higher), making the job valence of capital here very low. As a corollary, most of the cash flow is property income, not capital recovery.

As another example, we could lower the capital cost of buildings a good deal by shortening their service lives. This might seem like a bad trade, since to reduce the cost by one-third we would reduce the life about two-thirds. But we could then build 50 percent more houses each year with the same capital, increasing the annual service flow by 50 percent. We would increase jobs three times, since each building would be replaced in one-third of the time. This example is highly oversimplified, ignoring maintenance and rehabilitation as alternatives, but gives an idea of how many jobs we destroy by sequestering a nation's capital in forms that pay out slowly.

Long advance inventories and durable flowing capital are not bad in themselves. Deferral of recovery is the bad, and durability is the good that usually accompanies it. The point here is that this good is forced on us beyond our voluntary willingness to pay for it, and part of the cost is involuntary unemployment.

The life span of particular capital items is not to be judged in isolation. Durable capital like that in a barn, a sewing machine, or restaurant furnishings may complement and have a high valence for labor "in parallel," that is, labor applied in using and operating the equipment and short-term investments in maintaining it. And the aggregate capital needs of the overall operation, in a consolidated accounting, may be a modest share, if the material moving through the process is finished and sold quickly.

The point about capital turnover is not that all durability is bad for labor, but that capital which *appears* to drive labor off the land really *does* so, even though labor helps produce the capital. And opening new lands, seemingly so favorable to labor, may actually damage labor by pulling capital into forms where it turns slower than before and so has a low valence for labor.

Or it may be that an operation uses little labor in parallel with capital but a great deal downstream. Thus pulpmills use more capital per man than sawmills, yet paper requires little downstream capital per man, while lumber needs a lot. Newsprint turns over daily, while lumber in buildings ties up capital for decades. Looking upstream, too, pulpmills use smaller logs, and chips, and so require much less capital in timber than sawmills do. It is the price system that weighs these compensating factors in the same balance and lets us achieve an optimal total deployment and mixture of labor, capital, and resources.

Again, some durable capital may help labor by obviating even more durable capital. Thus utility cores and elevators in high-rise buildings may yield back capital slowly, but they use much less (for the functions performed) than one alternative, that of expanding the city laterally by extending streets and utility lines (they return it faster, too, and with taxes to boot). Also, high-rise helps labor by substituting for land, releasing a good deal for other uses. Of course, there may be still better alternatives in rehabilitating older houses, in low-rise garden apartments, and so on, depending on particulars. The price system is what supplies us with these particulars.

The point is not to regard capital as a threat. Labor needs capital, and labor suffers now from the shortage of capital available to invest where its job-creating efficiency is high. The point is rather to mobilize capital and redeploy it so that its valence for labor is higher. This means making it available to small businesses, especially, and others which combine a little capital with a lot of labor. And this means keeping capital out of sinks and traps. Of these, the worst are monuments, frontiers, and wars. Let us survey these three sinks of capital.

By "monuments" I mean things built with one eye on eternity, like the pyramids, and things that resemble them, like many works of governments and of other large organizations, the family seats of the very wealthy, and overmature timber.

Many monuments are built to make jobs. The intent is lost in the execution, for monuments soak up a maximum of capital per job created, and yield a minimum of subsistence to advance to labor for the next job. Public works to make jobs are one of history's great self-defeating, self-deluding, tragic ironies. There is only a one-shot payroll, after which the capital stops recycling for a long time, often forever. One of the great stupidities of all time, surely, was the English effort to relieve the Irish potato famine of 1845-49 by hiring Irishmen to build roads. A large fraction of the working population, 570,000 men, toiled for the Board of Works, while food prices took off like a bird and while half the people died of starvation.[74] The people needed subsistence for tomorrow morning, while public policy directed their effort to the next century.

An unrecognized self-defeating policy is the most dangerous concept imaginable, for its failure will be taken as a sign that more is needed. Could this be why some civilizations left such amazing tombstones as the pyramids of Egypt, the temples of Angkor Vat and the Aztecs and Greece, the Incan canals, and the famous Roman roads, aqueducts, and public buildings? It is grand to amaze future archeologists, but not at the cost of destroying a civilization.

The monument-building syndrome has many aspects. Generally, a monument is anything too far ahead of demand. A great deal of heavy construction and civil engineering is monumental, because tax-financed and tax-free. Advance extensions of transport-utility networks, sized for anticipated higher future needs, show monumental proclivities. They are often financed by cross-subsidy from the central system, and calculated to maintain the rate base, and/or internalize the profits. Excess capacity is often monumental, unless geared to reasonable forecasts of early need. Monumental excess capacity results from the use of capital as the ante in some of life's poker games, where it is used to claim quotas: a share in a cartel, a water right, a bank charter, an air route, an oil lease, or what have you. "Buying business" is the current phrase for it. Inventories of extractive resources are commonly excessive for a complex of reasons.[75] "Master plans" and "fully-integrated development" are usually monumental,' unless carefully staged; splendid examples are the California Water Plan, the California highway system, the U.S. Interstate Highway System, and the sterile city of Brasilia. "Internalizing externalities," "economies of scale," "planning for future expansion," and "foresight" are excellent catchwords for monument builders. Meanwhile, life is what happens while we are making other plans, and obsolescence is what happens to big plans under construction or soon after. Governments, world banks, and Wall Street all tend to favor monuments, for their publicity and promotional value. Hot-house "regional development," often promoted by local unions and contractors seeking jobs, has all the monumental traits. The headquarters and towers of large public and private organizations of every description tend towards the monumental, as do many of their other works. Every large organization seeks to internalize profits and keep the capital under control of the management.

There is massive inertia in all established agencies, so as capital grows scarce they shut their eyes to what the new parameter demands. It is still possible for the breeder reactor's spokesmen to abandon it because of its capital-intensiveness.[76] But FEA Administrator John C. Sawhill wants $500 billion for Project Independence, and does not regard capital as the prime constraint, but labor.[77] Barry Bosworth and James Duesenberry favor still pumping cheap capital into housing.[78] It is hard to plug a flowing drain of national capital.

Turning to "frontiers," these are the imperialistic variation of Henry George, getting access to land via conquest and expansion (a variation which reverses George's purport). There is some truth in the old idea of the frontier as a safety valve for labor, but a generation of revisionist economic historians now have established that the frontier attracted more than its quota of capital per man, much of it prematurely. This led to recurrent crises of capital shortage in the nineteenth century. We tap frontiers by building monuments like the canals of the 1830s, the premature western railroads, and the dams of the Army Corps of Engineers.

The payout from much developmental infrastructure capital comes in the form of increased land values. But to private owners this increment is income, most of which is normally consumed. Thus the capital is dissipated.

Frontiers of Science and Research and Invention are another Lorelei for capital. As Boulding has rhymed,[79] they yield "benefits hereafter." These are tax exempt because the capital cost is expensible. Yoram Barzel has shown that the patent system, too, hyperactivates research in the same way that an open range overstimulates grazing. Research in subsidized Agriculture Experiment Sations has gotten decades out ahead of dissemination and application. We need to embody faster in real capital what we already know, and adapt it more frequently to changing needs and scarcities, prices and costs, by replacing capital faster.

The energy frontier is the current vogue. Incredible figures like a trillion dollars are tossed off as capital "requirements" of pipelines, drilling, breeder reactors, fusion, tankers, ports, etc., requirements that will obviously never be met because the capital doesn't exist or can't be spared and won't be saved.

As a broad generalization, where we use capital to substitute for land, or open frontiers, the capital is very durable. It lies in close with land and resembles it and takes on some of its durability. Wicksell called such objects "rent-goods," because they so resemble land. Examples are surveying and exploring, cuts and fills, drainage, levelling, clearance, foundations, pipes, tiles, wells, pits, shafts, canals, tunnels, bridges, dams, and roadbeds. The permanence of land warrants building long life into capital that develops it. The rise of land values converts flowing into growing capital.

The upper levels of skyscrapers are also land-substitutes of long life, and high capital input. While intensive improvement of the best sites is generally desirable on balance all around, we suffer today from uneven improvement of sites, that is, high-rise sprawl or scattered hyperintensification. This pattern is more capital using, as a total system, than more uniform improvements at moderate densities.

Frontier governments often go overboard competing for seed capital. They put a high value on immediate payrolls from construction—an aspect of their high time-preference. They give away too much to get it: tax holidays, de facto pollution easements, resource leases on giveaway terms, land grants, charters, franchises, special services, and so on. These nonmarket fillips pull capital into premature and marginal development on frontiers. The form of the lure for capital, like borrowing a city's credit, often prompts excessively capital-intensive forms of investment. Granting pollution easements lowers the capacity of surrounding land to house labor and attract people generally.

During a boom, frontiers drain capital from older centers without doing much obvious immediate damage, but when it is time, as now, to renew the older centers, the frontiers do not return the capital. They demand more and more, having fallen into the seed-capital fallacy initially.

Subsidies to tap frontiers make land artifically abundant. This is supposed to help make outlets for labor, and in some ways does. But frontiering taps new land at the cost of sequestering capital. Frontiers soak up scarce capital and hold it so that it stops cycling and creating payrolls. Abundant land can still be badly used, and centuries of Caucasion expansion in the new world in a futile flight from unemployment have shown frontiers are not enough. Labor doesn't need great reservoirs of underused land so much as pressure to use the land we already have, and working capital to help labor use it.

The third great sink of capital is war, and the policies of mercantilism and imperialism that attend it. War combines the frontier fallacy and the public works syndrome and the waste-makes-jobs doctrine into a claim on the national treasure that can become greatly inflated above the simple cost of police protection. It costs money to win land—and one doesn't always win. Someone, indeed, always loses. Policing marginal outposts after they are supposedly "won" can be a continuing drain, as in Viet Nam. If and when land is won and secured, finally, the net benefits of the whole military outlay often accrue to a very few large owners of the land in question, as in California and Hawaii, or to foreign potentates like Mo-

hammed Reza Pahlevi or King Faisal who turn around and exploit us and
drain us of more capital, or to multinationals who reinvest mainly abroad
and bed down with the foreign potentates. Imperialism has generally been
an economic catastrophe for most of the players for the benefit of a few.

To keep capital from wasting into those sinks calls for massive institutional and attitudinal changes. Attitudes are surprisingly adaptable, and
we see evidence on every hand of eagerness to adapt life styles to scarcity,
even in advance of need. Institutions are something else. They are the
stubborn rear guard, shutting out the signals of the times and resisting our
efforts to budge them. But this, too, will pass in the coming time of
troubles, as the lag of institutions behind current needs creates overpower-
ing tensions. Here, we focus on tax policy. The question is, are we prepared, once the rear guards yield, to budge tax policy in the right
directions?

Rule One is to retain and strengthen the price system as much as possible, and be wary of rules couched in other terms. The price mechanism is
the only way we have of treating the economy as a total system and applying rules consistently in the same measure throughout.

The best tax on all counts is the part of the property tax that falls on
land values. The other part that falls on capital is far from the worst tax. It
is the surest way to tax capital without favoring longer lives over shorter.
So we should make greater use of the property tax at the same time that we
increase the share of it that falls on land.

The property tax on holding land presses landholders to use the land.
This employs labor and produces goods and services. It also abates the
pressure to waste precious capital developing new lands.

The land tax pressure should be applied with greatest force to land
already serviced by extant underutilized capital. There is a hard choice to
make when we know that some extant public works, roads and lines are
badly placed in terms of long-run good planning. The choice has to hinge
on particulars. Today one overriding particular is the crisis of capital
shortage, and the choice should often go to pressing into use land presently serviced. As there is a surplus, however, we have some choices and
can begin immediately an orderly retreat from the most remote submarginal extensions and outposts. But infilling of some good land bypassed by
public works may now wait a while until capital is cheaper. This calls for
land assessments more influenced by near than far future income. But
then, the high interest rates that signal the capital shortage will push
market values that way anyway. There is a lot to be said for having assessors simply follow that most useful of pilots, the market.

Added revenues from land taxes should be used to lower other taxes.
But the property tax on buildings and machinery and other capital should

be about the last to go. It is the only tax based on capital standing still instead of moving. It serves much like an increase in the rate of interest, to steer capital into forms cycling faster, with higher valence for labor. Realization or liquidation of capital, the base for income and excise taxes, is what feeds us as consumers and employs us as workers. Passive investment, the base for the property tax, employs no one.

We must prepare to accept the decline in investments of high capital intensity that a less-biased tax system would cause. For that is the whole point, to spare scarce capital and release it for higher uses. Even overmature trees, a form of extravagant monument revered by many otherwise thrifty and ascetic outdoors-persons, must yield, although it consoles some to note that capital shortage also dictates using more labor on each log after cutting, and fewer logs in each house.

The first tax to cut is the payroll tax. The major payroll tax is the personal income tax on earned income (wages and salaries). How far to carry this gets into value judgments beyond our present scope, but some first steps are clear enough. We should forget about revenue sharing, which substitutes federal payroll and other activity-based taxes for local property taxes. This taxes labor to relieve property. Federal grants to local people should go to persons, not governments, and what better way to do this than lower the personal income tax on earned income?

Among other benefits, this would help make localities more hospitable toward workers as residents. Now, central government taxes individuals to subsidize local governments, which turn around and zone out poor individuals because their disposable after-tax income is so low they might dilute local property tax bases. Ideally, central governments would relate to individuals as their net benefactors, instead, and localities would compete to attract persons. Lowering payroll taxes increases the incentive both to work and to hire, and a secure employed worker would be as good a neighbor as one usually finds.

We should decline current proposals to widen income tax loopholes for property. This can only shove more burden onto payrolls and make our income tax resemble more that of England, the sick man of Europe.[81] Labor is supposed to benefit from the greater investment, but our analysis has shown that labor needs faster *re*investment. Ignoring this central truth is one of the truly great and damaging economic fallacies, leading us to think we must spoil capital to employ labor. It is, rather, payroll taxes that slow down reinvestment, by making labor look artificially dear to employers and motivating them to substitute capital and land for it. Special tax favors for capital almost all favor deepening capital and slowing reinvestment. The only exception is the investment tax credit, stripped of the present sliding scale.

Instead, we should plug the loopholes for land and capital so that we can lower the tax rate, relieving payrolls. It would be a good idea to reinstate a generous lower rate on earned income as well, for we will be a long time plugging a hundred clever loopholes, some subtle and others complex beyond easy reform.

We should remove biases that favor long over short investments. It is too much to expect that we could tax accruals and imputed income annually, as the Haig-Simons logic would have it, and the more workable alternative is to strengthen the property tax, which reaches the same end by a different route. But we could remove all explicit biases granting lower rates to longer investments. Capital gains treatment is the greatest of these, with all it implies, and we could also do away with all the sliding scales that apply higher rates against shorter investments.

Although we cannot easily tax appreciation other than by the property tax, we can and do deduct depreciation, and a neutral tax policy here will key tax depreciation to real asset value depreciation, removing biases against shorter-lived capital described in section B, above.

Having turned the income tax back into a tax that includes property income, we could abate the corporate income tax, with its powerful bias for internalizing new capital. A progressive rate might be very helpful to break up the largest corporations which, as we have seen, employ the fewest workers per unit of capital. Undistributed profits should be taxable to stockholders on the same basis as dividends.

Public works are major sinks of capital. They need to pay property and income taxes, and the agencies in charge should show these in the budget, if only as shadow costs, along with interest at full market rates. Here we need tread carefully, remembering the logic of marginal cost pricing, and remembering that the right works in the right place, like subways in New York, can save much more capital than they consume. Let us look last to the subway for revenue, and first to the capital and land in highways, cars, trucks, terminals, gas stations, parking lots, garages, refineries, and car lots.

A decreasing-cost distribution system is ideally priced to yield a deficit, according to a rationale now familiar. The value is imputed to the land served, and that is the proper tax base. The deficit-yielding subsystem has no value and should pay no property tax, but receive a subsidy. That is a good principle in its place, but it is hard to keep it there. Cross-subsidies and submarginal extensions become the rule, wasting capital. Here the solution is user charges, especially peak pricing and area rates, which force users to economize on the capital and serve as substitutes for excess capacity. Fortunately there is a wide literature on this subject to supplement these spare and summary words.

Another needed change is the tax treatment of income from offshore. We cannot suddenly create much new capital, but we can summon back a great mass of it now lost to us offshore by removing the egregious special loopholes for U.S. capital invested abroad.

These are some steps toward a tax system less biased for monuments and frontiers, more geared to help make jobs by mobilizing and activating wealth. If we do this, and like the results, we can go further. Meantime, these steps represent substantial progress.

They will help us find full employment on our present land base, permanently, freed from the compulsion to grow and expand that we inherited from generations of ancestors who had not yet learned the finite limits of the Earth. We can continue to create capital, and we can apply new ideas more quickly than now as faster replacement lets us embody new techniques in capital in a shorter time. Thus we can grow in every good sense by substituting real progress for the random lateral expansion of the past. We can find full employment in peaceful labor on our share of this small planet, and doing so, drop the burden of imperialism that may otherwise destroy us.

Appendix 1. Share of Labor in Claim on Total Output as Decreasing Function of Life of Capital: Identity of Single-cycle and Going-concern Models

Flowing (Depreciating) Capital

The text shows (fig. 6.1, table 6.4) that the share of labor in revenues from the service flow of a building or machine (flowing capital) is a decreasing function of life. Here we show the rule, and the mathematics are exactly the same in a "going concern" model where an investment in machines is normalized or staggered.

There is one machine of every age. We build or buy one new machine each year, and scrap another one. The number of extant machines is n, where n is the number of years each machine lasts. As in text equation 1, each one yields a flow of $1 per year, so the yearly flow is n.

The yearly labor input is no more than the warranted investment (I) in one machine when new. Dividing this by the yearly service flow (n) we arrive at the same result as when we analyze one machine over life, that is, labor's share is

(2) $$\frac{I}{n} = \frac{1 - e^{-in}}{ni} \quad [\text{same as text eq. 2}]$$

The share going to capital as interest must be the complement of (2), of course. To check this, let us derive it directly.

The capital value remaining unrecovered in each machine at the start of every year, y, is the present value (V_y) of future cash flows from that time until scrapping.

(3) $$V_y = \frac{1 - e^{-i(n-y)}}{i}$$

Total unrecovered capital (K_y) is

(4) $$K_y = \sum_{y=0}^{n} V_y = \frac{1 - e^{-in}}{i} + \frac{1 - e^{-i(n-1)}}{i} + \cdots + \frac{1 - e^{-i(n-n)}}{i}$$

$$\frac{1}{i}\left[n - e^{-in} \sum_{y=0}^{n} e^{iy} \right] = \frac{1}{i}\left[n - \frac{1 - e^{-in}}{i} \right]$$

Interest on K_y as a share of total output flow is

(5) $$\frac{iK_y}{n} = 1 - \frac{1 - e^{-in}}{in}$$

Q.E.D.

In the going concern, capital recovery is the excess of cash flow (n) above interest cost (Ki). Rearranging (5)

(5A) $$n - Ki = \frac{1 - e^{-in}}{i}$$

But the right side of (5A) is I, the warranted investment to build a new machine. So capital recovery from all the machines together is just enough to finance one new machine each year.

Now we add land to the inputs. The capital is a building on a good site. The yearly service flow is now \$1 plus \$a, where a is the annual value of the site. Fig. 4 shows the share of land:

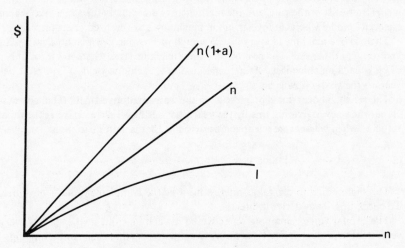

Figure 6.4—Division of value of service flow of n houses of evenly staggered ages among warranted investment (I), rent (a), and interest.

K remains the same as before. So does I. Only service flow is greater. The shares of labor and capital are accordingly smaller.

The share of land is

(6) $$\frac{na}{n(1 + a)} = \frac{a}{1 + a}$$

(6) is not a function of n, i.e. it is unaffected by life (under the present simplifying assumption of level service flow). Accordingly, the share of land rises relative to labor, and falls relative to capital with increasing life of capital.

The last point seems a little surprising, because in the last years of an old building the cash flow covers little more than land rent. In part, the surprising result comes from my artificial simplifying assumption of level cash flow over "life." In fact, there is a geriatric terminal life of old buildings, after the service life is over, when the carcass survives and yields just enough cash flow to give a return on the site. When we include this terminal period in "life," the share of land rises with life, and more so when site value rises over time.

But that is not the whole story. In the main, the surprising result represents a real phenomenon: to build for long-sustained service flow of capital calls for heavy inputs of capital from the beginning of life, inputs which must be paid from the beginning. Note that we are not here treating what happens from year to year to the individual building as it ages and the unrecovered capital approaches zero. Of course, capital's share then also approaches zero. We are treating of shares over the whole life of buildings, and, what amounts to the same thing, shares generated from a normalized collection of buildings of every age.

The share of labor falls with increasing life. But land tempers this effect by claiming a share of the product even when life is short, like the life of corn plants in rich Champaign County, Illinois; or when there is little capital, as on a parking lot. Appendix 3 develops this aspect further.

Growing (Appreciating) Capital

Assume that we plant a tree on marginal land, at a cost of \$1, and harvest it n years later (when the growth of its stumpage value as a percentage of the base equals the rate of interest). Stumpage revenue (R) is e^{ni}. Labor's share is no more than e^{-ni}, and less if planting cost is not all wages. e^{-ni} is a decreasing function of n. Labor gets a lesser share when life is longer.

This conclusion does not depend on using a single cycle as an example. Let the operation be normalized by staggering the cycles to keep a constant flow of input and output through a going concern. Each year we plant one new tree, and harvest the oldest one. The number of trees in our inventory must equal n, an increasing function of n. In addition, the average tree must be older and contain more capital. The capital stock (K) is the sum of the value of all the trees:

(7) $$K = e^i + e^{2i} + \cdots + e^{ni} = \sum_{n=1}^{n} e^{ni} = \frac{e^{ni} - 1}{i}$$

The share of capital in receipts is

(8) $\dfrac{Ki}{e^{ni}} = 1 - e^{-ni}$

(8) is an increasing function of n, and of course the complement of labor's share, e^{-ni}, a decreasing function of n. This is exactly the same result as for a single cycle.

Now we add land. Let the tree grow on a good site, of value S. Now growth must cover interest on S as well as on capital in the tree, by reaching at maturity a value on the function:

(9)[82] $R_n = e^{ni} + S[e^{ni} - 1] = (1 + S)e^{ni} - S$

The share of labor is no more than $1/R$, obviously a decreasing function of n since R grows with n.

The share of land is Sin/R. We will see ahead that this is an arcade function, an increasing and then decreasing function of n. The increase comes first because labor's share drops almost inversely with n for low values of n. The decrease comes later because K increases logarithmically with n so that Ki takes nearly all.

The share of capital is the sum of interest on planting cost plus interest on ground rent, divided by R.

Interest on planting cost is $e^{in} - 1$

Interest on ground rent is $S(e^{in} - 1 - in)$[83]

The share of capital is

(10) $\dfrac{e^{in} + S(e^{in} - 1) - 1 - Sin}{e^{in} + S(e^{in} - 1)} = 1 - \dfrac{1 + Sin}{R}$

(10) is also the complement of land's and labor's shares, as we would expect.

To normalize the single cycle, assume a fixed piece of land divided into n cells or tracts. Each year we plant trees in one cell, and harvest another. Payroll to plant one cell is $1/n$. Receipts each year are R/n. Yearly land cost is Si, and for each cell is Si/n.

The capital stock at all times is

(11) $K_y = \displaystyle\sum_{y=1}^{n} \dfrac{(1 + S)e^{yi} - S}{n} = (1 + S)\dfrac{e^{ni} - 1}{ni} - S$

Receipts each year are

(12) $\dfrac{R}{n} = \dfrac{(1 + S)e^{ni} - S}{n}$

Labor's share is

(13) $\dfrac{1/n}{R/n} = \dfrac{1}{R}$

(13) is the same as the single cycle case.
Land's share is

(14) $$\frac{Si}{R/n} = \frac{Sin}{R}$$

(14) too is the same as tne single cycle case.
Capital's share is

(15) $$\frac{Ki}{R/n} = \frac{(1 + S)(e^{ni} - 1) - Sin}{R}$$

But (15) is the same as (10), the share of capital in the single cycle case.

So we have normalized tree-growing operations and shown that the shares of land, labor, and capital are the same as when we look at one cycle over its life.

Now let us get a better idea of how the shares vary as functions of life (n). Table 6.5 is an example worked out for assumed values, with $i = .05$, and $S = 800$. Instead of assuming the original investment is \$1, as in the algebra above, it is \$200, assumed to be all payroll (P).

Applying the principle of leverage, it is evident from table 6.5 that a slight rise of interest rates will screen out or shorten long cycles, as we would expect from the simpler earlier demonstration. A rise of wage rates will screen out or lengthen short cycles—we economize on labor by using it less often. For very long cycles, interest cost dominates everything. Such long cycles are, however, unusual outside of forestry, and often pathological there, permitted only by sheltering from real interest costs. For most growing capital, cycles are under fifteen years, and land cost is a powerful force. High land rents screen out or shorten medium cycles. An example that the model partly fits is cattle breeding, a very land-using business. High interest rates are not enough to pry land away from cattle and sheep and feed grain, the great historical depopulators of farm land. High holding costs must be brought directly to bear on the tenure of land.[84]

Historically, farm labor has had to clear away trees to find jobs working the land, and then to push back sheep and range cattle. These organisms of slow maturity create virtual economic deserts for labor. Even the capital in them is mostly geogenic (land derived). Now for some decades forests and livestock have been repossessing land formerly tilled, while farm labor has left for the cities, and food prices have risen. Something is scrambling the market signals; we have seen that tax bias is part of that something.

Aside from the intuitive leverage principle, how do higher rents and interest rates shorten life? It is geometrically obvious that any tree is mature financially in equilibrium when its growth curve touches the R function, where it has the same slope. Differentiating (9):

(16) $$\frac{dR}{dn} = ie^{in}(1 + S) = i(R + S)$$

(16) says that a tree is mature in the year when its growth just covers interest on its achieved value (iR) plus rent (iS). Raising rent and interest thus results in shorter cycles.

TABLE 6.5
Factor Shares as Functions of Life of Trees, Normalized Operation

n	Interest factors		Receipts	Wages		Land rent		Interest on cap. stock		Sum of shares (check)	Intensive-ness
	e^{ni}	$\dfrac{e^{ni}-1}{i}$	$\dfrac{1000\,(2)-800}{(1)}$	Am't	Share	Am't	Share	Am't	Share	$(6)+(8)+(10)$	$(6)+(10)$
					$\dfrac{(5)}{(4)}$		$\dfrac{40}{(4)}$		$\dfrac{(9)}{(4)}$		
(1)	(2)	(3)	(4)	(5)	(6)	(7)	(8)	(9)	(10)	(11)	(12)
1	1.05	1.00	250	200	.80	40	.16	10	.04	1.00	.84
7	1.41	8.14	87	29	.33	40	.46	20	.23	1.02	.56
14	1.97	19.6	84	14	.17	40	.48	30	.36	1.01	.53
21	2.79	35.7	94	9.5	.10	40	.43	45	.48	1.01	.58
28	3.92	58.4	111	7.1	.06	40	.36	65	.59	1.01	.65
35	5.52	90.3	135	5.7	.04	40	.30	90	.67	1.01	.71
42	7.76	135	166	4.8	.03	40	.24	120	.72	.99	.75
49	10.9	198	206	4.1	.02	40	.19	160	.78	.99	.80
56	15.4	288	261	3.4	.01	40	.15	215	.82	.98	.83
63	21.5	410	328	3.2	.01	40	.12	285	.87	1.00	.88
70	30.4	588	423	2.9	.007	40	.09	380	.90	1.00	.91
77	42.7	834	544	2.6	.005	40	.07	500	.92	1.00	.93
84	60.2	1184	707	2.4	.003	40	.06	665	.94	1.00	.94

Notes by column numbers:

(1) Life.

(2) Amount of 1 at compound interest, 5%.

(3) Amount of annuity at 5%.

(4) $\dfrac{(P+S)\,e^{ni}-S}{(1)}$

(7) $S_i = 800 \times .05 = 40.$

(9) $K_i = .05 \cdot 1000 \cdot \dfrac{(3)}{(1)} - .05 \cdot 800 = 50 \dfrac{(3)}{(1)} - 40.$

(11) Discrepancies due to rounding.

(12) Intensiveness.

$P = 200$

$S = 800$

Appendix 2. Investor's Rate of Return after Tax on Realization of Income from Growing Capital[85]

The rate of return after tax, (r), is an increasing function of life, (n).

$$(17) \qquad e^{rn} = e^{in}(1 - t) + t = \theta$$

where t is the nominal tax rate.

To prove: $dr/dn > 0$

$$(18) \qquad g \equiv \frac{d \ln \theta}{dn} \text{ is } \frac{\theta'}{\theta}, \text{ the growth rate of } \theta(n)$$

$$(19) \qquad \ln \theta = \int_0^n \frac{d \ln \theta}{dn} = \int_0^n g \, dn$$

but from (1), $\ln \theta = rn$, so that

$$(20) \qquad r = \frac{1}{n} \int_0^n g \, dn$$

By inspection of (4) and the Theorem of the Mean, r must be rising if g is monotonically rising, i.e., if $dg/dn > 0$.

$$(21) \qquad \frac{dg}{dn} = \frac{d}{dn}\left[i - \frac{ti}{\theta}\right] = \frac{ti\,\theta'}{\theta^2} > 0$$

$$\therefore \quad \frac{dr}{dn} > 0$$

Q.E.D.

Appendix 3. "Intensity" of Land Use and "Labor Intensity" of Land Use

"Intensity" of land use and "labor intensity" of land use are two different things. Capital on land may displace more labor than it requires to produce it. Much capital is partly geogenic (earth-derived), by the operation of compound interest.

We will compare the overall Intensity Quotient (Q) and labor-intensity (Q_w). We begin with a point-input-point-output (PIPO) model, and easily modify it to cover all cases.

We invest $\$I$ at the beginning of year one, on land worth $\$S$, and realize $\$R$ after n years.

In equilibrium

$$(22) \qquad R = Ie^{in} + S(e^{in} - 1)$$

$$(23) \qquad \text{Labor input} \leq I$$

$$(24) \qquad \text{Land input} = Sin$$

(25)   Capital input $= I(e^{in} - 1) + S(e^{in} - 1) - Sin$

(26)   Labor intensity, $Q_w \leq \dfrac{I}{R}$

(27)   But total intensity, $Q = \dfrac{R - Sin}{R}$

$$= 1 - \frac{R - Ie^{in}}{e^{in} - 1}\frac{in}{R} = 1 - \frac{R - Ie^{in}}{R}\left[\frac{in}{e^{in} - 1}\right]$$

The coefficient on the right in (27) (in brackets for easy reference), is the ratio of simple interest to compound interest. Call it θ. For low values of n, $\theta \to 1$, and $\therefore$ $Q \to Ie^{in}/R$. But $e^{in} \to 1$ also, so $Q \to I/R$. That is, $Q \to Q_w$ and intensity and labor-intensity are the same, virtually, for short lives.

But for higher values of n, i.e. longer lives, $\theta \to 0$ and $\therefore$ $Q \to 1$, even if labor-intensity, I/R, is low. This reflects the buildup of geogenic and autogenetic capital that occurs whenever recovery of principal is deferred.

To adapt this definition of intensity to flowing capital, we need only date all inputs, discount them to year 0, and add these present values to I. Similarly compound all revenues to year n and add them to R. Most investors above the lowest level of sophistication go through some such analysis whatever they may call it. Cash-flow analysis, annualizing, present value analysis, land appraisal, etc., all involve this kind of intertemporal commensuration.

Normally w, the share of I paid out for onsite workers, is much less than one, so true labor-intensity

(28) $wI/R < \dfrac{I}{R}\cdot$

There is on a priori grounds a strong negative relationship between w and n, because building durably calls for heavy materials, of high resource content.

(27) is based on deriving site value, S, from the current use, which is to assume the site is in its highest use. Often it is not, in which case (27) overstates intensity. If we have reason to put an opportunity cost value on S higher than $R - Ie^{in}/e^{in} - 1$, then we should not substitute this in (27), but stop at

(27A) $Q = 1 - \dfrac{Sin}{R}$

(27A) gives a lower value which can easily even be negative when R fails to cover simple interest on S, or rent.

The only good reason for managing land this way would be to save it for a higher future use. Yet the foregone revenues of these n years must then be regarded as plowed back into the site as "intangible geogenic capital." The present property tax is biased by virtue of failing to tax such capital, thus favoring it over buildings.

Landholders, like some government agencies and corporations who are sheltered from social opportunity costs, are doubly disinclined to turn over their capital fast enough. The land cost itself is a pressure to shorten cycles; but so is interest on the intangible geogenic capital which they do not feel. The last point has been entirely neglected and is very important.

Appendix 4. Inflation, Phantom Profits, and Tax Bias against Shorter Investments

We compare two PIPO investments, one maturing in one year, the other in ten. $i = .07$, and there is annual inflation at 7%. $t = 50\%$.

	I	R	$R - I$	$R - Ie^{.07n}$	$(R - I)t$
$n = 1$	100	114	14	7	7
$n = 10$	100	400	300	200	150

When $n = 1$, half the profit of \$14 is phantom, and the 50% tax rate consumes the the other half.

When $n = 10$, only one-third of the \$300 profit is phantom, so the tax leaves \$50 of real profit after tax.

More generally,

(29)   Taxable income $= R(n) - I_0$

(30)   Adjusted basis $= Ie^{jn}$

where j is the rate of annual inflation.

In equilibrium

(31) $R(n) = Ie^{(i+j)n}$

Income adjusted for inflation is

(32) $R(n) - Ie^{jn} = Ie^{(i+j)n} - Ie^{jn} = Ie^{jn}(e^{in} - 1)$

Taxable income as a multiple of adjusted income is

(33) $\beta = \dfrac{I[e^{(i+j)n} - 1]}{Ie^{jn}(e^{in} - 1)} = \dfrac{e^{(i+j)n} - 1}{e^{(i+j)n} - e^{jn}}$

β is a decreasing function of n, ranging from a high of $\beta = (i + j/i)$ when $n = 1$, to a low of one when $n = \infty$.

The case is often made that it is the opposite, that inflation hits the longer investments harder. The argument is that the short investment lets principal be recovered at a lower price level, while it is worth more. It is an unbalanced argument, overlooking the larger fact that the long investment lets revenue be taxed later, in softer dollars. That is, when $n = 1$, the \$7 phantom profit is taxed in year one and paid in dollars worth twice as much as those of year ten. When the phantom profit merely *accrues* in year one it is not taxed until year ten, when the dollar is worth half as much.

As we have seen, most long investments are written off faster than they actually depreciate. The intertemporal bias here is magnified because costs are deducted from hard dollars and taxes are later levied on soft ones.

Notes

1 *Business Week,* Sept. 9, 1972, p. 114, citing data from U.S.B.L.S. Wage rates have risen faster in Japan, Italy, Germany, Britain, and France. The data are for wages before taxes. U.S. payroll taxes have also risen in this period.

2 Paul A. Samuelson, *Economics,* 3rd ed. (New York: McGraw-Hill, 1955) p. 336.

3 Ibid., p. 350.

4 "Nixon Must Alter His Game Plan," *Washington Post,* Aug. 23, 1970, p. G1.

5 *Inflation* (Washington, D.C.: The Brookings Institution, 1970), p. 9.

6 *New York Times,* Dec. 1970.

7 *Newsweek,* April 20, 1970, p. 91.

8 "The Budget is the Spur," *Newsweek,* Jan. 31, 1972, pp. 63-64

9 "Resharpening the Tools," *Business Week,* Jan. 5, 1974, p. 56.

10 "Capital Shortage, or Glut?" *Newsweek,* Aug. 1974, p. 73.

11 John Kendrick, *Productivity Trends in the U.S.* (Princeton: Princeton University Press, 1961), pp. 148-49, table 39.

12 Cited in "The Push to get More from Men and Machines," *Business Week,* Sept. 9, 1972, pp. 80-81.

13 Jack Stockfisch, "Investment Incentive, Taxation, and Accelerated Depreciation," *SEJ* 24 (1), 28-40 (July 1957), p. 38. Since land is not depreciable, these tax preferences theoretically do not apply to land income. In practice, however, land income is as sheltered as capital income. (Mason Gaffney, "The Treatment of Land Income," *Economic Analysis and the Efficiency of Government* [Joint Economic Committee, Congress of the U.S., 91st Conress: 1st Session, part 2, 1970], pp. 405-15.) Keynesians have not been at all alert to this problem.

14 They are simply financed with owned instead of borrowed capital. The relevant "term" is how long the capital sunk is tied up before being fully recovered. "Recovery" is the residual after deducting interest from cash or service flow, and may be very slow and even negative when interest rates are high and cash flow low.

15 Norman Ture, *Tax Policy, Capital Formation, and Productivity* (New York: National Association of Manufacturers, 1973). The whole case made by Ture rests on assuming that capital complements labor, an assumption built into the Cobb-Douglas function. See his p. 14, "The Law of Diminishing Returns."

16 Knut Wicksell, Lectures on Political Economy, Trans. E. Classen (New York: The Macmillan Company, 1938), pp. 194-96.

17 The research group at Resources for the Future has devoted years to belaboring this point in respect to pollution control. The object here is to generalize the point to the whole economy.

18 Adam Smith, *Wealth of Nations* (New York: Random House, 1937), pp. 538-40.

19 Ernst R. Berndt and David Wood, "Technology, Prices, and the Derived De-

mand for Energy," preliminary draft, December 1973, 28 pp. A most perceptive and more general treatment is Sanford Rose "The Far-reaching Consequences of High-priced Oil," *Fortune,* March 1974, pp. 106-12, 191-96.

20 Mason Gaffney, "Diseconomies Inherent in Western Water Laws," in *Economic Analysis of Multiple Use,* Proceedings of Western Agricultural Economics Research Council, Range and Water Section, 1961, pp. 55-82, 75 ff.
See also Irvin H. Althouse, "Water Requirements of Tulare County," Report
to Tulare County Board of Supervisors, January 1942 (mimeographed), map
in back pocket.

21 This is simplified. The commensurable combining of labor and capital inputs
is formularized in appendix 3.

22 G. W. Dean and Chester O. McCorkle, *Trends for Major California Fruit
Crops,* California A.E.S., Extension Service Circular 448, 1960.

23 William Shrader and N. Landgren, "Land Use Implications of Agricultural
Production Potentional," in L. Fischer, ed., *Shifts in Land Use* (Nebraska
Agricultural Economics Service, 1964).

24 John Riew, "Assigning Collection of a Statewide Uniform Rate Land Tax," in
R. Lindholm, ed., *Property Taxation and the Finance of Education* (Madison, Wis.: University of Wisconsin Press, 1974).

25 Morton Paglin, "Surplus Agricultural Labor and Development," *American
Economic Review,* September 1965, pp. 815-33.

26 Albert Berry, "Presumptive Income Tax on Agricultural Land," *National
Tax Journal,* June 1972, pp. 169-81.

27 Jon Udell, *Economic and Social Consequences of the Merger Movement in
Wisconsin* (Madison: Bureau of Business Research, 1969).

28 Richard Muth, "Capital and Current Expenditures in the Production of Housing," in L. Harriss, ed., *Government Spending and Land Values* (Madison:
University of Wisconsin Press, 1973).

29 A collection of such cases is documented in U.S. Congress, *The Analysis and
Evaluation of Public Expenditure: The PPB System,* (Joint Economic Com-
mittee, Subcommittee on Economy in Government. Washington, D.C.: U.S.
Government Printing Office, 1969).

30 David Weeks and Charles West, *The Problem of Securing Closer Relationship between Agricultural Development and Irrigation Construction,* University of California, College of Agriculture, Agricultural Economic Service Bulletin 435 (Berkeley: University of California Printing Office, 1927).

31 An example of such thinking unrelieved by any apparent doubt of its
adequacy is Bert G. Hickman, *Investment Demand and U.S. Economic
Growth* (Washington, D.C.: The Brookings Institution, 1965). Nor could I
name any Brookings economist who takes a different view. Close to power and
the application of economic ideas to policy, Brookings plays a central role in
defining the orthodoxy that has dominated policy to date.

32 Mason Gaffney, "Adequacy of Land as a Tax Base," Daniel Holland, ed.,
The Assessment of Land Value (Madison, Wis.: University of Wisconsin
Press, 1969).

33 If the buyer pays on the installment plan at 8% interest over n years, he pays the full n, the entire service flow, because

$$n \times \frac{i}{1 - e^{-ni}} \cdot \frac{1 - e^{-ni}}{i} = n.$$

34 Martin Bailey, *National Income and the Price Level* (New York: McGraw-Hill, 1962), p. 111.

35 Hans Brems, *Output, Employment, Capital, and Growth* (New York: Harper & Bros., 1959), pp. 212-26.

36 C. Harry Kahn, *Employee Compensation under the Income Tax* (Princeton: Princeton University Press, 1968).

37 If this word doesn't exist, it should.

38 It often helps the fund manager most of all. Companies can, for example, borrow from their own pension funds, as the U.S. Treasury borrows from the Social Security fund. The borrower gains from inflation, while the pensioner is exploited. Pensioners are also exploited by managers taking bad risks, and some funds are unable to meet their obligations.

39 There is a wide literature on this, including Holland, ed., *Assessment of Land Value.*

40 Mason Gaffney, "Tax-induced Slow Turnover of Capital," *WEJ* 5 (4): 308-23 (September 1967). An expanded version ran in *American Journal of Economics and Sociology,* from January 1970 to January 1971. The material on land income is in vol. 29 (3): 409-24, and is much more fully treated than in the *WEJ*. A more institutional approach is used in Mason Gaffney, "The Treatment of Land Income," *Economic Analysis and the Efficiency of Government* (Joint Economic Committee, Congress of the U.S., 91st Congress: 1st Session, part 2, 1970), pp. 405-15.

41 Before World War II, *salaries* paid by state and local governments were free of federal income tax. Then salaries became taxable, while the cost of hiring capital remained exempt.

42 The best source on this is in a series of studies sponsored by Ralph Nader, available from the Tax Reform Research Group, Washington, D.C.

43 Alfred Kahn, "The Depletion Allowance in the Context of Cartelization," *American Economic Review* 54 (June 1965), pp. 286-314.

44 Gaffney, *Extractive Resources,* pp. 391 ff.

45 Mason Gaffney, "Benefits of Military Spending," unpublished MS., 1973.

46 Rose, "Far-reaching Consequences."

47 Ellis T. Williams, *State Forest Tax Law Digest,* 1967, U.S.D.A. Forest Service, Misc. Pub. No. 1077, 1968.

48 Ellis Williams, *State Guides for Assessing Forest Land and Timber,* U.S.D.A. Forest Service, Misc. Pub. No. 1061, 1967.

49 A proof is in Gaffney, "Tax-induced Slow Turnover, p. 318, and a more general one by Vickrey and Consigny is appendix 2 of the same title, AJES 30 (1): 107-8 (January 1971)

50 For more detail see Robert Evenson and Finis Welch, "Taxation of Farm Income," MS., n.d., 22 pp., available from authors.

51 Dale Hoover, "An Economic Analysis of Farmland Development," *Agricultural Economics Research* 22 (April 1970), pp. 37-44, p. 42. See also "One Man's Poison," *Forbes,* Aug. 15, 1965, p. 27, showing how housing builders can expense water supply systems. William Condrell, writing in the *Timber Tax Journal,* October 1970, also discusses how Section 175 of the Internal Revenue Code lets "farmers" expense soil and water conservation, and Section 182 lets them expense land clearing.

52 Via defaulting on non-recourse loans. *Forbes,* Aug. 15, 1974, pp. 40-41. "The Numbers Game."

53 "Combining with capital" refers to producing durable improvements. These might be for personal use or for later resale with capital gains treatment. Both are common.

54 James W. Thompson and Edgar N. Johnson, *An Introduction to Medieval Europe* (New York: W. W. Norton & Company), 1937, pp. 293-95.

55 An exception may be poultry. That is, however, very unusual. It is part of a general bias for agriculture inherent in cash basis accounting allowed for livestock.

56 I.R.S., Tax Guide for Small Businesses, Pub. No. 334, (1965 ed.), p. 26.

57 There are several points in tax law, besides those already noted, where excess depreciation is recaptured using a sliding scale where the amount recaptured declines with the number of years before sale.

58 A good popular summary is Jeanne Dangerfield, "Sowing the Till," *The Congressional Record* 119 (1974); 59247-55 (May 16, 1973). A more establishmentarian but less forthright statement is National Planning Association, *The Effect of Federal Income Taxes on the Structure of Agriculture* (Washington, 1972).

59 Hendrik Houthakker, "The Great Farm Tax Mystery," *Challenge,* Jan.-Feb. 1967, pp. 12-13, 38-39.

60 Liquor of course is highly taxed outside the income tax, by excises, but the excise tax levied upon sale has a bias for longevity, and greatly favors Scotch, maturing in 10 years, over Vodka, which can age in the bottle in as little as 10 days.

61 In fairness to Terborgh, many of his writings advocate faster replacement.

62 *The Warren, Gorham and Lamont Report,* Sept. 9, 1974, sec. 2, p. 3; "Pensions: The Reformation Begins," *Newsweek,* Sept. 24, 1974, pp. 98-99.

63 Adam Smith, *Wealth of Nations,* pp. 338, 341, 349.

64 J. S. Mill, *Principles of Political Economy* (Boston: Lee S. Shepard, 1872), pp. 41-63, passim. See also J. S. Mill, *Essays on Some Unsettled Issues of Political Economy* (London: Longmans, Green, Reader, and Dyer, 1874), pp. 55-59.

65 Wicksell, *Lectures on Political Economy,* pp. 194-96.

66 K. Wicksell, *Value, Capital and Rent,* trans. S. H. Frowein (London: G. Allen & Irwin, 1954), p. 127.

67 Ibid., p. 160.

68 He credited it to Böhm-Bawerk, who however expounded it very roundaboutly, if not obscurely.

69   7.273 years, to be more exact.
70   Instead of K = FP, the proper formula is now

$$K = F \frac{e^{Pi} - 1}{i} > FP$$

71   "Why Ma Bell Constantly Needs More Money," *Business Week,* March 25, 1972, pp. 57-58.
72   Ibid.
73   In Practice, "investment" is used very loosely by macroeconomists for spending on durables, without careful distinctions of net and gross, as the logic would require. No careful effort at all is made to estimate real depreciation, the problem being buried by using GNP instead of national income.
74   Cecil Woodham-Smith, *The Great Hunger* (New York: A Signet Book, 1964), pp. 137-60 and passim.
75   These are covered in Gaffney, *Extractive Resources and Taxation,* pp. 391 ff.
76   "Second thoughts that threaten the breeder," *Business Week,* Aug. 24, 1974, p. 21.
77   "Project Independence Will Cost a Bundle," *Business Week,* Aug. 24, 1974, p. 24.
78   "Why Housing Still Feels the Crunch," *Business Week,* Aug. 17, 1974, p. 50.
79   In modern industry, Research
                      Has become a kind of church
                      Where rubber-aproned acolytes
                      Perform the ceremonial rites
                      And firms spend funds they do not hafter
                      In hope of benefits hereafter.
                                              —K. Boulding
80   Yoram Barzel, "Optimal Timing of Innovations," *RE&S,* 50(3):348-55 (Aug. 1968).
81   Ironically, the data come from Joel Barlow of Covington and Burling that British taxes bear lighter on capital than do those of other major capitalist nations. Joel Barlow, "The Tax Law Bias against Investment in Production Facilities," NTJ 26 (3): 415-31, at pp. 432-33.
82   (9) may be derived from $(1 + S) e^{nl} = R + S$, which simply says we put in land at the beginning and get it back at the end, along with the mature tree.
83   Note in passing that when S is large relative to planting cost (here equal to one), most of the capital is geogenic (land-derived). Some reforestation is entirely voluntary and geogenic, representing no labor at all.
84   The lives of cattle are foreshortened in the U.S.A. as compared with Argentina, where rangeland and cash grain are cheaper, for example. But in Western Europe and Japan, lives are even shorter, if cattle are grown at all.
85   Matthew Gaffney, Jr., John Hoven, and Steve Hanke helped refine this proof. Further discussion of this and related points are in the writer's "Tax-induced Slow Turnover of Capital."

7 *Douglas N. Jones*

Property Taxation, Land Use, and Environmental Policy: The Alaska Case

Introduction and Scope

A topic as broad as Property Taxation, Land Use, and Environmental Policy requires some limitation of scope even to worry about it—to say nothing of analyzing it. Accordingly, in this paper I have chosen to treat these three subjects as they bear on Alaska.

The choice of focusing on the Alaska case is not a casual one, and several ends are served. First, I know a fair amount about it—a necessary (though not sufficient) condition to a respectable paper. I was the economist member of an obscure three-man presidential committee for developing Alaska created by President Johnson and the governor of Alaska in the aftermath of the 1964 Alaska earthquake. More recently I served as economist and legislative assistant to the junior senator from Alaska. And most recently, in the Economics Division of the Congressional Research Service, congressional inquiries on the economics of Alaska are among those inquiries that come to me for resolution. Second, the Alaska case is a peculiar and interesting one in that land and land resources dominate nearly everything about Alaska—its physical features, its institutional characteristics, its unfolding development, and its public policy needs.

The views expressed are those of the author and do not necessarily represent the views of the Congressional Research Service or the Library of Congress.

167

Sixteen years into statehood, Alaska in many ways is at the stage of our western states of, say, eighty or a hundred years ago. This, of course, provides opportunities as well as problems.

Third, as the most idle reader must note, issues about Alaska are very current, and almost all of them have to do with land use and environmental preservation—the trans-Alaska oil pipeline and now the proposed gas pipeline, underground nuclear testing, taking of sea mammals, the clearcutting of timber, the construction of new towns, minerals extraction, the elaboration of a transport system, the creation of a park system, state and Native land selection, to name a few. In short, Alaska has become the arena where the forces of environmental and social and economic development are being played out in a major "high stakes" fashion with the outcome of obvious significance to the state and of substantial consequence to the rest of country. The Alaska case may not be so peculiar as to preclude generalizing from it. Further, since such a large proportion of Alaska is still public land, it is a legitimate occasion for "outsiders" to look in on what is happening there.

Finally, it seems logical to ask what part property taxation as one instrument of public policy might play in all this. As a new entity faced with old and new problems Alaska and its localities have the opportunity at least for innovation and fresh directions, or at a minimum for avoiding pitfalls and mistakes of the past. It is the advantage of "coming last."

The task, then, is to say something of the likely future of the property tax in Alaska and assess how far it may be a useful device in reconciling environmental and developmental considerations there.

Land and Land Use in Alaska

Some numbers and magnitudes are perhaps helpful to recall. Alaska's sheer enormity has many implications. It is about 375 milion acres in area (over two and one-half times the size of Texas), it spans 17 degrees in latitude and 40 degrees in longitude. Said another way, the expanse of the state equals that of the forty-eight contiguous states from coast to coast and border to border because of the great length of the Aleutian Chain and southeastern Alaska projecting from the great land mass of the state. Its boundary is 3,200 miles long and its coastline is half again as great as the total coastline of the conterminous forty-eight states.

The present population of Alaska is 357,000, and it is therefore the least populous of the states both in absolute terms and in density. It is in fact at the very early stages of development, with its communities confined to coastal areas and along rivers. One city, Anchorage, has almost half the state's population. A major push inland awaits the development of a surface transportation system which in turn awaits the need for developing Alaska's vast land, mineral, and recreational resources.

When the U.S. bought Alaska a century ago the population was about 35,000, of whom only a tiny fraction (perhaps 500) were non-Native. The population doubled by 1940, doubled again by 1950, grew by another 80 percent by 1960, and by almost 40 percent over the last dozen years. Meanwhile the percentage of Native population (Aleuts, Eskimos, and Indians) fluctuated as non-Natives came and left Alaska in boom and bust periods, until Natives now comprise about one-fourth the total (some 85,000 people).

At the granting of statehood, about 96 percent of Alaska was public land. Even after state and Native land selection (discussed next) is completed, the federal government will still own 59 percent of Alaska, which continues to be the largest public land state. Most of the state is now un-incorporated and is part of no organized local entity. There are no counties in Alaska, but rather eleven boroughs which perform a similar function. These boroughs taken together make up 161,000 square miles, ranging from 1,200 square miles in the case of the Bristol Bay Borough in southwestern Alaska to 88,000 square miles for the newly formed North Slope Borough in Arctic Alaska. Nor is there any ready correlation between area and population of the boroughs, as can be noted in a glance at table 7.1.

TABLE 7.1
Alaska City and Borough Populations and Areas

Locality	1970 census*	Estimated square miles
City and Borough of Juneru	13,556	3,100
City and Borough of Sitka	61,109	2,900
North Slope Borough	3,322	88,281
Bristol Bay Borough	1,147	1,200
Fairbanks North Star Borough	30,618	7,500
Greater Anchorage Area Borough**	102,994	1,500
Kenai Peninsula Borough	15,836	25,600
Ketchikan Gateway Borough	10,041	1,250
Kodiak Island Borough	6,357	4,500
Matanuska-Susitna Borough	6,509	23,000
Haines Borough	1,351	2,200

Source: *Alaska Taxable Municipal Property Assessments and Full Value Determinations,* Department of Community and Regional Affairs, State of Alaska, Juneau, 1972.

*Exclusive of military residents.

**At the end of 1974 the Eagle River Chugiak Borough was formed out of the Greater Anchorage Area Borough as separately incorporated.

At the next unit of government, Alaska has only 14 cities which are empowered (along with the boroughs) to levy the property tax. These range in (population) size from North Pole, Alaska, at 265 people, to the city of Anchorage. In addition there are about 180 Native villagers, ranging in size from 25 to 2,500 people, scattered generally in coastal and rural Alaska.

In understanding the importance of what is going on in land policy issues in Alaska two crucial milestones must be treated in some detail. One is the provision in the Alaska Statehood Act for state selection of public lands and subsequent state behavior; the other is the 1971 "full and final settlement and extinguishment of any and all claims" for the lands of Alaska by the aboriginal citizenry.[1]

Under the Statehood Act Alaska was granted the opportunity to select for itself 104 million acres of land over a twenty-five-year period (i.e., by 1984). The idea was that the new state should be launched on its way with the chance of "succeeding" fiscally, enhanced by being allowed to choose "the choice land." Some selections were easy, but it was soon seen that knowing which lands were choice and which were not depended on information—what was under the lands and what was on them. It also depended on what land management improvements federal agencies were willing to pursue in the performance of their regular programs.

State selection was slow, and by 1970 only about 17 million acres had gone into state hands, with perhaps another 11 million acres applied for. Besides the tendency to delay land selection until more was revealed about the value of the land resources, there were several other reasons for slowness on the part of the state. The transaction itself was a major one, dealing with such immense magnitudes, and not a simple process. Further, certain federal aid formulas applicable to Alaska (e.g., highway assistance) were tied to the amount of federally owned land in the state, and therefore each acre that went over to the state eroded away the total dollar contribution of the federal government. Also, the cost of managing massive amounts of land is very considerable (the Bureau of Land Management budget for Alaska is about $20 million annually), and as long as the feds owned it the state didn't have to carry this burden. Finally, Native groups in the late 1960s began filing protests to further state land selection, fearing that as more of the land passed to state (and other) hands it would become all the more difficult to gain a favorable settlement of their claims to the land. State selection does not mean continued state holding of the land, because much of it presumably would be sold or leased to private parties. Increasing industry attention and exploration activity on the land resources of Alaska and the dramatic North Slope oil discovery served to heighten these concerns.

Recognizing that these interests had to be reconciled, the Secretary of the Interior issued a "land freeze" order that stopped all public land transactions until these conflicts could be resolved and titles to the land cleared. Subsequently, the federal courts ruled that nothing should happen to the lands of Alaska wherever Natives had filed claims, until the Congress sorted out the ownership problem.[2] The advent of a great oil find became not only the proximate cause for bringing to a head the issue of Native claims to the land, but as it turned out, a crucial part of the solution.

This, then, was the situation. The State of Alaska was anxious to proceed with its "rightful" selection of land; the Natives were increasingly active in pressing their claims to the land (almost all of Alaska was claimed) with a focus on what might be under it; the oil industry (and other development interests) were anxious to have the uncertainty of clouded titles to land alleviated; and the federal government was ready to resolve once and for all the lingering Native claims issue, prodded in part by the societal forces flowing in favor of all American minorities. The environmental forces were at that time only dimly aware of what a Native claims settlement might mean to their interest.

Legislation was introduced in 1969 to settle the Alaska Native land claims. The Senate Interior Committee held extensive public hearings on the several bills proposed, and the House Interior Committee did the same. Intensive Executive Sessions of the Senate Interior Committee followed in which the major concepts of the bill were agreed to after sustained debate and many record votes. The result was that on June 11, 1970, the Senate Interior and Insular Affairs Committee favorably reported for consideration by the full Senate S. 1830. After two days of debate on the Senate floor the bill passed 76 to 8, with relatively minor amendments.

For our purposes here the key provisions of the Senate bill were:
1. $500 million payable over twelve years with no interest;
2. a 2 percent royalty upon leasable minerals, not including lands "tentatively approved" for state selection or bonuses already paid to the state from the $900 million oil lease sale on the North Slope in 1969, until $500 million would be reached;
3. approximately 11 million acres of land, primarily around villages under the formula of one township (23,040 acres) per village, plus an additional township for every increment of 400 people;
4. real property interest conveyed under the Act to be exempt from state real property taxes for twelve years, except that municipal taxes, real property taxes, and assessments could be imposed upon real property within the jurisdiction of any Native village incorporated as a munici-

pality. Also rents and profits derived from leasing or other business transactions with the land would be taxable.

For its part the House Interior Committee held further sessions on the legislation, but failed to report out a bill before adjourning in December.

With the convening of the new Congress the identical bill that had passed the Senate in the 91st Congress was introduced as S. 35 by Senators Jackson, Gravel, and Stevens on January 25, 1971.[3] This time, however, the Senate Interior Committee decided not to act on the bill until the House acted—or at least showed definite forward movement on the matter. Meanwhile the Secretary of the Interior kept extending the Alaska land freeze a few months at a time in order to allow the Congress time to act on the land claims legislation.

Subsequently, the Alaska Natives had their own bill introduced, demanding 60 million acres in the land package—up from their previous call for 40 million acres. Further, through skillful lobbying efforts the Alaska Native organizations were able to persuade the Administration to actively back a provision for a 40-million-acre settlement.

The diverse forces for settlement reached a crescendo in the early fall of 1971, and the House Interior and Insular Affairs Committee reported favorably (with one dissenting view) its bill H.R. 10367 on September 28, 1971. After a moderately tough floor fight involving several conservationist amendments the House passed the bill 334 to 63 on October 20, 1971.

The key features of the House bill were: a $425 million cash award over ten years; acceptance of the 2 percent royalty idea until $500 million accrues; a land package totaling 40 million acres around villages, of which about 18 million could be selected ahead of the State of Alaska and the remaining 22 million selected *after* the state had finished its statehood selection.

Spurred on by the House action, the counterpart Senate Interior Committee held additional public and executive sessions on the several bills before it and on October 21, 1971, favorably reported S. 35 with certain important changes. Compensation was again set at $500 million, and timber revenues were added to mineral revenues from the land resource in contributing to the $500 million revenue-sharing pot.

But by far the most important change was in the land package, it having become clear that the obstacles to settlement centered not around money but around land. To the surprise of everyone the Senate committee provided two alternative land provisions from which the Natives could choose in a statewide referendum vote. The first option was 40 million acres in fee, the bulk of which would be contiguous to the Native villages. The second option was a land grant of 20 million acres, to be selected for their economic potential as mineral, timber, or recreational lands; and permits to use 20 million acres for subsistence purposes (hunting, fishing, trapping, berry picking, and fuel gathering) under a revocable permit system.

The bill passed the Senate as H.R. 10367 on November 1, 1971, by a vote of 76 to 5.

As the two committees went "to Conference" this meant that any one of three alternatives (or combinations thereof) might emerge as the final settlement. The Natives had to decide for purposes of their own lobbying efforts what weight to give "time preference," that is, 40 million acres now *vs* half now and half later; how to evaluate larger contiguous selection rights around villages as against smaller free-floating selections in search of valuable subsurface resources; whether to prefer a smaller land package in fee to a larger total land package with only part of it in fee; etc.

Racing against the holiday adjournment schedule again the House-Senate Conference Committee began a series of nine executive sessions on November 30, 1971. On December 14, 1971, both Houses passed H.R. 10367 and the 104-year issue was at least legislatively over. President Nixon signed the bill into law four days later.

In the final outcome the law provides that Alaska Natives will receive title to 40 million acres around 220 villages selected from 25 townships withdrawn around each village. The cash compensation settled at $462.5 million, and the revenue-sharing remained at $500 million. The tax-exemption provision for undeveloped and unleased real property held by Natives was retained and extended to twenty years.

The Alaska Native Land Claims Settlement necessarily altered a number of existing relationships. Relationships between the state and federal governments were placed under strain and altered by the land claims settlement process. The settlement was by definition an ethnic one based on aboriginal rights and directly impacted on only 20 percent of the state's population. Perhaps more important, however, was the impact on the land resource and therefore the rest of Alaska. Prior to the settlement, the federal government had withdrawn from general use about 151 million acres for various purposes. Overall, the Department of the Interior managed about 330 million acres of the federal lands in national parks, national monuments, wildlife refuges and ranges, and unappropriated public domain. Other federal agencies holding significant acreage are the U.S. Forest Service and the Department of Defense.

Perhaps the most serious conflicts, and the conflicts that came closest to delaying the settlement, came in the relationship between the state government and the Alaska Natives. Both parties were competing directly for the most valuable land in Alaska. Resolution of the conflict came at the eleventh hour of negotiations, and three years into the implementation of the act's provisions things may yet flounder on this point.

Of course the principal question was one of priority. Who would have prior selection rights to land? Secondly, but closely related, was the question of which lands. The natives were insistent that some portion of the land settlement be "free-floating"—that is, with unrestricted selection rights in the federal domain. The state opposed this concept. The state wished to restrict the areas eligible for Native selection to land contiguous to villages rather than permit Natives to select at will for economic potential.

This argument ran directly counter to the one made by most Native leaders. They argued that to force the principle of contiguity would be tantamount to creating super-large reservations. There was no valid reason, they argued, to foreclose their selection right to land that might not have as great an economic value.

The settlement compromised these positions generally closer to the state's viewpoint. The Natives have a prior selection right to 22 million acres of land contiguous to the villages named in the Act. Following village selection, the regional corporations will select from townships remaining within a withdrawal area that approximates 25 townships surrounding each village. These selections need not be contiguous. Thus the areas of withdrawal and selection are defined by the Act. Again the implementation of this provision has not been as clear of conflict as the authors intended. Withdrawals and selections have been challenged by both sides and by the federal government as well.

Two other provisions important to our land-use story deserve mention.

The state had opposed creation of a federally chartered land-use corridor that would generally follow the 800-mile route of the pipeline from the Arctic Slope to the Gulf of Alaska. The state believed such an action would create a type of Panama Canal Zone, where state authority could not be exercised. Environmentalists supported the federal position, feeling that the feds would be easier to deal with than the state. This issue was compromised (more in principle than in practical effect) by removing the direct establishment of the pipeline route from the Act and conveying the authority to the Secretary of Interior to establish it, if he so desired.[4] The Secretary did.

Toward continuing management of Alaska's land resources, the federal and state governments established a Joint Land-Use Planning Commission. Language creating the commission was incorporated in the land claims bill, and counterpart legislation was passed in the state legislature. This commission was directed to undertake comprehensive land-use planning for public lands, including lands to be conveyed to Natives. It was charged with reviewing all proposed federal withdrawals, making recommendations on proposed land selections, recommending patterns of usage, and helping resolve conflicts. The commission was given no enforcement authority, but commands considerable public attention, and therefore has become an important factor in land-use decisions in Alaska.

From the public policy point of view it was important that in the pushing and hauling over ownership of the lands of Alaska the character, or at least the outcome, of the legislation not be a land *disposal* transaction but have a land-*use* emphasis. The Federal-State Land-Use Planning Commission has the chance of achieving that hoped-for result. In August 1973 the commission made its initial recommendations to the Secretary of the Interior on a major land-use issue in the aftermath of the Native Land Claims settlement and has since met periodically with the Secretary and with the House and Senate Interior committees on easement and other issues.

In order to protect the public lands of Alaska and provide for an orderly sorting out of these large quantities of land the Act directed the Secretary of the Interior to withdraw "from all forms of appropriation" up to 80 million acres of unreserved public lands which he deems are "suitable" for addition to or creation as units of the National Park, Forest, Wildlife Refuge, and Wild and Scenic Rivers Systems.[5]

The Secretary had nine months to make his initial withdrawals and had two years to make formal recommendation to the Congress for classifying these lands in one or another system. Those areas not recommended are available for appropriation. Those areas recommended by the Secretary but not acted upon by Congress within five years become available for appropriation. Initial withdrawals were made in September 1972 by Public Land Orders 5250 through 5257. Recommendations for classifying these lands were made in December 1973 as S.2917 but had not been acted upon by the Congress by the end of 1974.

These provisions too were compromises, but in favor of the environmentalists. They wanted all of Alaska lands withdrawn and a five-year

TABLE 7.2
Legislative Proposals* for Classification of National Interest Lands in Alaska
(in millions of acres)

Additions to	Bill	
	S. 2917 (Administration's)	S. 2918 (Citizens')
Park system	32.26	59,76
Wildlife refuge	31.59	43.19
Forest system	18.80	1.60
Wild & scenic rivers	.82	1.59
	83.47	106.14

*In addition to S. 2917 and S. 2918, Congressman Dingell has proposed setting aside 133.5 million acres in Alaska for wildlife refuges, in H.R. 2295.

moratorium on land transactions there: the state, for economic and financial reasons, wanted a smaller withdrawal and a shorter period. Having
had the lands "frozen" for five years already, the state did not look
forward to the prospect of an additional five-year "delay."

As mentioned, the two-year period for recommending what to do with
the 80-million-acre withdrawal expired in December 1973. Pending before
the Congress are the contents of two bills—S.2917, the Administration
proposal, and S.2918, a citizens' proposal introduced by Senators Jackson
and Fannin by request. The major categories and the amounts of delin-
eated acreages in each bill appear in table 7.2. Besides the obvious importance of land classification to the simple matter of how much is added to
which systems, is the crucial and controversial issue of the nature and extent of mining activity that can go on in Alaska *as a result of being* classified under one system rather than another. For its part, the Land-Use
Planning Commission recommended that some 60 million acres or three-
fourths of the classified lands be open to exploration and extraction of
minerals.

The present situation is that the Alaska Natives are moving ahead in
selecting 40 million acres of their allotted land while state selections are
impeded in areas around each village; after four years, state land selections around the villages will be unimpeded; state land selection outside
these areas is now proceeding toward the balance (76 million acres) of its
104 million acreas statehood promise; except that neither party can select
any of the 80 million acreas which the federal government withdrew as
mentioned above.

What's beginning to unfold in Alaska in the resolution of its land issues
seems to be a good example of what has been elsewhere called "the quiet
revolution in land-use control."[6] There is an increasing awareness of
scarcity and limited supplies. There may even be a changing concept of
land, indicated by the distinction between land *as a resource* as opposed to
viewing it as merely a *commodity*. The earlier philosophy of land regulation as narrowly a matter of maximizing private property values is grudg-
ingly giving way to a broader notion of social and environmental considerations.

Also there remains the question of federal/state and state/local relationships regarding land use regulation, though these are in part being
worked out by the novel commission previously described. The tough
question of knowing just what the really big land decisions are and which
ones to address continues to be perplexing. Finally, there lurks in the
background in a constitutional system such as ours (coupled with an
economic system based on property rights) big unresolved questions of the

limits of regulation, for example, when do regulations, restriction, or prevention of a particular land use become "taking?"

Environmentalism and Alaska

It seems fair to say that, flushed with a victory over the Supersonic Transport, the environmental movement has made Alaska (particularly with the oil pipeline issue) the next arena where the national guilt feelings can be vented. And there are, of course, legitimate environmental concerns about what happens there.

For the purposes of this paper, environmentalism is roughly equated with pollution control and pollution abatement. The kind of pollution to be considered is of the eye-car-nose-and-throat variety, that is, scenic, noise, air, and water pollution. With this in mind it is helpful to survey sector by sector the specific environmental degradation issues associated with each of the major elements of Alaska's economy.

Oil and Gas

In the exploration phase the problem is one of damage to the land—especially in permafrost areas—through vehicle movements and campsite construction in support of drilling activity. During the construction phase the culprits are haul roads, major work camps, waste material disposal, digging and filling (about half of the proposed oil pipeline will be buried), and destruction of wildlife.

At the operations stage the pollution control problems largely shift from a terrestrial to a marine context. While the spectre of a ruptured 48-inch-diameter pipe spewing oil over the fragile tundra is a haunting one (and even here the concern is mostly the messing up of watersheds), the main considerations become damage to the fisheries should spillage occur at the terminal port facilities and spills from tanker collisions and ballast operations. No significant refining activity is seriously contemplated for Alaska, though the appearance of a petrochemical derivative industry is quite possible.

Mining and Minerals

The minerals that are likely to be exploited in Alaska in significant amounts are coal, copper, fluorspar, tin, and tungsten. Of these only coal is now actively mined. The environmental worry in these cases centers on strip mining, stream pollution, dredging, waste material disposal, and access road construction. This sector is one of the two most controversial (the other being forestry) with respect to implementation of the multiple-use concept. Here is where the hardest lines are drawn between the environmental and the developmental forces. As mentioned, the Land-Use Planning Commission in its recommendations tries to walk the tightrope by allowing 60.8 million acres of federally withdrawn land for mineral exploration and extraction but qualifies this in several ways. On 2.7 million acres only oil and gas exploration and extraction would be permitted; on 294,000 acres only geothermal exploration and production would be allowed; on another 910,000 acres only exploration for inventory purposes (no production) would be permitted; and on about 14 million acres mineral exploration and extraction would be allowed "but only under careful regulation."

Forest Products

Unlike the mining sector, the forest products sector is currently an economically active one, though geographically limited (with few exceptions) to southeastern Alaska. Pollution control problems are pulp mill effluents, the practice of clear-cutting timber, haul road construction, and salmon stream degradation. The multiple-use concept is in contest in this sector as well. When and if the forests of interior Alaska become commerically feasible, presumably most of these problems will occur there.

Fisheries

In this important sector of the Alaskan economy the main pollution problems are oil spills and fish waste disposal around the coastal canneries. This is one of the few sectors where significant pollution damage is already being experienced in Alaska.

Tourism and Recreation

The tourism and recreation sector makes up perhaps 15 percent of the state's economy and can be expected to grow markedly in absolute if not relative terms. Pollution control issues obviously are central to the establishment and management of national and state forests and park systems, wilderness areas, fish and wildlife refuges and preserves, and wild and scenic rivers in Alaska. A complicating factor peculiar to the Arctic and sub-Arctic regions is the limited level of utilization that particularly fragile areas (for instance, the tundra) are able to stand without undue damage.

Utilities and Communities

As might be expected in an underdeveloped region, the utilities sector in Alaska is just emerging—transport, power, communications, and community facilties systems. In the transportation field only the airport system is well developed; in the power generation field hydroelectric is a major component, and the small population and limited manufacturing sector mean that the total power requirement is small in any event. Gas-, oil-, and coal-fired plants are in existence in the populated areas. Two military petroleum and petroleum product pipelines operate in Alaska, the private trans-Alaska oil pipeline is now being constructed, and a national gas pipeline has been formally proposed.

Community development in any frontier region always presents pollution problems of the visual variety. Zoning requirements tend to be minimal, architectural and planning attention slight, when the primary object seems to be to subdue the land and establish footholds for community development.

In sum, then, Alaska is not presently faced with the whole range of pollution problems bearing in on the rest of the country. Air and noise pollution is minimal, scenic pollution coincides with the few major communities. Water pollution is the main danger and centers on the two industrial sectors—oil and forestry activity.

Property Taxation and Alaska

Turn now to the third strand of this story—the property tax in Alaska.

For a glimpse of magnitudes, table 7.3 was constructed to give selected general revenue data for the state in 1973. Only $41 million of property tax

TABLE 7.3
Selected General Revenue Data for Alaska, 1973
(in millions of dollars)

	Total general revenue*	All general revenue from own sources	Total tax revenue	Property tax revenue
Alaska	$538.5	$334.5	$163.0	$41.5**

Source: *Government Finances in 1972-73*, U.S. Department of Commerce, Bureau of the Census, from table 17.

*Includes federal payments.

**The next lowest states after Alaska are Delaware at $60 million and Wyoming at $87 million in receipts from the property tax.

TABLE 7.4
Property Tax Data for Alaska and the U.S., 1972-73

	Per capita amounts	Percent of total tax revenue	Percent of all general revenue*
U.S. average	$215.78	37	30
Alaska	$125.85	25	12

Source: *Governmental Finances in 1972-73*, U.S. Department of Commerce, Bureau of the Census, from tables 17 and 22.

*From state sources only (exclusive of payments from the federal government).

receipts were collected out of a total tax take of $163 million. These are the lowest amounts for any of the states. Table 7.4 compares the Alaska case to the national average in per capita amounts for the property tax and dependency thereon.

Note that the per capita amount collected in Alaska is substantially below the national average—$125.85 vs. $215.78. Note too that while nationally the property tax provides 37 percent of total state and local tax revenue, in Alaska the figure in 25 percent. Further, for states generally, receipts from the property tax comprise almost one-third of all General Revenue, while in Alaska only 12 percent is attributable to property taxation. And this differential would be even greater if figured against all general revenues the state receives *including* federal assistance, because per capita federal payments are $618 as against $187 on a national average. The point of all this is simply that Alaska has not so far become unusually dependent on the property tax, despite the way in which land dominates its behavior and its future.

There is no statewide property tax (except in the case of the oil industry), and no state-level tax assessment review agency. The property tax is contained in the Alaska constitution and is rated as "middle range" in the amount of detailed spelling out.[7] The basis for assessment is full and true value, and assessment-sale ratio studies are conducted annually. Municipalities collect ad valorem taxes on nonbusiness vehicles, aircraft and boats, of which there are many. Intangibles are exempt from ad valorem taxation. Mobile homes are taxed.

As of January 1974 the full-value determination of taxable property in Alaska stood at $4.85 billion. Of this amount 82 percent was real property and 18 percent was personal property.[8] Combined assessed values (as distinct from the full value) totalled $4.47 billion or about 92 percent of the full-value determination—local exemptions and exclusions accounting for the difference. Somewhat less than half the assessed value is in the Greater Anchorage area.[9]

The growth of the property tax base in Alaska has average 17 percent annually over the past ten years, increasing from just over a billion dollars full-value determination in 1964. Even this rapid growth can be expected to increase dramatically as the land ownership issues of state and Native selection and pipeline developments treated in the earlier sections clarify in the near term.

At an earlier time Alaska had on the books an Industrial Incentive Act which involved forgiveness of property taxes. This was, happily, stricken from the statutes in 1971. Alaska is, however, one of seventeen states which have provisions for preferential assessment of farm use land designed to encourage preservation of open space land.[10] The law was carefully drafted to avoid abuse through land speculation for nonfarm use, a considerable danger in Alaska. Even at that, the tax cost in Alaska (as elsewhere) of holding land remains lower than the tax cost of holding other assets that might be bought by the sale of land. This widespread special advantage for landowners follows what has been called "the tendency of all twentieth-century tax systems to snoot anything that moves and to spare anything that stands still." Motion is penalized and inertia rewarded. The Alaska landowner sits on his property while the economy grows (or inflates) around him.

While Alaska's earlier approach was tax preferences for industry, it is fashioning an aggressive tax policy in dealing with the oil industry. As yet this has not included considering the tax instrument as an environmental control device.

Not surprisingly, each session of the Alaska State Legislature has before it property tax legislation treating the oil and gas industry specifically. Faced with the prospect of all the individual local governments in the oil areas and along the 800-mile pipeline route moving to get "a piece of the action" by taxing its chunk of the line and the construction equipment and permanent structures associated therewith, the state moved in 1973 to preempt the field. The oil industry, though not ecstatic over the state's aproach, had an understandable preference for the certainty and uniformity it expected would result.[11]

Effective January 1974 the state's legislation (1) while not precluding local taxation of the pipeline severely constrained it, (2) taxed all property used in the exploration, production, and transportation of oil and gas at a 20-mill rate[12], and (3) exempted from property taxation oil and gas leases and oil and gas in place. A "final certified assessment role" as of the statutory commencement date for construction of the trans-Alaska oil pipeline (April 1974) was set at $723 million. The numbers get large very quickly.

If the 48-inch pipeline is valued at cost, for example, a $5 billion line works out to $6.25 million per mile. A 20-mill rate would produce a tax of $125,000 per mile or $100 million annually over the whole line. If the estimated construction equipment and materials are valued at cost, the additional $1 billion assessment would result in $20 million more. These taxes will apply whether or not the equipment or pipeline is located on federal land.

I start with the proposition that as between state and local government in Alaska, taxation of the oil industry should be allowed both, with the severance tax, gross receipts tax, and the income tax the *main* tax sources for the state, and the property tax and the sales tax the *main* sources for local governments.

The state's move into property taxation in the case of the oil pipeline may have merit on administrative grounds, but the revenues secured from partial preemption of property taxation along the pipeline should in the main be returned to the governmental entities the line traverses. A fair division of the revenues might be one-third for the state's general fund, arising out of its role as a collection agency and the fact that much of the pipeline route lies in state lands, and two-thirds for the local governments along the route. This latter apportionment could be allocated among the particular boroughs (now two) and cities (now two) using the existing formula embodied in the Federal Revenue Sharing program for distribution of funds to localities. The advantages of this are that the formula is increasingly familiar and comprises three factors—population, general tax effort, and a relative income factor.

The property taxes thus apportioned would be (as mentioned) substantial, but not huge. For purposes of exposition, if the $120 million annual total take suggested above were to be the number and if two-thirds of that were to be rebated to the four present areas of origin along the pipeline route, the amounts are not overwhelming. Moreover if, as would seem likely, new boroughs and old municipal boundaries would be extended into the pipeline corridor in order to participate in the proceeds of the rebate, the portions would be still more modest. This would still be a force toward fostering local governments—perhaps four more if Native regional corporation boundaries were approximated and three if census division lines were followed.

On the question of whether property tax receipts from the pipeline should accrue to the state as a whole or should at least in part go to local governments along the route, several points come to mind. One is that the property tax is, as we know, a revenue source traditionally left to local governments. Another is that the windfall aspect of the "happenstance" that the line traverses certain subdivisions and not others has long been honored in property taxation. And finally, unless there is a conscious state policy against it, the encouragement of local government formation and the broadening of the revenue base would seem to be desirable.

Conclusion

What can be said, then, about property taxation as an instrument of environmental control in the Alaska case in particular and in the nation at large? I believe that the use of property tax as a major pollution control device will not come to Alaska nor be widely used elsewhere, for both pragmatic and theoretical reasons.

Recall that the whole question arises at all because of three facts. First, the environment which has traditionally been a common-property resource and freely usable by anyone has taken on the properties of an economically scarce resource. Second, the situation is characterized by the familiar phenomenon of externalities—costs generated, with no direct consequences for the one giving rise to the costs. In economic terms, the statement is that firms operate on private cost functions which are less than social cost funtions where the production of a good or service entails pollution damage. The object of a tax here would be to make the private and social cost funtions converge by forcing up variable cost and hence prices of the polluting firm's product to the point where marginal costs equal marginal price, including taxes. Third, taxation is one of only three main methods of control open to government, subsidies and grants and direct regulation being the other two.

Recall too that for whatever reason there have been relatively limited efforts to apply tax policy as a pollution control device. The federal government and seven states offer accelerated depreciation for control facilities. Control facilities are exempt from sales taxes in twelve states, an income tax credit is allowed in six states, and property tax exemption (the most favored tax approach) is allowed in twenty-four states.

Arguments in favor of using the property tax for environmental preservation are, of course, not to be dismissed out of hand. The cost of cleaning up is high, competitive positions can be altered by affecting average cost; abatement does serve the general good; and there is ample precedent for resorting to taxation to influence various kinds of behavior.

But for me the arguments against are more compelling. The tax structure already suffers from too much social engineering, and encouraging one more foray seems to me the wrong direction. Large segments of polluters would be missed by such a tax, that is, the municipalities and state and federal enterprises. This is especially significant in Alaska, where the public sector is so important. Economies in pollution control through cooperation of firms regionally toward securing large-scale equipment and facilities is discouraged by a system which encourages individual action to take advantage of tax-assistance schemes.

Property tax forgiveness may encourage firms to focus on pollution abatement efforts at the expense of devising changes in the production process itself toward lessening pollutant generation. R & D attention thus may also be distorted toward pollution control technologies, and where government underwrites this, that technology or process which is more socially expensive may be chosen because it is less expensive to the firm. Furthermore, consumers (or other parties to the production process) should stand the cost of pollution control and abatement by industry through higher prices, rather than having the burden fall on taxpayers. This substantially alters the distributional effects of particular pollution control solutions.

Then there are severe practical difficulties in throwing the property tax into the environment control battle. Presumably the focus must be on improvements, since they occasion the damage, not on the passive land itself. Presumably, too, consideration of intangibles doesn't apply. How can one really demonstrate the relation of tangible personal property, say, land, improvements, and machinery to environmental degradation? Does more property mean more pollution, and if so, in what proportion? Or is pollution damage a function of the *value* of property rather than the amount? Or is land neutral with respect to pollution? Finally, admitting that the occasional instance can be found where imposition (or forgiveness) of the property tax might be appropriate and effective, how well suited is it to the task compared to alternative approaches?

The answers to these and similar questions will doubtless be emerging as the sparse literature is elaborated on this topic. Tentatively my answer to the last one is that the tax laws generally and the property tax in particular should not be a strong force in environmental clean up and protection. Direct regulation is the preferred path to follow.

Notes

1   *Alaska Native Claims Settlement Act,* H.R. 10367 92nd Congress, 1st Session, passed December 14, 1971, sec. 2 (a).

2   Native Village of Allakaket, et al *v* Alyeska Pipeline Co., et al., Supreme Court State of Alaska, 3rd Judicial District. Also Civil Action 706-70, Native Village of Allakaket, et al. *v* Rogers C. B. Morton, Secretary of the Interior, U.S. District Court, District of Columbia.

3   *Congressional Record* of January 25, 1971, volume 117, no. 3 Proceedings and Debates of the 92nd Congress. Subsequently the Alaska Natives had their own bill introduced demanding 60 million acres in the land package—up from their previous call for 40 million acres. Further, through skillful lobbying efforts the Alaska Native organizations were able to persuade the Administration to actively back a provision for a 40-million-acre settlement.

4   On March 15, 1972, the Secretary withdrew 5 million acres for the "utility corridor," along with 1.22 million other acres.

5   *Alaska Native Claims Settlement, op. cit.,* sec. 17(d)(2)(A).

6   *The Quiet Revolution in Land Use Control,* prepared for the Council on Environmental Quality by Fred Bosselman and David Callies, U.S. Government Printing Office, Washington, D.C., 1971.

7   *Status of Property Tax Administration in the States,* prepared by the Subcommittee on Intergovernmental Relations of the Committee on Government

Operations, U.S. Senate, 93rd Congress, 1st Session, March 23, 1973, Government Printing Office, Washington, D.C., p. 19.

8   *Alaska Taxable Municipal Property Assessments and Full Value Determinations,* Department of Community and Regional Affairs, State of Alaska, Juneau, 1975, p. 23.

9   Ibid., p. 28.

10   *Alaska Statutes,* 29.53.035.

11   The newly formed North Slope Borough which encompasses the Prudhoe Bay field was quickly moving toward both a real and a business property tax that would cover both equipment and the pipeline itself. The North Star Borough (which includes Fairbanks along the pipeline route) on the other hand found itself with neither a personal nor a business property tax.

12   Experience across neighboring Canada for existing pipelines indicates a tax of not over 20 mills is typical.

8 *Frederick D. Stocker*

Property Taxation, Land Use, and Rationality in Urban Growth Policy

Any attempt to link taxation, land use, and rationality in urban growth policy must be regarded as presumptuous. Who, after all, can say what is "rational" in urban growth policies? Economists tend to equate rationality with economic efficiency. But even this is an elusive criterion. The typical American pattern of urban development, with a high degree of decentralization and fragmentation, is grossly inefficient in its use of land, its transportation requirements, and its high cost delivery system for both public and private goods and services. Yet by the economist's own concept of efficiency—the conformity of outcomes to citizens' basic preference patterns—there may be room to argue that this pattern of development is not merely a result of twisted and misguided subsidies (though to some extent it doubtless is), but that it really reflects the consumer's preferred pattern of urban development. Perhaps it is true, as the political scientist Daniel Elazar has recently suggested, that ". . . in view of the goals of decentralization implicit in the development of these variegated metropolitan land-use patterns, this so-called urban sprawl is what makes living tolerable to many (if not most) Americans." (Daniel J. Elazar, *The Metropolitan Frontier: A Perspective on Change in American Society* [General Learning Corp., 1973], p. 11.)

It is not my purpose to argue that view one way or the other. I do want to suggest that it is no easy matter to define what is a rational urban growth policy. The objectives of such a policy remain undefined and the subject of much dispute.

Nor is the cause and effect relationship between taxation and patterns of land use and development as well understood as we might like. There exists, I judge, a fair measure of agreement on the *direction* of these effects, but not much evidence on their strength. Economists know a lot more about the signs of the coefficients, in other words, than about their values, but probably not enough about either to enable us to be very effective in pressing major policy recommendations. We lack the firm evidence on causes and effects that is necessary to any consensus, even among professionals, as to the proper uses of tax policy in shaping urban growth. And, lacking professional consensus, we are farther still from being able to build that high degree of unanimity in the general public that in turn is necessary before any major, radical policy shift can occur.

A posture of diffidence, therefore, is becoming to the economist who would address himself to questions of urban growth, land use, and property taxation. With that in mind I have decided in this paper to be content with discussing three ways in which property taxation seems to influence urban growth in directions that, at least on a prima facie basis, would seem to be non-neutral and inefficient. In each, I hope to suggest property tax reforms that might move us a step toward more rational urban growth policies.

The Level of Property Taxes: Too High or Too Low?

Perhaps the most obvious feature of the property tax as it influences urban development, as well as the most potent, is the application of the tax at uniform rates to improvements as well as to land. This topic has not been totally overlooked in other TRED conferences, and I shall not dwell on the cause and effect relationships except to note that the practice of taxing land and improvements (and certain other kinds of property as well) at uniform rates results in a tax that is at the same time *too high* on reproducibles and *too low* on land. Yet the practical obstacles to differential taxation of land and improvements, also explored in previous TRED conferences, appear formidable.

The question I would pose is this: If we must continue to live with a property tax that applies equally to land and improvements, would the cause of rationality in urban growth be served by reducing the emphasis on the property tax in our total fiscal system, or by increasing it? The ACIR in its various reports, for example, has pointed toward a reduction in the role of the property tax. Dick Netzer has argued the same point in his paper at the Hartford conference last May.[1] Yet such a policy could lead us toward what Mason Gaffney has sometimes referred to as "latin-americanization" of the property tax, especially if reductions were to occur in states and localities where property taxes already are low, or where underassessment of land is especially pronounced.

Which way should we be going with property taxes, if we are concerned with reducing adverse tax influences on urban growth and development? All might agree that there are some areas where property taxes are too high and should be reduced, and other areas where increases do little harm and might do some good. All might agree also that better (i.e., higher) assessment of land relative to improvements is very often in order. All might agree that changes in the quality of assessment, exemption practices, interarea rate differentials, etc., have an important bearing on the answer.

But rarely are policy issues posed in a framework where a "yes-if" or "no-but" answer is possible. The practical policy issue, as it arises in state legislatures and in countless city halls, is whether the tax as it now exists should be scaled down through increased use of alternative sources, or left about where it is, or increased. In facing the issue of effective rates of the property tax as it exists, particularly its equal application (in principle, if not in practice) to land and improvements alike, I wonder if there can be any consensus on "how high is high enough." Leaving issues of equity aside, the answer requires a judgment of the strength of the deterrent effect of the tax on improvements relative to the positive incentive effects of the same level of taxation on land.

A 1973 study by the Arthur D. Little Company, done for the Department of Housing and Urban Development, offers some empirical evidence on the strength of the deterrent effect of the property tax on residential improvements. The effects of the property tax on housing investment, according to that study, depend on assessment practices. In "upward transitional" neighborhoods "the rate of return on such investments and, consequently, the probability of their taking place, is highly sensitive to tax policy." In "stable" neighborhoods, especially the older ethnic and elderly neighborhoods "the rising level of property taxes threatens buildings maintained primarily out of pride of ownership and neighborhood cohesiveness. Increases in the property tax could seriously undermine these noneconomic incentives for rehabilitation and maintenance." In both cases, however, the possible adverse effects of the tax are largely negated by the failure to reassess building improvements.[2]

In blighted or downward transitional areas, the study suggests a more potent effect for the property tax. "In those blighted and downward transitional neighborhoods, where property taxes account for up to 20 to 25 percent of gross income, the chance to generate a substantial positive cash flow from properties has been effectively destroyed." Again, "failure to reassess properties downward, in line with depreciating capital values, undermines the ability of current owner-occupants to retain ownerships, thereby placing considerable financial pressure on the areas' most stable households."[3]

While the evidence is far from clear and conflicting interpretations of the findings are possible, the conclusion I draw is that the deterrent effects of the property tax as it now operates and at present levels constitute an important problem in most American cities, and reductions would ease this problem.

On the other hand, any such reductions would weaken whatever pressure the property tax places on owners of undeveloped property to put their land to more profitable use. It would reduce holding costs and tend to encourage speculation. Through the capitalization process, it would enhance capital gains, thereby converting explicit tax costs into implicit interest. Higher land prices in turn would produce deterrent effects on development. How serious are these problems? I know of no empirical evidence on the strength of the incentive effect, but intuitively I cannot believe that an annual tax of two, three, or even 3.5 percent of the market value of a tract of undeveloped land in an urban area would constitute much of an inducement to prompt development, especially if the property has speculative potential. Certainly annual interest costs of 8 to 10 percent would be far more potent. If my hunch is correct, it follows that reductions in property taxes would not sacrifice any significant advantage.

Of course, many other things need to be considered in making any broad judgment of the proper role of the property tax. Among these are the equity aspects of the property tax; the possibility of recouping capital gains from tax reduction, perhaps through a local land increment tax or through the federal income tax; the effects of alternative revenue sources to which local governments might turn in lieu of property taxes;[4] the effects of interarea property tax differentials. Considering only its contribution to a rational pattern of urban growth and development, I come to the tentative conclusion that the property tax, at typical urban rates, is likely to do more harm than good and on balance our urban areas would be better off with lower rather than higher property taxes.

Preferential Tax Treatment of Underutilized Land

A second feature of the property tax with implications for urban development patterns is the preferential treatment that is systematically given underutilized land, sometimes legally, more often extralegally. Much has been said and written on the tendency of the assessment system to value land at a lower percentage than improvements and to undervalue vacant lots, suburban acreage, and farmland in general. Most of us, perhaps all, would agree that this is a deplorable practice that is of dubious equity and tends to distort land-use patterns in antisocial ways. Most of us would agree that assessment practices should be strengthened to produce more accurate valuations of undeveloped land and a more realistic assignment of value to land in developed areas. Most assessors, I suspect, would agree that the pattern of tax preference to underutilized land is an unfortunate, though perhaps inevitable, result of the inherent difficulties in the assessment process.

What is especially alarming is the growing acceptance by the public at large of the idea that the property tax *ought* to be designed to favor low-intensity land uses. There has been a continuing spread of what are variously called "preferential" or "use-value" assessment laws, under which farmland (and sometimes woodland, recreational land, airports, golf courses, etc.) are valued for tax purposes at the "value they have in that particular use" (whatever that may mean) rather than the market. There are at present some thirty states in which this form of favoritism to low-intensity land uses has been written into either the statutes or the constitution. Ohio is about to join the list with a constitutional amendment which will almost certainly carry by a wide margin in the coming election.

While those who favor such legislation base their view partly on equity, it is the supposed effect on land use that is relevant to the present topic. It is argued that the property tax, if applied on a strict ad valorem basis, places an intolerable burden on the land owner (typically depicted as an elderly, low-income dirt farmer), forcing him prematurely to sell or develop his land. "Premature" in this context presumably means development in a form that is *socially* suboptimal—strip development or scattered subdivisions with water wells and septic tanks—and not merely development that occurs too early for the owner to realize his maximum speculative profit. Property tax abatement is seen as a way to remove that incentive, head off premature development, and thereby preserve open spaces.

How are we to judge such a policy from the standpoint of rationality in urban development? For the sake of the argument let us assume that the public interest requires that open spaces be preserved in and around our urban centers. The question then becomes one of whether tax abatement contributes significantly to this objective. Having indicated earlier that property taxes at present urban effective rates are probably not a major force impelling development, I likewise doubt that tax abatement does much to prevent or delay the process. The really irresistible impetus to development comes through the market and the opportunity it affords the landowner to become a millionaire. Compared to that, and to the pressure created by high interest rates, the pressure of a 2 to 4 percent a year property tax must surely be a relatively insignificant carrying cost.

Moreover, those tracts that are held in an undeveloped state because of tax preference are not necessarily of the type or in the location to be socially useful as "open space." Surely not all tracts are equally valuable as open space. Some no doubt ought to be developed. But preferential assessment laws typically do not distinguish areas as to their suitability. They are not, as uncritical observers seem to believe, a cheap and painless substitute for land-use planning and for public purchase of property for social purposes. Nor do these laws offer any assurance that property on which such tax preference is granted will remain undeveloped any longer than the owner sees it as being to his private advantage to do so.

Rational use of the property tax in urban development policies should avoid conferring blanket tax subsidies on owners of underutilized land. To the extent that urban land-use plans call for preservation of open spaces, property tax abatement is an unreliable tool.

Interarea Disparities and Tax Exporting

A third way in which property taxes distort urban development patterns is through spatial disparities in property tax levels. This of course is not a problem that is uniquely associated with property taxes. Interlocal differences in other taxes have similar effects. But the property tax is the principal levy used by local governments. And the points I want to make do pertain to property tax policy.

Property tax disparities (or disparities in local taxes generally) cannot be viewed in isolation. To the extent that interlocal variations in tax levels are matched by variations in expenditure on public services, there is no necessary distortion of development patterns. Where this matching does not occur, the result is a pattern of positive and negative subsidies that tends to influence urban development. In the absence of any good reason to believe that these distortions reflect some conscious social policy, we would have to assume that they produce a worse pattern of land use rather than a better one.

One common situation in which variations in local taxes are not accompanied by service differences is that in which local governments have access to a property tax base that includes substantial amounts of what can be called "nonlocal" property, meaning property that is either owned by nonresidents or, in the case of business property, is used to produce somthing that is sold to nonresidents in a market in which forward shifting is possible. In either case, local taxes are exported. Viewed another way, the taxes local voters impose on themselves are supplemented by a matching grant from the rest of the world. The result is to drive a wedge between the marginal valuation of benefits and cost such as to underprice and oversupply services in such a community. Although the property tax is the best example, it should be clear that the same argument applies to other local taxes to the extent they are exportable.

The effect of this system of local taxation is to create an inequity—the same expenditure for public services requires different tax prices in different communities, depending on the amount of nonlocal property in their tax bases. More relevant here, it becomes a source of distortion in local development patterns, as some areas present a favorable public expenditure-tax cost ratio and others an unfavorable.

The remedy would seem to lie in denying local governments the right to tax those forms of property (or other tax bases) that permit a high degree of tax exporting. Railroad and public utility property are the most obvious examples. Industrial property is also a logical candidate. Commercial property seems less so. Those classes of property removed from the local tax base might appropriately be subjected to a state property tax at a rate, for example, equal to the state average local rate.

Conclusion

In dealing with only three property tax issues, this chapter has only nibbled at the large subject implied by the title. It has, for example, totally ignored those issues relating to the proper division of financing responsibility between the state and its urban local units, although they obviously have much to do with property tax levels and differentials and therefore with urban development. Yet the problems discussed represent three significant ways in which our present property tax distorts urban growth patterns.

The property tax, even in its present form as a tax that falls equally on land and improvements, would seem to be potentially a highly effective tool for deliberately influencing urban development. But before it can be brought fully into play in that unaccustomed role, there needs to be a fairly clear, unambiguous, and generally accepted view of what a rational pattern of urban growth is. Until then, it seems wiser and safer for policy makers and those who would influence policy makers to be content with the less ambitious task of reducing distorting effects.

Notes

1   Dick Netzer, "Is There Too Much Reliance on the Local Property Tax," paper presented at the Conference on An Agenda for Property Tax Reform, spon-

sored by the Lincoln Foundation and the Urban Institute, Hartford, Conn., May 20-22, 1973.

2   Arthur D. Little, Inc., *A Study of Property Taxes and Urban Blight,* Subcommittee on Intergovernmental Relations, Senate Committee on Government Operations, April 23, 1973, pp. 6-9.

3   Ibid.

4   User charges would deserve emphasis here, along with greater reliance (in many states) on state aids financed from state-level taxes on personal income.

III. PUBLIC POLICY ALTERNATIVES

Introduction

Part III considers public policy alternatives and includes chapters by C. Lowell Harriss, John Shannon, and Dick Netzer. Harriss examines the complex interrelations between property taxation and other fiscal issues, as well as reviewing a considerable variety of property tax redesign options. Against this rich background he notes the complexity and merit of direct action in land-use planning.

In the second chapter of this set, John Shannon registers grudging but growing appreciation of and for the contribution of the old property tax to operative fiscal federalism. He notes the characteristics of the tax and their derivative political significance in the formation or deferral of intergovernmental tax policy. Shannon concludes that as far as federal action about the property tax is concerned, Congress will make haste slowly.

The final chapter in this trilogy is by Dean Netzer on property tax reform and public policy reality. Noting the gap between what scholars prescribe and what policy makers in fact adopt, he catalogues the apparent policy objectives suggested by public action and then seeks to uncover the thrust of change that would tend to achieve the results desired. En passant, Netzer suggests that the capital tax theory of the property tax has intellectual rather than practical value and concludes that an appropriate intermediate term goal is the development of an explicitly classified property tax system in which land as such is taxed more heavily than either nonresidential or residential property other than land. Netzer would use percentage credits rather than variations in assessed value levels to implement the proposal. Finally, he endorses fairly generous use of appropriately constrained tax deferrals.

9 C. Lowell Harriss

Property Tax Redesign Options: Productive or Counterproductive?

The pace of change in property taxation may, or may not, be unprecedented. But it *is* rapid. It *does* challenge analysis and evaluation.

Diversity Calls for Caution in Generalization

Today's systems of taxing property differ widely among, and within, the fifty states and the District of Columbia. A change which would clearly constitute progress in one place might be of dubious merit or even retrogressive elsewhere. The diversity which is relevant to our topic includes (1) not only this tax[1] but (2) other elements of the tax system as well and (3) government finances more generally, including especially the amounts and "structure" of governmental expenditures. Social and economic conditions also differ among areas in ways that are relevant to an evaluation of changes in property taxation.

In combination, the differences create a presumption against simple generalizations and conclusions. Certainly, one must exercise caution in thinking about recommendations for changes to apply nationwide.

Broad theories and policies will have general validity. All implementa-

Assistance from the John C. Lincoln Institute, University of Hartford, helped in the work underlying this chapter. The views expressed are the author's own and not necessarily those of any organization with which he is associated.

199

tions and applications, however, will consist of specific elements in environments which differ significantly. A "package" which serves well in one place may be far from optimal elsewhere and actually ill-suited in some cases. Interrelations in a complex society cannot be appreciated fully.

Value Judgments

My assignment calls for evaluations. To some extent they must rest on personal judgments. Space does not permit adequate explanation of the reasons for my views—for example, the desirability of shifting tax burdens from one group to another or of changing the degree of local government independence. A spelling out of the reasons for our opinions would help to clarify elements of fundamental significance—the philosophy which underlies conclusions.

The "redesign options" which I shall examine will be (1) "circuit breakers"; (2) extension (enlargement) of state government participation; (3) relief for owners of farm land on the urban fringe; (4) use charges and greater use of elements other than value as a base for taxation; (5) land increment taxes; and (6) income as a base. Major possibilities *not* considered here are (1) major reduction in burdens on reproducible (man-made) capital and increases on (pure) land values; (2) improvements in administration; (3) reduction or elimination of tax on machinery and other personal property; and (4) reducing the scope of exemptions. First, however, a general matter deserves explicit comment.

Role of Property Taxation Relative to Other Revenue Sources

A reduction in the *relative* role of property taxation would probably not be "redesign" in the sense intended for this program. Nevertheless, since some possible redesigns might alter the importance of property taxation, a few comments are in order. The suggestion of President Nixon (1972) to replace much of the residential tax with a levy on value added (with relief for lowest income groups) would have reduced the relative position of property taxation.

Property taxation has a "bad press": frequent assertions repeat misconceptions. As a result, many persons who comment on taxation—from observers with only casual, superficial knowledge to some who have claims to competence in tax matters—would probably endorse redesigns to reduce the role of the property tax. Although some might expect such a change to slow the rise in government spending, most would probably envisage a shift to income and consumption taxes.

The proper concern in appraising any such shift would not be property versus income or consumption taxes in a broad sense. At issue are marginal or *incremental* results of the taxes as they *actually* exist with both their merits and defects. Have we not heard much recently about weaknesses of income taxation—on the one hand, gaps, shelters, loopholes, and on the other, excessive burdens, economically distorting rates, capital-eroding failures to recognize inflation, double taxation of dividends, and so on? Many defects do exist; few are likely to be modified significantly. Even though state (and local) income taxes may not be so subject to criticism as is the federal tax, they, too, suffer from deficiencies.

Existing differences in tax structures over the country require us to be cautious in generalizing. Of course, federal taxes—income, payroll, excise, and estate—do apply over the country as a whole. A family with $x income pays the same federal income tax wherever it lives. But the state taxes which might be increased to offset a decline in property taxes vary greatly. So do property taxes. Therefore, judgments about altering (reducing) the role of property taxation which would apply in some places, such as the older cities of the Northeast, would hardly be valid where burdens are much lower.

Without presuming to settle the matter, I note two points: (1) heavier relative use of income or sales taxation would accentuate the marginal effects of their defects; (2) property taxation has merits (such as utilization of land values as a base and slight compliance cost) which are often underestimated when it is being criticized.

Circuit Breakers

The speed of adoption of the relief features known as circuit breakers must be almost without precedent. For so many states to act so quickly (without compulsion from "outside" in the form of a tied grant-in-aid or a federal tax credit) testifies to something. To what?

Reasons for Adoption

1. For one thing, a "need" did exist, something about as clearly indicated as this often-vague concept could mean. Some older persons with little income did have a justified claim for relief from the obligation to pay as much as was being required from them toward the costs of government.[3] Persuading lawmakers to act could be done on grounds arousing little debate. *Extreme cases permitted of no real dispute.* Humane values of commanding influence in American attitudes toward the distribution of taxes—and the proper treatment of senior citizens—supported some relief. And, it was asked, why should the oldest generation pay for schools for the children of others?

2. (a) Much or all of the tax on the aged few in real need could be forgiven without large revenue loss. Pinpointing relief could make this an *efficient* means in the sense of concentrated benefit for the needy, with little "wastage" in the form of misdirection to persons with no truly justified claim. (b) The burden increases on others are spread widely; on average they are tiny. No sense of heavier burdens on taxpayers in general exerted appreciable counteraction from voters. (c) State governments could provide some offset aid to localities.

3. The administrative problems have apparently not imposed serious obstacles. Extra costs of administration and compliance seem to be minor. Abuses to discredit the system and to complicate administration are not yet, so far as I know, arousing concern. Extension to renters can be administered by using arbitrary rules. The results may be more rough and ready than refined, but in dollar amounts the crudities can be kept within safe bounds.

4. The relief is *personal.* It is not in a form which is likely to be capitalized in higher land prices.

So we can credit states with design innovations which are applauded widely and with justification. The specific features differ considerably. Some must be better than others. Analysis of accumulating experience can lead to improvements which embody the more satisfactory features. But no such progress is inevitable. And moves in the "other direction" can be expected. It is not perfectionist carping over failure to reach an unattainable goal that leads me to raise some questions.

Doubts and Possible Criticisms

1. Present plans do not comprehend everyone who may seem about as worthy of relief as those getting it. The relief for low-income renters, for example, may be relatively inadequate in some states. Or it may be excessive, if some or all of the property tax is not really shifted to renters.

2. Some relief in fact goes for tax which must have been capitalized when the house was purchased. Present owners do not really suffer to the extent (or at least in the way) assumed.

3. The use of age as a dividing line can be questioned as arbitrary. Young families may also be hard up. Why not, it may be asked, ignore age and rely on income alone in granting relief? In response, one may note (not necessarily with full agreement) that this question implies greater reliance on income as the proper base for taxation, to the exclusion of assets, than may be appropriate.

4. Definition of "family," or the unit to be exempt, will not be fully satisfactory. If much becomes involved per case, then incentives to abuse must be expected in a world of human beings.

5. How many families (persons) fail to get relief to which they are entitled? Can administration be developed to keep such shortfalls at an absolute minimum?

6. The family's tax relief declines as income rises. Eventually the relief disappears. This feature will discourage work and thrift a little. It adds another to a considerable list of disincentives. In doing so, this new form of relief aggravates the difficulties of improving the public welfare system by overcoming the high marginal "tax" rates.

Acceptability of Property Tax Increased

One result of the circuit-breaker movement has probably been to enlarge the acceptability of property taxation, or more accurately, to reduce the number of voters who are strongly opposed. A revenue source subject to considerable criticism has been spared some condemnation which might impede the financing of schools and other local services. Elected officials are freer from pressure of popular reluctance to burden retired persons, especially those who suffer from inflation and whose pension and other incomes are less than "adequate."

Tendency to Enlarge Relief to "Undue" Extent

As one thinks of cases not now getting circuit-breaker relief, or too little, uneasiness appears—at least for me. The present may be better than the past in freeing the poor and near-poor from governmentally created deprivation through taxation. But distress remains. Ought not society treat more members less harshly, reducing burdens created by the public (taxes)? An obvious "solution" suggests itself: move the frontiers outward. As lawmakers respond, I ask, "Where will the movement go?" Will aspirants to office, and those holding positions, feel pressure to do more—the "what-have-you-done-for-me-recently" aspect of political rivalry?[4] If so, with what results? Any good thing can be overdone.

The circuit-breaker concept does not have within it inherently limiting factors. No *principle* sets boundaries—to coverage, to amounts, or to refinements and complexities. If a little is good, why not more? Incremental changes from one year to the next may in themselves involve rather little (1) revenue loss and (2) burden addition for others. Impulses to "do good" and to capture votes can reinforce each other—altruism enlisted in the cause of selfishness, including the search for political power. And over a few legislative sessions the increments of relief could cumulate to totals of enough substance to produce something almost different in kind.

One result should be expected with increases in the amounts of relief in individual cases. Unless human nature changes, incentives to abuse will rise. The intrafamily and other conditions which determine both *eligibility* and the *amount of relief* will need more policing. Taxpayers will have economic reason to try to evade the law. Even though dollar amounts for the individual or family will be small, relative to the taxpayer's affairs the temptation could be enough to create some pressures. Demands on administration may pass from the minor to the consequential unless society will tolerate abuse which, though probably not large relative to old defects of property taxation, would not mark progress. Perhaps the laws can be drafted to forestall serious difficulty. At best, however, is there not solid reason to believe that strains on honesty will increase?

Ignoring assets as an element of "ability to pay," where such is the case, seems less than fully logical in principle. Today, of course, the money amount of relief is so limited per case that practical aspects may well override principle. That is, making an effort to adjust for wealth would seem hardly justified. But if relief gets larger, then so will problems.

Moreover, the amount of relief granted to renters needs examination in light of recent thinking about incidence of the tax. To the extent that final burdens fall not on occupants but on the suppliers of capital, the circuit-breaker "relief" for the occupant must be something other than remission of taxes.

"Government must be paid for," an observation so trite that merely saying it once again may be embarrassing. When "we" (the community generally, as in the state legislature) decide that some of the public will be freed from obligations to bear certain taxes, then (1) others must pay more, (2) expenditures must be less than otherwise, or (3) greater reliance must be placed on revenue sources which in fact the initial group (persons to be aided) must help to bear, such as hidden taxes paid through business.

Perhaps added income and sales tax burdens are generally preferable to some of the property tax. Yet in my opinion the arguments are not so overwhelmingly adverse to property taxation as is frequently asserted or assumed.[5] I would hate to see the argumentation which supports relief in *exceptional* cases extended to discredit property taxation more generally. Nothing compels such an extension of assertion, but political "debate" can include oversimplification and even error which is not corrected. One tendency seems highly probable: Relative increases in tax on business property. With what results? Not those which on balance will improve effectiveness in production or wisdom in political economy.

What is now only a "tiny cloud on the horizon" may warrant mention. As more and more members of a community are relieved of more and more taxes, the burdens on the remaining taxpayers increase. Something of a vicious cycle may develop. The amounts of change in typical burdens in the foreseeable future appear too small for immediate concern. But a projection of the trend of the last two or three years for a few more might be sobering. Such a projection may seem entirely unjustified. But when appetites for tax relief, on the one hand, and for votes, on the other, are to be satisfied, what may happen? The results may differ materially from those predicted on the basis of past experience or scholarly logic.

Another caution: freeing a portion of the public from evident and obvious obligation to share the cost of government must have some effect on (the growth of) government spending. With what results? One seems probable. (Older) voters qualifying for the relief will tend to be less opposed to higher school budgets and other local spending. This outcome provides one argument for the policy. But as other taxpayers must pay more, some of them may put up more resistance to enlarging budgets. As long as the increases in burden are not really large in total and are spread widely, the net effect of these forces would probably be some relaxation of resistance to expenditure increases.

As state governments bear costs of circuit-breaker relief, in what ways and by how much will effective local influence on government finance decline? With what results? These and related questions lead into the second of the "redesign" elements.

Greater State (or Large-Area) Participation in Property Taxation

New property tax roles for some governments seem certain. The extent and the form, however, are by no means clear. The court cases on school finance have raised possibilities which a few years ago would not have seemed deserving of serious attention. The U.S. Supreme Court in the *Rodriguez* decision ruled against an extension of federal court jurisdiction over school finance which could have required greater state concern over property taxation. But other forces work in the direction.

The reasons which led states to give up property taxation do not necessarily have validity today. Much state withdrawal from property taxation (notably in the 1930s) resulted from a desire to "free up" revenue for localities from the one tax source which localities could administer. States then developed other sources, chiefly income and consumption taxes. But nothing inherent in the nature of things compelled this set of changes. For one thing, continued or enlarged state use of the property tax could have been coupled with enlarged grants to localities or shift of functions from them to the state level.

The return now to state taxation of property would *not* be, somehow, a simple reversal of past actions. Such a return would not grow out (1) of need to deal with an "excess" of local revenue rate reduction obviously being possible or (2) of inability of states to make substantial use of other tax sources. Nor is there likely to be a general belief in the superiority of property taxation over income or consumption taxation for state financing.

The chief reason likely to be operative—one with merit—would be a belief that the distribution of property (in value terms) is highly unequal relative to expenditure obligations. In consequence, it is argued, especially as regards school financing, exclusive local taxation has results which are less desirable than if larger areas imposed the tax and disposed of the revenue. The potential merits of some such action are considerable. The new area might be the whole state. Or a set of new enlarged (consolidated) districts might be established by state decision. Such extension of state participation may naturally, but inevitably, be coupled with a bigger part in administration.

The large industrial or public utility establishment which is now taxed exclusively by a single school district, town, or even county yields revenue for particular units of government (groups of people) which can hardly be justified on equity or other grounds. Burdens are not appropriately related to either benefits from the spending or need in some meaningful sense. Less striking cases exist.

Whether the tax on business property (especially that on reproducible capital) is eventually paid by customers or by the suppliers of capital to the enterprise, many of those who pay live outside of the present taxing and spending jurisdiction. "Taxation without representation" may be deplored or (silently) praised, depending upon the position one has or hopes to get. Reducing it appears to me the desirable direction of policy. But the apparent principle involved in such an argument probably carries less weight than more pragmatic reasons.

To some extent, however, the local government services do benefit the "property." For this reason their cost is properly a charge on the establishment (its customers or owners). I am led to this conclusion, not only by equity considerations but also by the probable effects on resource allocation of so tying cost and outlay. Beyond this reason, however, the concentration of tax base as unequally as in some places today seems subject to powerful criticism.

"Fiscal zoning," "tax enclaves," and distortions and abuses associated with those terms have more or less scope, depending upon the size of taxing jurisdictions. A state with a multiplicity of small taxing units will include more opportunities for misallocation (whether or not deliberate) and abuse than will a state with fewer but larger units. On this score alone, it seems to me, some states have opportunity to improve matters.

Although setting up taxing jurisdictions larger than now exist in most states has appeal, the entire state itself is not obviously the most logical.

What guidelines might apply? Distinction might be made by type or size of property (industrial and utility), leaving other types (residential, small houses) for local control.

Something to retain considerable local autonomy has merit. The discussions of school finance illustrated differences of views about the amount of freedom appropriate to groups to do more and less than others. I for one prefer a society in which groups (as well as individuals) are not held back (excessively) by others. Majority rule has its "proper" place in our affairs, but that does not necessarily embrace all of what today is, or by the wishes of some might be, the coercing (governmental) elements. More precisely, groupings of various sizes have roles to play. And the role of freedom as *protected* and *served*—as distinguished from being restricted and confined—by political processes does not always flourish best within big government.

No clear principles seem to me to indicate the "proper" scope of *local* taxation of the people on the basis of their ties to (tangible) property. (1) The land, it seems to me, would belong in the local base of jurisdictions which are not "unduly" small. The "best" size would probably be smaller than many counties but larger than many present school and special districts. (2) The man-made capital might more logically be taxed according to the "market area" served; but the latter is not easily defined. Moreover, if one looks not to the market for output but to that supplying capital, then no boundaries less than the nation or the world may seem clearly defensible. Perhaps for taxing plant and equipment of large manufacturing and utility properties something as large as the state has merit—with some local freedom to go above the state rate.

Agricultural and Urban-Fringe Exemptions

Special tax exemptions for land on the urban-rural fringe (freezing rates as for value in agricultural use) have become common. Conceivably, they can help toward constructive, long-run planning of land use. Before commenting on this possibility, let me deal briefly with another aspect.

Future Food Concerns

Perhaps agricultural policy can be aided by retaining the land in use for farming—with offsetting effects in places to which development is shifted. The possible advantages seem to me rather modest, less than small. The portion of total potentially useful land affected must be slight. If some such purpose is to be served, that is, retention of urban-fringe land as part of the source of supply of the country's food and fibers, a national rather more than state-local interest seems to be involved. The policy and planning ought, in principle at least, to be national. The costs should presumably be borne in ways other than those involved in the form of property tax exemption, which will tend to fall on others in the area. Perhaps some interest in garden or dairy products produced locally to save the costs of transport (and perhaps for better quality) may justify exemption. The means-end relation potentialities call for analysis which I have not seen. The result would probably not provide meaningful support for many, if any, present exemptions.

Land Use

The larger potential merit—as an aid to improved land-use planning—can hardly be related to the many exemptions now existing. The provisions of laws and the conditions under which they apply differ greatly. The requirements to qualify, the amount of tax saving, racapture provisions, and other elements vary so much that the "package" in one place may be quite a different total from those elsewhere. Do not most plans benefit the few (those whose land has *risen* in price!) at the expense of the many?

One thing generally involved is community action to deny itself (1) the more intensive use of land and (2) the revenue based on a realizable alternative to existing use. A basic element of the property tax is set aside. Market forces would put a higher value on the land, one that would be the source of greater revenue to share the costs of local government. Does it not seem foolish for the public to deprive itself of the best potential use of land? Land, we recall, is (a) physically, to a large extent, the creation of nature and, (b) economically, to large extent, the creation of community and general economic forces. The "proper" rights of private ownership in land, therefore, differ from the "proper" rights in man-made capital.

One result will be an alteration of the "natural" pattern of land development. Individual owners will have more power to decide on uses without responding to market forces which reflect the ability to pay and the willingness to pay by others in the area. Nothing apparent to me suggests that in general the total for the community will be better than if "normal" forces operate. To the contrary, in fact. True, by some worthy standards the results in particular cases will be more desirable because the decisions were made under the "protected" ("distorted"?) tax laws. But in the majority of cases the interests of those owners of land who are offered tax exemption will not obviously conform to those of the community.

The withholding of some land from a new use can, of course, fit into a longer-run program for community development. Coordination of the tax exemption with land-use planning can contribute to a total result which is desirable in terms of future needs—near- or long-term. The tax advantages can at times be large enough to have a meaningful effect in altering behavior. The nature of a reasonably well planned system to adapt tax exemption at the choice of the owner of land to planning for land use would require more thought than I have given. Details, of course, would depend upon local characteristics. Do any existing plans approximate a set of coordinated features generally well designed to advance the general public interest? At most, I expect, only a small minority. It is not my impression that states permitting the special exemptions generally *require* integration with land-use planning. Local implementation may somehow induce conformity in one way or another. Postive accomplishments, I suspect, are haphazard, infrequent, and rarely economical (benefits relative to costs).

Where do forces exert their effects when tax exemptions redirect them? What reasons can there be for believing that, by reasonable standards, the new results are not inferior?

To some extent the lesser availability of land on the fringes will retard the outflow of population and business. Compactness will be encouraged—congestion, perhaps, in some cases. Some land values within the city will tend to be higher because of the "artificial" alteration of demand. And on the outskirts demand for land, especially for specific parcels, will be different from what it would be if the growth and movement of population were not diverted from the most natural. Some landowners will benefit from larger increments of land values because the land of others is being withheld from the market.

Settlement and development on the outskirts will, in some cases, be less compact because some land is not made available for new use. As a result, streets, water supply, and utility facilities must cover a greater area. The cost per unit (per person) served will almost inevitably be higher. The community will bear heavier real as well as money costs. The exemption policy enlarges the disadvantages associated with "sprawl," "leapfrogging," and "checkerboard development."

Of course, conditions attached to qualify for exemption may bring benefits. Access to open space, use of green areas, may perhaps have some advantages to (a part of) the public.

Equity

On the grounds of equity in sharing the costs of government, the exemptions seem to me to move away from rather than toward goals of fairness. Certainly, the granting of economic favors to some owners of land will be arbitrary. In my personal view, the results will be more in conflict than conformity with acceptable standards of equity. The persons benefiting will almost always be those who have already enjoyed increments of land price, increments which have resulted from community development rather than owner investment and effort. By keeping tax below what it would otherwise be, the exemption enables the landowner to hold land for more capital gain. The exemption reduces the (current) sacrifice required in waiting. The community grants opportunity to profit from (more) "unearned increment" at lower cost than when the tax operates normally. In doing so, the general public must be subjecting itself to considerably greater costs than can be identified and related to general benefit. Many taxpayers bear heavier burdens (or receive fewer benefits from government spending) so that a few may be aided in receiving more capital gains.

From the point of view of equity, is there not a perversity in forcing users of land to bear financial and other burdens so that some owners can seek (larger) gains by withholding land from better use?

Some plans do require that upon shift from agricultural to other use, the unpaid tax, or a portion, be paid to the government, perhaps with some interest. The community then recaptures a part of what it gave up. But any such compensation will be only a portion of the full *real* cost. Better land use during the interval has been sacrificed. Computing the *net* cost of differences in land use, the many alterations of use, will defy the best of measurement.

User Charges

The arguments favoring greater reliance upon user charges have substantial economic merit. (1) Equity as among various owners and users could be advanced by adaptation of payment to cost (and/or benefit) of service. (2) Inducement for more efficient land use could be increased if private costs were related more closely to those of government.

In principle, there seems to me reason to favor more of the financing of streets, sewers, garbage collection, water, and perhaps some other local services by charges related to physical characteristics, such as location and size, or to the amount of use, rather than to value.

At this time I have neither new arguments nor empirical evidence about possible amounts. But one point does call for attention. The largest item of local spending, education, does not seem to lend itself to such financing. At least for the near future, application of user charges to payment for schooling at the elementary and secondary level seems improbable. Therefore, the maximum result of any change would involve only a modest alteration in the total effect of property taxation. Marginal differences in some cases could be of significance.

Deductibility for income tax purposes, or lack thereof, imposes constraints which may have no basis in rational tax policy.

Land Increment Taxes

Federal and state income taxes capture some of the fruits of increases in land prices. (Owners suffering declines can get some offset against tax on income.) The amounts of tax can be one-fourth or more of the gain, but, in the majority of cases any offset will probably be appreciably less. By no means all gains and losses are realized for income tax purposes. For years or decades, ownership can be retained without payment of tax on capital gains. Property held till death can pass with no income tax on the capital gain.

Capital gains taxes have not been designed to deal specifically with land prices as such. The results can hardly conform to a rational plan for using increments of land price to help in financing local government. The tax system does have one element of what might be considered an appropriate system—the recipients of some gains must hand over a portion of what they realize (by sale) to help pay the costs of government. But present taxes do not have other elements which would seem to belong in a desirable plan.

For one thing, the revenue obtained does not go to the particular localities involved. Most of the increments in value taken in taxes seem to me more properly to belong to the local government than to either the state or the federal treasury. Differences in local government spending will tend to have something to do with changes (and differences in changes) in property prices.

A second deficiency of present capital gains taxes is that they create some deterrent to changing land use—sale to shift to use based upon higher values. This feature works against what would be one desirable element—the tax should encourage improvement in land use, or certainly not discourage shift to more productive use.

Although I would not foreclose the possibility of designing a generally desirable tax on increments in land value (or property prices more generally), the problems are greater than may appear—valuation, incorporation and sale of shares of stock, use of complex financing, division and consolidation of parcels, more-or-less-arbitrary provision for income tax, depreciation, and, especially, inflation.

Income as a Base

The capital value of an item of property depends upon the estimated benefits (income) which it will bring (discounted, of course). Taxing on the basis of "income," therefore, would presumably be the same as getting the same dollar revenue by taxing on capital value. Why not, therefore, tax explicitly on the basis of income? Perhaps data are more readily available. Perhaps there is better relation to ability to pay as somehow conceived.

A big difference exists in reality. The "income" used as a basis of annual property taxation in parts of the British Commonwealth where this method is used is *not* income in the full sense of *all* of the benefits for an owner (or user). When the income capitalization bases of assessment valuation is used in this country, the income flow used can be less than the total of expected benefits. Specifically, (prospective) increases in value accruing from time to time are not considered as part of the income normally included. The latter is likely to be money income or some close approximation.

Yet the benefits of owning property can exceed rents or other annual income as ordinarily conceived. One need only refer to holding of land as a speculation. Some of the widespread and in some cases substantial underassessment of vacant land results from the use by assessors of an income concept which fails to include important elements.

Use of money income may have an apparent appeal in that the tax is related to the funds which can be used for payment. Property, such as vacant or grossly underutilized land, which yields little or no cash will not require much cash for payment of tax. (Borrowing on the basis of potential use may be distasteful.) This arrangement not only deprives the local government of revenue properly belonging to it. In addition the practice aids the underutilization of land. Speculation in the form of delay for more remunerative use is eased. The community taxing on the basis of money income would in effect deprive itself of some of the best use of a resource. The public must alter what would presumably be the best pattern of land use, one reflecting more fully the realities of demand and supply. Where the free play of private forces seems likely to lead to less than the best results, the method of improving would be some direct action in land-use planning. As property values are affected—as by restriction on usage which would yield most income—the effects should, of course, be reflected in assessed values.

Notes

1   For a convenient reference showing one of many kinds of diversity see Tax Foundation, *Facts and Figures on Government Finance,* 17th Biennial Edition, 1973, table 122, tax per capita by state. The 1971 figures ranged from $41 in Alabama to $296 in California. The absolute amounts have risen, but the disparities remain large indeed.

2   The reasons why such a shift would seem to me highly desirable appear in many places; for example, C. Lowell Harriss, *Innovations in Tax Policy and Other Essays* (John C. Lincoln Institute, Univ. of Hartford, 1972), pp. 170-96.

3　The definitions or concepts of "income" used in most states are generally much broader than for income taxation. Social Security benefits, for example, are included. Imputed value of occupancy, however, does not get included. As to wealth (distinguished from income), those persons now qualifying for circuit-breaker aid are not likely to have enough to cause concern that tax relief goes to non-needy.

4　Perhaps young voters—in college towns—will see opportunity to use their political influence to garner rax relief.

5　To the extent that property taxation falls on pure land values, this tax deserves high praise indeed—to be preferred over another "twist" of the income or sales tax where they are now on the "high" side. Such considerations are of an order of magnitude which is quite different from those which are relevant to circuit-breaker relief. At today's amounts they seem to me too small to warrant attention as relevant to current decisions. But attitudes do seem to be affected.

10 *John Shannon*

Property Taxation: Federalism and Federal Policy

An analysis of the role of the property tax in our federal system can raise many issues; however, in this chapter I shall try to answer three questions:

1. What has the property tax contributed to our system of fiscal federalism?
2. What has federalism done for (or to) the property tax?
3. Should the Federal Government become directly involved in local property tax relief and reform efforts?

The Property Tax—Its Contribution to Fiscal Federalism

As one who might admit to a strong bias in favor of decentralized decision making, I now believe that if the property tax did not exist, fiscal federalists would have had to invent it. Moreover, as inventors, we might well be advised to construct the property tax in the same massive and rough mold we actually see out there in the real world—quite an admission for someone who has urged others for many years to tidy up the local property tax.

Four Significant Attributes

My grudging and growing admiration for the "inequitable property tax" can be traced to the fact that this levy has four characteristics that strengthen or complement fiscal federalism:

1. *A massive revenue-generating capability* that enables this local levy to serve as a primary underwriter for most counties, cities, and local school systems, thereby insuring a considerable degree of local fiscal independence.
2. *An onerous reputation* that has enabled many state leaders in recent years to win grudging approval for the adoption of state income and sales taxes as trade-offs for partial local property tax relief. The creation of many strong and diversified state revenue systems, in turn, stands out as a most heartening development for those concerned about the centralization of fiscal power in Washington.
3. *A unique budgetary flexibility* that permits local policymakers to make small incremental adjustments in the tax rate and base—a "fine tuning" capability that is not found at the federal or even at the state levels, but which is necessary to promote the diverse needs of local constituencies.
4. *An ad valorem character* that makes the property tax the only major levy in our federal-state-local system that taxes unrealized capital gains—an attribute that both endears it to most economists and makes it repugnant to most taxpayers.

Federalism—Its Contribution to the Property Tax

While the property tax has made a substantial contribution to fiscal federalism, our system of shared powers has probably done far more for the property tax. To be more precise, the politics of fiscal federalism may go a long way in explaining the property tax paradox—a levy characterized by both a powerful revenue-generating ability and a very poor administrative reputation.

The nostrum that an old tax is a good tax comes easily to mind when one attempts to explain why the property tax, despite its administrative shortcomings, continues to dominate the state-local fiscal landscape. If one probes beneath the surface, however, he will quickly discover that it is the politics of our federal-state-local fiscal system that keeps this poorly administered levy alive and well. To be more specific, there are at least six intergovernmental factors that have combined to sustain and nurture the local property tax.

First, most state legislators are reluctant to authorize widespread local use of state income and sales taxes for fear of impairing state use of these two taxes. Despite the fact that the use of local income and sales taxes is growing, authorization of local nonproperty taxes has met heavy resistance in many state legislative chambers. The arguments usually cited in opposition to local income and sales taxes are that they would magnify interlocal fiscal disparities and impose undue compliance costs on tax-payers. Recent state experience indicates, however, that it is possible by means of state piggy-backing to resolve most of the compliance programs associated with local income and sales taxes, and there is no logical reason why state revenue-sharing programs could not be designed to offset local fiscal disparities caused by the imposition of these two taxes. The bedrock opposition, therefore, to local income and sales taxes can be traced to the fear that if authorized at the local level, they would impair the revenue-raising capability of the states.

Second, state legislators generally wait until the local property tax be-comes very heavy before they evince any willingness to pull the local fiscal chestnuts out of the fire, and by that time the situation has become so difficult that it is almost impossible to cut local property tax levels dras-tically. As in the case of most major issues, public officials must wait for a crisis situation to develop before they can generate sufficient public con-sent for a significant departure from the status quo. This political fact of life is especially apparent in our federal system, where officials at higher levels have no desire to take the blame for higher taxes just to ease the fiscal pressure on local policymakers. As a result, most of the income and sales tax statutes now on the books came only after the cry for property tax relief became too strident to ignore.

Ironically, by the time the public is ready to accept higher state taxes, the property tax load has become too massive and too deeply ingrained in the economy to work out an easy substitution of state income and sales tax dollars for local property tax revenue. In most states, it would take an unacceptably high level of income or sales taxation or both to do the job.

There is also the vexing problem of windfall gains to owners of land and buildings. As the Commission recently pointed out, "The so-called land speculator is twice blessed by property tax reduction. First, his vacant land, like all taxable realty, has more value in the market, and second, his cash costs of holding land off the market are sharply reduced."[1] Because of these fiscal and economic obstacles, state policymakers can achieve only limited substitution objectives, and have been more successful in using their newly adopted income and sales taxes in slowing down the growth of the property tax than in rolling back this venerable levy.

Third, the proliferation of local fiscal authorities and the resultant dif-fusion of political responsibility make it difficult for many property owners to pinpoint political responsibility for increases in the local property tax. When a governor proposes a new tax or is successful in the hiking of an existing levy, he runs the likely risk of defeat at the next election. In sharp contrast, it is ordinarily far more difficult for a local property tax owner to fix responsibility for an increase in his property tax, because the tax rate may be raised by the county, the city, one or more of the special districts, or in many cases by the independent school board. There is also the assessor. He may be held responsible for heavier tax loads, if the local rate makers fail to cut back their rates commensurate with their decision to hike assessed valuations. In any event, this diffusion and misdirection of political responsibility tends to act, albeit imperfectly, as a "heat shield" that partially protects local tax policymakers from the full blast of irate taxpayers.[2]

It should also be noted that local school board members appear to be less concerned about their political futures than most other tax policymakers, and this fact also militates against the operation of the normal political sanctions against those who raise property taxes.

Fourth, the link in the public mind between home rule and the local property tax is still strong, particularly in the case of the local property tax for school purposes. Virtually every time state policymakers have suggested a quick state takeover of educational financing responsibility in recent years, the proposal has gone down to defeat—Michigan, Oregon, New Jersey, California, Colorado, and Washington. While there were many factors working against these state takeover proposals, the fear of loss of local control certainly played a part both in defeating these proposals and in sustaining heavy local use of the property tax.

Fifth, as previously noted, the local property tax possesses an unusual degree of fiscal flexibility—a characteristic ideally suited to the diverse constituencies of local governments. As Glenn Fisher has pointed out at this conference, de facto tax base adjustments help local policymakers maximize revenue while minimizing political stress, much to the dismay of most property tax reformers. This phenomenon is most visible in the not uncommon practice of assessing farmers and homeowners at lower percentages of assessed value than downtown department stores, utility property, or out of state property owners.

Sixth, the property tax is the "residual" tax in our federal system—it is usually called upon to finance everything and anything that the Congress or the state legislators will not underwrite. President Harry Truman used to say that the buck stopped at his desk—an observation that is undoubtedly true in matters pertaining to foreign relations and national economic policy making but not applicable to our domestic public finance world. If a locality wants to set up a well-baby clinic, pay higher firemen's salaries, or hire psychologists to provide guidance to their high school students, it is usually the property tax that is called upon to underwrite these ventures, because the localities cannot obtain the necessary dollars from the State Capitol or Washington. Thus, the residual character of the property tax remains an important factor as long as this levy serves as the primary means for financing local government.

TABLE 10.1
Itemized Property Tax Deductions on Federal Individual Income Tax Returns, 1972

Adjusted gross income class	Number of returns (thousands)	Taxable returns with property tax deductions (thousands)	Amount of property tax deductions (millions)	Cost of property tax deductions to gov't (millions)	Average property tax deduction per return with itemized property taxes	Value of property tax deduction per return with itemized property taxes
$ 0- 2,999	15,470	55	$ 14	$ 2	$ 260	$ 36
3,000- 4,999	8,740	595	184	29	309	48
5,000- 6,999	7,970	1,450	457	79	315	54
7,000- 9,999	12,610	3,890	1,274	238	327	61
10,000-14,999	17,230	6,725	2,784	580	414	86
15,000-19,999	7,100	3,920	1,984	485	506	124
20,000-49,999	4,375	2,980	2,396	785	804	264
50,000-99,999	415	345	483	246	1,399	712
100,000 and Over	90	81	208	117	2,562	1,446
All incomes	74,000	20,041	9,782	2,560	488	128

Source: ACIR staff estimates.

TABLE 10.2
State Action on Property Tax Relief Plans for the Elderly

	Number of states on January 1		
Kind of relief	1970	1973	1974
State-financed, circuit-breaker	4	13	22
State-financed, other plans	8	11	8
State-mandated, locally-financed	12	15	14
State-authorized, locally-financed	4	6	6
Total	28	45	50

Source: ACIR staff compilation.

The Property Tax Relief Issue

Any discussion of the intergovernmental aspects of the property tax relief issue should note the presence of a most curious division of labor between the federal and state governments. Currently, the federal government is operating an *indirect* residential property tax relief program with benefits that become progressively more generous as family income rises (table 10.1). In sharp contrast, a growing number of states are operating *direct* residential property tax relief programs with benefits that become progressively less generous as family income rises—the so-called cirucuit breaker programs (table 10.2).

The real issue confronting the Congress is whether it should supplement or supplant the state-finance circuit breaker programs, and there is no lack of conflicting advice on this issue.

At one end of the advisory spectrum we have the "academic revisionists," who assert that the property tax bears down more heavily on the rich than on the poor. As might be expected, these revisionists take a rather dim view of either state efforts or federal aid proposals designed to shield low-income homeowners and renters from property tax overload situations.[3]

Moving across the spectrum, we find the "state activists"—clearly a majority of the Advisory Commission would be numbered in this group. While they take the position that there is a real problem—that the residential property tax does bear down too heavily on many low-income families—they argue that there is no need for federal incentive grants to induce states to do something that is highly popular, morally right, and relatively inexpensive. They point to the impressive elderly homeowners from property tax overload situations and to the gradual evolution of state circuit breaker plans to cover the nonelderly poor as well. Thus, they argue that the Congress would be well advised to hold off any action for at least a few more years in order to give the states enough time to place their own property tax relief houses in order.[4] Of special note is the fact that

Wilbur Mills, former chairman of the House Ways and Means Committee, also argued that the Congress should not rush into this area, in view of the remarkable progress registered on the state front.[5]

Moving still farther across the spectrum, there are to be found the "federal activitists," who urge the national government to use incentive grants in order to hurry state circuit-breaker history along. They come down hard on the fact that there are still great gaps in state circuit-breaker coverage—that only a handful of states shield the nonelderly poor homeowners and renters from excessive residential property tax burdens. While they acknowledge that the states are moving in the right direction, they contend that progress is still too slow—justice delayed is justice denied. Senators Muskie and Percy represent this point of view.[6] They have introduced S. 1255—a measure that calls for the use of federal aid sticks and carrots to accelerate state action on both the circuit-breaker and assessment-reform fronts.

At the extreme end of the spectrum, we have the "federal hyperactivists," who dismiss state efforts as inadequate and urge the Congress to finance and administer its own circuit-breaker program of residential property tax relief. Curiously, the Nixon Administration fell in this category, and Secretary Shultz urged the House Ways and Means Committee to enact legislation designed to provide circuit-breaker protection for all elderly homeowners and renters below the $25,000 income level.[7] Thus, whereas Senators Muskie and Percy would simply have the national government give the state circuit-breaker bandwagon a push, the Administration urged Congress to jump on the wagon and push the states off this popular vehicle of property tax relief. This is hardly an exercise in intergovermental comity and certainly cut against the decentralization grain of the Administration's "New Federalism."

Confronted with this great and growing divergence of opinion on this issue, only one policy inference can be drawn—in framing a property tax relief policy for low-income homeowners, Congress will make haste slowly.

Notes

1 ACIR, *Financing Schools and Property Tax Relief—A State Responsibility* (Washington, D.C.: G.P.O., 1973), p. 13.
2 This same diffusion of political responsibility also partially explains the pervasive conflict between local assessment practice and state valuation law. See John Shannon, "Conflict Between State Assessment Law and Practice," *Property Taxation U.S.A.* (University of Wisconsin Press, 1967), pp. 49-51.
3 Henry Aaron, "What Do Circuit-Breaker Laws Accomplish?" *Property Tax Reform,* ed. George E. Peterson (Washington, D.C.: Urban Institute, 1973), pp. 53-64.

4 ACIR, *Financing Schools and Property Tax Relief* (Washington, D.C., 1973), pp. 4-7.
5 Wilbur D. Mills, "The Essential Federal Role in Reform of the Property Tax," *Property Tax Reform* (seminar sponsored by International Association of Assessing Officers, Chicago, 1973), p. 6.
6 Hearings Before the Subcommittee on Intergovernmental Relations of the Committee on Government Operations, United States Senate, Ninety-Third Congress, First Session, on S. 1255—Property Tax Relief and Reform Act of 1973, pp. 233-39.
7 Ibid, p. 264.

11 *Dick Netzer*

Property Tax Reform
and Public Policy Reality

I

This paper is an effort to cope with the apparent gap between what seems to be happening in the real world of policy making with regard to the property tax and the prescriptions for property tax reform that emerge from the work of scholars. In the literature of American public finance over the years, the property tax has been anything but neglected: it accounts for a large fraction of the total pages published in the last hundred years. True, there was a period of relative scholarly neglect, but during the last decade there has been renewed attention and a fair amount of high-quality scholarly work on the property tax, as evidenced by the papers presented at the TRED conferences in particular.

Meanwhile, in the last few years, the property tax has received a great deal of political attention—largely in response to high and rising tax rates that often amount to taxation of unrealized capital gains, which public finance economists alone consider to be a proper subject for taxation—and marginal legislative reforms of the property tax have been adopted in a large number of states. The difficulty is that, aside from improved assessment administration, the reforms that policy makers are considering and implementing are for the most part rather remote from the reforms that might seem suggested by the work of scholars. This is not to say that the scholars have been totally ignored; indeed, there are cases in which legislature and the courts have been frighteningly attentive to propositions that scholars advance with the usual qualifications on the basis of all sorts of simplifying assumptions. Nonetheless, it seems fair to say that the systems of property taxation likely to emerge from current legislative trends will strike most scholars as not just unsound but actually perverse, in that the reforms appear to reduce equity and increase efficiency losses.

No doubt this is partly explained by the customary time lags between the output of academic scribblers and public acceptance of these notions (often, when they are no longer valid, if they ever were) and by the difference between our notions of equity and those of legislatures attempting to reflect the views of the median voter. Another explanation lies in the inherent difficulty of persuasively expounding economic propositions that are superficially implausible, like economists' definitions of income and wealth, the conditions for efficiency in resource allocation, and the incidence of taxation. But one suspects that, in addition, there is a problem in our own inability to marry our conceptions of what is theoretically proper to the immediate concerns and practical capabilities of policy makers.

There is, of course, a fundamental difference among us as to the essential nature of the property tax, which relates to disagreement about its incidence. Recently, the capital tax theorists have reminded us of the contributions of Harry Gunnison Brown, and thus provided a solid analytical basis for the long-standing posture of most public finance economists, the view that general and uniform taxes are better than partial and nonuniform ones. In the older literature on the property tax, public finance economists appear as strong opponents of exemptions, classification, tax rate limits, selective relief devices, and extralegal differentials in assessments, on the presumption (usually implicit) that the more uniform and general the property tax is, the less distorting its economic effects and the more likely it is to have a distribution of burden that conforms to ordinary notions of equity. Simultaneously, most public finance economists accepted the theory of incidence of the property tax that is the conventional wisdom, a theory that treats the tax as if it is a set of partial taxes appropriately handled by partial-equilibrium analysis.

The recent revisionist writing on the incidence of the property tax—the leading figure is Peter Mieszkowski, who explicitly acknowledges Harry G. Brown as the Founding Father—provides an explicit and sophisticated support for the longstanding hostility to nonuniformity. The essence of the case, of course, is that if the supply of savings is interest-inelastic, then a truly general uniform tax on all forms of physical capital will have only one significant economic effect: it will reduce the rate of return on capital. It will not change the level or composition of real investment, nor will it affect product or noncapital factor prices or the spatial distribution of economic activity. The ownership of capital being progressive with respect to income, such a tax will be progressive in incidence.

To the extent that the property tax is not uniform (and no one argues that the existing tax is completely uniform), it has excise tax effects. Product and factor prices *are* affected, as are the composition of investment and the spatial distribution of activities. Tracing all this through is an extremely complex business, and it is hard to make flat-footed statements about the pattern of incidence that results from the extent of nonuniformity that does exist. However, one can say flatly that a nonuniform tax is very unlikely to be as progressive in incidence as a truly uniform tax on capital and that nonuniformity does result in significant efficiency losses. Thus, the theory provides a case for resisting policy moves that would increase the extent of nonuniformity and for favoring policy moves that work in the reverse direction. The latter would include, in addition to improved assessment administration, intergovernmental transfers for equalization purposes and to deal with geographic externalities, even to the point of statewide or metropolitan-area-wide financing of some activities; elimination of the most egregious exemptions and other legal property tax preferences; coping with the problem of income tax deductibility; and so on.

II

This is not the place to contest the revisionist view of property tax incidence. Other papers at this conference address the issue, and I have dealt with it at length elsewhere.[1] In general, my view is that the existing tax is so nonuniform that it makes no sense to treat it as other than a collection of partial taxes for which excise tax effects dominate. Moreover, nonuniformity is clearly attractive to elected officials, otherwise we would not have the near-universal practice of systematic differentials in assessment levels among property types and the very widespread adoption—increasingly so in the very recent past—of legal measures to provide differentially favored treatment of specified types of property or taxpayers, including partial and complete exemption, tax credits, tax abatements and postponements, preferential assessment, and fully elaborated classification schemes like Minnesota's.

It can be argued that, once it was decided to exempt publicly owned capital and capital owned by private nonprofit organizations and used for eleemosynary purposes and agreed that many types of nonrealty capital are so difficult to discover and/or value that they too should be exempted, the opportunity to have a property tax that is economically beneficent and convincingly progressive in incidence was gone.[2] In this light, the further steps that resulted in even more nonuniformity can be interpreted as efforts to make an already imperfect tax into one that conforms more closely to the notions of equity that are politically effective and also matches politically effective resource allocation objectives. That is, given the degree of nonuniformity that seems inherent in the American variety of the property tax, even more nonuniformity is necessary to make it socially tolerable.

If one accepts the argument that the persistence of the doctrine of governmental tax exemption, the constitutional attractiveness of subsidizing eleemosynary activities via tax exemption, the administrative difficulties in taxing most personal property, and myriad other well-entrenched tax preferences make it right to view the property tax as a collection of partial taxes, then the case for a classified property tax makes economic as well as political sense. Both the equity and efficiency of partial taxes can be improved by judicious differentiation, as economists acting as tax policy advisers frequently point out. This is not to say that the differentiation that actually exists in any state has been judiciously chosen and begins to approach an equitable and efficient solution. Instead, in most states, the property tax system constitutes an almost incomprehensible set of differentials that are unwieldy, complex, sometimes erratic, and often far from effective in achieving the relative tax burdens policy makers are seeking.

Thus, there is great scope for property tax reform designed to produce a system that matches public policy objectives, even though these objectives will not—and in my view, should not—produce across-the-board uniformity. The need to rationalize the system is compounded by the increasing judicial impatience with extralegal differentiation via assessment differentials, an impatience only evident in the past dozen years or so. There is a lot to be said for this judicial posture, for it is extraordinarily difficult to avoid substantial within-class disparities that no legislature intends, if administrative classification by the assessor's fiat is grafted on to the statutory classification devices that exist. However, real reform in assessment administration does change the allocation of property tax liabilities by property class, and often by considerable amounts. The typical losers from assessment reform are single-family houses and farm property, classes that rank highest in legislative esteem.

III

It is worth trying to catalog the explicit and implicit policy objectives that legislatures and governors seem to be aiming at, in their current and recent property tax reform efforts. I exclude here the most obvious such objective, geographic equalization of effective property tax rates, since it is much more a question of reforming intergovernmental fiscal relations than reforming the property tax itself. Policy makers seem to be trying to:

1. generally encourage housing investment and consumption by reducing the tax component of the recurring costs of housing to consumers, particularly consumers of owner-occupied housing, who predominate in most housing markets;

2. specifically encourage maintenance and improvement of older housing, typically that located in central parts of urban areas;

3. relieve all or some (e.g., elderly) low-income taxpayers from property taxes that are high in relation to their low current incomes;

4. generally relieve farmers from the increasing taxes that reflect the increased real property values that in turn are a result of the increased application of reproducible capital to agricultural land, and more recently, the worldwide increase in agricultural commodity prices;

5. specifically reduce the temptation to convert farm land (or other open space) on the urban fringe to urban uses, by not taxing such land at its market value in anything other than its present use.

6. encourage, generally or selectively, economic development in the form of business investment in plant and equipment;

7. export tax burdens to people in other jurisdictions by high taxes on business property;

8. disguise the tax burden borne locally, by collecting a high fraction of property taxes from business property, with the tax shifted to consumers, employees, and owners in ways that are close to invisible;

9. encourage or discourage higher-density urban development by changing (or retaining) the ratio of taxes on improvements to taxes on urban land as such;

10. preserve an ancient American tradition, the opportunity to make a killing on urban land, as values rise along with population growth and collective investment in social capital.

Obviously some of these objectives are irreconcilable, and others can be reconciled only if public revenue from some other source replaces revenue from the property tax. Economists *qua* economists have no brief to denounce the legislative objectives. They do have a responsibility to speak out loudly and clearly about the conflicts among the objectives, the efficacy of specific measures proposed to achieve the objectives, and the noxious economic by-products that either the specific measures or the achievement of the objectives may produce. It is best to be hard-boiled about all this, in particular by heavily discounting long-term effects and being properly cautious in the presence of uncertainly, like all successful politicians.

This is particularly so in the case of proposals designed to reduce the relative tax burden on residential property, which, *ceteris paribus,* must increase taxes on nonfarm business property. It is reasonably clear that higher taxes on local firms producing for export that have major competitive advantages in their present locations are likely to result mainly in lower location rents to the factors employed by those firms, especially to land, and under some demand elasticity conditions might be exported in higher product prices. In the long term, if and when the location rents have been fully absorbed by higher taxes, the consequences for the taxing jurisdiction are more equivocal.

Higher taxes on export firms that compete on reasonably even terms with those located elsewhere and on firms selling to local final consumers cannot be exported, of course, but will be borne locally, by the least-mobile factors of production and, for locally traded goods, by local consumers. It is difficult to specify the distribution of economic burdens, but it is easy to argue that the short-term burdens are likely to fall much more heavily on owners of capital, relative to land, labor, and local consumers, than are the long-term burdens. But given time preference and uncertainty, policy makers ought not to be criticized out of hand as prodigal with the economic patrimony, for giving in to political expediency and favoring housing vis-a-vis nonfarm business property.

This is also relevant to one of the two major concerns with regard to the form of tax preference accorded residential property. Those two concerns are the relative treatment of owner-occupied and renter-occupied property and the income-distribution effects of alternative tax preference devices. They are important concerns simply because legislatures generally have granted much more favorable treatment to owner-occupied residential property than to rental housing and because many of the existing tax preferences seem perverse in their income-distribution consequences. It is possible to argue that both these conditions are a result of inadvertence, convenience, and simple-minded head counting (all of these in turn reflect either poor staff advice or mindless ignoring of good advice), rather than carefully calculated policy choices. That is, it is much easier to devise tax preferences that are not conditioned by any taxpayer economic characteristic save his ownership of the type of property in question and that apply to homeowner properties than to design property tax preferences that accurately reflect differences in the economic circumstances of individual households and extend equally to tenants and owner-occupants. Moreover, renters *are* a distinct minority that is easy to overlook, especially since their property tax burdens are invisible to them as voters.[3]

Of course, the discrimination against rental property is not always accidental or innocent. Politicians and their advisers not infrequently distinguish between homeowner and "income-producing" property, with rental housing in the latter category. They thereby reject the economists' contention that capital is capital and housing is housing, capable of producing money or imputed income, regardless of the form of ownership. Differential taxation of assets that are partial substitutes for one another is likely to have wealth effects, but it can be argued that the effects may be of no great practical consequences. A more important issue, if the objective of the tax preference is to encourage housing consumption, is the extent to which taxes on renter-occupied housing are shifted forward to the occupants. If the tax is fully shifted, then tax preferences that discriminate against rental housing deserve unqualified condemnation by economists, as very imperfect means to the end sought. If, however, much of the tax is not shifted, the criticism must be more qualified.

An efficient set of housing preferences would exactly reflect the extent of forward shifting to occupants as occupants, for both classes of housing property. Thus, in both cases, there would be no need to grant preferences to the land underlying the housing structures, since a reduction in land taxes does not increase housing consumption but only serves to increase the value of the land. Abstracting from cyclical fluctuations in mortgage credit conditions, the supply of single-family houses appears reasonably elastic with respect to price, even in the short run, which means that a tax preference to owner-occupied housing (93 percent of which is single-family) is likely to be largely shifted forward to consumers. The evidence at hand now suggests that the supply of rental housing is very price-inelastic in the short-run, still relatively inelastic in the medium term, and perhaps quite elastic in the longer run. So, taking into account time prefer- and uncertainty, residential property tax preferences that appear to discriminate moderately against rental property are not necessarily inefficient. However, this surely does not justify the extreme disparities in taxation of the two classes of housing property that frequently exist. Considering what is surmised about the relative ratio of land to building values for the two types of property and the supply elasticity evidence, I would guess that on the average rental housing preferences should be about two-thirds as great as homeowner tax preferences (in effective rate terms), in a system of housing tax preferences designed to encourage housing consumption in general (or alternatively, to treat all housing consumers alike).

The circuit breaker aside, nearly all housing tax preferences are quite insensitive to the economic circumstances of housing consumers. The typical forms include preferential assessment ratios (by law or otherwise), exemptions of specified dollars of assessed value, and credits or exemptions that are percentages of tax liability or assessed value. The latter two forms usually have dollar ceilings, which means that the tax preference becomes a declining fraction of income or wealth once the ceiling is reached. But within the ceiling, the size of the tax preference varies directly with economic status. Moreover, for all the housing tax preferences, not excepting the circuit breaker, the more wealth one has in the form of housing, holding income constant, the more tax relief one gets. This, of course, is a major strand in the scholarly critique of the "populist" proposals to reduce property taxes.

However, unless one believes that the property tax is a true capital tax, this last argument is logically powerful but irrelevant. It *is* objectionable, in the absence of some overriding public purpose (like reducing consumption that is environmentally damaging) to tax people with similar incomes differentially, depending upon whether they spend more or less of their income for housing, rather than other goods and services; and the property tax, in the absence of well-designed housing tax preferences, does just that.

In this light, the circuit breaker appears an attractive instrument for providing housing tax preferences. However, two caveats are in order. First, the circuit breaker may be a good tax relief device, but it is a poor measure as an instrument of general antipoverty policy. It is far too uneven in its effect among the poor to consider it otherwise.[4] Second, the senior citizen variety of circuit breaker does enrich heirs at the expense of everyone else by not recapturing the relief at death; heirs surely are the principal monetary beneficiaries, although the benefits from an undisturbed residential status are very important to the immediate beneficiaries, the senior citizens themselves, and may be considered an important social benefit as well.

The record of scholars with regard to tax preferences for agricultural property is a good one: we are virtually all strongly opposed, especially to preferential assessment of urban-fringe land without strong provisions for recapture of the preferences at the time of land conversion, provisions that simply do not exist. Where there is a recapture provision at all, it tends to be so limited in time and extent that is amounts to a modest realized capital gains tax that falls to zero after a holding period that is not terribly long. We have not been at all effective in persuading policy makers of their error, but we have an obligation to continue to speak out. Moreover, we should speak out more clearly on the question of generalized preferences for agricultural property. The historic basis for the preferences is obvious: in the 1920s and 1930s, farmers had low incomes and often negative net worth. Sometimes they owned real property of significant positive value, but more often they were subjected to burdensome property taxes because assessors continued to markedly overassess property with extremely low market value. These circumstances do not exist today, nor have they existed for a generation, so generalized preferences for farmers amount to making up to today's farmers for maltreatment of their fathers and grandfathers.

Earlier in this paper, it was suggested that rising values of farm real property are in good part a result of the increased application of other forms of capital to the land. A convinced land-value taxer might be persuaded that this is one of the exceptions to the case for land-value taxation, in that the land value increase in this instance is a result of the actions of individual owners, not a result of external forces, and to tax the land more heavily will have adverse effects on how it is used. However, this would be an unnecessary stipulation. Farm land values will rise as long as it is technically possible and economically desirable to apply more capital to farm land, whether or not the individual owner of a given piece of land does so. Essentially, the situation does not differ from that prevailing with regard to urban land: the land tax is neutral with respect to the use of individual parcels of land, and low taxes simply mean higher land values.

There is a common thread running through many of the more popular forms of tax preference, especially those for farmers and senior citizens, the notion that the property tax should not be among the economic incentives that induce or compel people to change their economic behavior. That is, governments should do nothing to add to the pressures we all face to make changes in consumption patterns, work habits, places of residence, or life styles, over time. When put so baldly, this is an extraordinary idea, one that dominated Europe in the first half of this millenium but disintegrated in a modernizing world and had no currency by the eighteenth century. It reminds one of the British Labour Party view that no one should ever be "forced" to move by changes in the price of housing services, a view that calls for rigid rent controls. The implications of general application of the notion that governments should assure economic stasis are truly mind-bending.

There is a set of property tax preferences about which reformers talk much and policy makers worry: wholly tax-exempt property. The great bulk of this is publicly owned property, with another large element consisting of the property of eleemosynary organizations; a small fraction is composed of property owned by ordinary private parties whom legislators wish to favor, like veterans. Although policy makers worry a good deal about tax-exempt property, little action results. This is fortunate, for the case against tax exemption, as it is usually put, is a very poor one, based on a series of fallacies about the consequences of removing tax exemption.[5] Scholars do have an obligation not to repeat conventional foolishness, without inquiry, just because it is superficially plausible and seemingly well-meaning, lest a generation hence our present students and auditors act on our words, along the lines described in the celebrated passage by Keynes about the power of defunct economic ideas.

At a TRED conference, it should not be necessary to belabor the virtues of another form of property tax preference, the untaxing of all improvements in favor of heavier taxation of site values. There is an issue worth mentioning, however: our inability to persuade policy makers of the case for heavier taxation of land. That inability is striking, and it is difficult to explain convincingly. A partial explanation surely is that a major shift in the direction of land value taxation will occasion such widespread changes in the distribution of tax liabilities (and, therefore, widespread capital gains and losses) that policy makers are frightened. This in turn suggests that the best policy payoff from additional research on land value taxation lies not in global studies, but in empirical work that is specific to the conditions of time and place in which the tax policy change is proposed. We must be able to let policy makers see that this particular radical reform is not a recipe for political defeat, but one that entails politically acceptable risks in the short run, risks to be run in the prospect of very substantial longer-run political and economic gains.

IV

In this paper, I have tried to uncover a direction for property tax reform that is not utterly at variance with what policy makers seem to be seeking and, at the same time, not wholly at odds with what economic reasoning suggests about the consequences of their acts. The underlying rather presumptuous purpose is to suggest how we as scholars might best work to be effective in affecting policy without doing violence to our intellectual convictions.

My own convictions are that the intermediate-term goal should be an explicit classified property tax system (operated by percentage credits rather than manipulation of assessed values, which cannot help but debase the valuation operation), in which there are heavy taxes on land, somewhat lighter taxes on other nonresidential property, and still lighter taxes on residential structures (with only modest, if any, distinctions between owner-occupied and renter-occupied housing). Considerable caution is in order with respect to further distinctions and classifications, especially among types of business property (although there is surely a long-term case for taxing business activity on the basis of value added rather than on the basis of the value of selected types of physical assets).

Fairly liberal use of genuine tax deferrals is warranted; indeed, there is a case for rather general access to a deferral option, provided the recovery is complete and the rate of interest on the taxes deferred is high enough, say, something like two or three percentage points above the market rate of interest on low-risk private obligations. If the tax rate on housing structures is a relatively low one, then the need for low-income relief in the form of the circuit breaker will be less. A circuit breaker to deal only with truly extreme cases might still be appropriate; alternatively, there is some case for a device akin to the sales tax credit, a per capita credit operated through the income tax system which provides everyone with a uniform dollar exemption.

As is evident, this prescription is really at odds with current policy trends in only two major respects: heavier taxation of land and the failure to be kind to farmers. It is very much at odds with the policy implications of the capital tax theory of the property tax, but that theory, in my view, has intellectual rather than practical value.

Notes

1 See "The Incidence of the Property Tax Revisited," *National Tax Journal,* 26 (December 1973), 515-35.
2 That is, unless the tax were to become one on site values only.
3 In 1970, owner-occupied housing units were 60 percent or more of all occupied units in forty-one states and 55-59 percent in six other states. In Alaska, Hawaii and (even) New York, owner-occupied units comprised just about half the total. The owner-occupied proportions declined during the 1960s.
4 Some of the defects that are accentuated when the circuit-breaker is extended from the elderly to all ages are explored in Marc Bendick, Jr., "Reforming Homestead Tax Relief in Wisconsin," *Institute for Research on Poverty Discussion Papers,* no. 170-73, University of Wisconsin—Madison, July 1973.
5 This is elaborated in my paper "Property Tax Exemptions and Their Effects: A Dissenting View," *Proceedings of the Sixty-Fifth Annual Conference on Taxation, 1972,* National Tax Association, 1973, pp. 268-74.

Summary Discussion and Evaluation

After the eleven papers in this volume were presented, the conference devoted a final session to general discussion, for which Daniel M. Holland served as Provocateur and Eli Schartz as Editor. An edited transcript of the discussion follows.

Mr. Daniel Holland: Our present discussion will be summarized and will appear in the published document. Over most of this conference, gems of extemporaneous thought and insight have been dropping from you with unwanted frequency. Nonetheless, we have captured none of them for the record. The assumption now is that these gems will revive. So please do not be afraid to repeat what you may have said before; the fact is that the published volume has no memory of it, as of now.

Our purpose is to go beyond the prepared papes if we can, to develop a consensus if we can, or to point out where this conference has suggested the need for additional work. Generally, academicians are obsessed with the fear of unemployment. In this session we may point up the need for more work.

The conference has disclosed a number of areas where we agree (these may not be that interesting), and a number of interesting areas where there seems to be a good deal of disagreement. These may be especially worth exploring. I intend to follow the procedure of not injecting prejudices or preferences but simply giving each of you the opportunity to do so.

We can proceed in a variety of ways. Had a Mr. Risen from Jamaica shown up here, he would have perhaps directed our initial attention to the difficulty of implementing tax reform. Mr. Risen wrote to me about a week ago (probably as the last man in the world who would still talk to him) complaining of the problems of instituting land value taxation in Jamaica. He wondered if I could suggest some sources containing a few painless approaches. His letter was full of graphic examples of the difficulties of instituting land tax reform.

Apparently his difficulties overwhelmed him or took priority over other activities, and he did not get here.

However, I guess the most serious thing running through our discussions, and one that may or may not be settled sufficiently for operational purposes, is the question of incidence. We have had both traditional and revisionist views presented. Dick Netzer told us, and I am not quoting, "The property tax is so nonuniform that the capital theory of tax incidence is not useful other than as an intellectual exercise."

George Break, who like Jesting Pilate, did not wait for an answer (I am trying that again—last time it appeared in the notes as P-i-l-o-t [laughter]) wrote that since the two opposing views of tax incidence are not likely to be reconciled in the near future and since each view has some strong arguments behind it, the best that the policy maker can do is to avoid relying entirely on either. And he must be fully aware of the different policy implications of each. That means move softly and carry two statistical tables. [laughter]

Incidence of the Property Tax

Bill Vickrey, I know from his previous propensity to compromise polar cases, suggested that incidence is in the eye of the beholder; where the beholder is a relatively small decision-making unit, he can take one of the tables or one of the views of incidence as useful for his deliberations. And if the decision maker is the federal government, seeking to influence all the small decision makers, he can take the other view.

William S. Vickrey: Nevertheless, even if the decision maker is only influencing a small number of other decision makers, he must consider incidence relative to the country at large. He can say, in effect, that if a single community increases the tax in improvements, this will shift burdens to consumers and renters in town *A* and away from the consumers and renters in *B,* who will now gain the benefit of a greater concentration of capital in their area. However, from the view of the country as a whole, consumers and renters in the aggregate neither gain nor lose. Nevertheless, in the country as a whole, property owners lose.

Arthur Lynn: Which theory are you identifying yourself with?

Vickrey: Well, the Mieszkowski theory[1] is correct for the country as a whole, if you talk in terms of aggregate classes across the country. However, within each class there will be a shift. If, for instance, the areas southwest of the Rockies do one thing and the eastern states do something else within the given class, there could be a shift of burdens from the portion of the class that is west of the Rockies to the portion of that class that is east of the Rockies.

Lynn: Is that our consensus? Do we leave it at that?

I thought I understood Dick (Netzer) to have a view that there were not merely two possibilities, given the realities of the nature of property tax.

Dick Netzer: However, one can proceed by logical stages, and what Bill

has interjected is this additional stage. Suppose one takes the pure Mieszkowski case of the central government imposing a national uniform property tax, one could say it will have these effects.

Now let's go to the next stage. It is no longer central government
making the decisions, but thousands of local governments. Even if they
end up with a uniform tax, the impact will be felt differently.

The next stage is to assume that the local governments will not make the
same decisions. That is another range of differences. Moreover, empirically, 40 percent of tangible capital is not subject to the property tax at all.
The whole capital theory really becomes extremely questionable; opera-
tionally, the tax does not really work with any degree of uniformity. The
assumptions that make the capital theory work just are not present. Thus
I am far apart from the capital tax theory of Mieszkowski, in that I don't
think it is possible to make a short-cut statement about national aggregates as if the property tax were a true capital tax. I think it is necessary to
look at the tax in quite specific terms.

Not being able to make a statement about the national aggregates has
certain negative policy implications. If you can't say what the incidence of
the tax is, you can't call with certainty for a national policy to replace the
tax with something else. You don't know what you are calling for. You
don't have sure equity grounds for your argument.

Vickrey: I would disagree with that to some extent. Let us suppose that
the tax—this unequal tax is achieved in two stages. First, a uniform tax is
enacted on all capital at an average level, and then secondly, a subsidy is
enacted to pay some forms of capital out of taxes levied on the other forms
of capital. Assume that the second stage changes the allocation of capital,
and the effects are in terms of forward shifting. However, the incidence of
the first stage would be in terms of backward shifting. Then, I think, you
have something of a reconciliation of the two points of view.

Netzer: Yes, I think so. However, when you consider the layers of geographic nonuniformity, you have to then start looking at differentiated
markets, and this changes the outcome.

Nevertheless, from the policy view, I don't think that most of the people
who have written along the line of the capital theory of incidence or
adopted its position have argued that the theory proves that there is no
case for massive federal replacement of the property tax. But my agnostic
view of the property incidence approaches the argument from a different
angle. There is no case for massive federal replacement of property tax
revenues, because in view of the complexity of things, we don't know the
exact outcome of its removal.

Secondly, I quite agree that there is a lot of backward shifting of the
property tax even where excise effect prevails. However, the backward

shifting will not necessarily be on owners of capital. Some of the backward shifting of taxes on reproducible capital will also be on labor. One can't be sanguine about the equity characteristics of that.

Not that there is no forward shifting; the simple case that the portion of the tax on land rests on the owners but that all the rest is forward shifted just doesn't ring true.

Vickrey: Nevertheless, you have to be careful if you argue that the tax on improvements rests on the landowners. As a matter of fact, in some of the models that I have played with, the aggregate ground rents are actually increased by an increase in the tax on improvements. However, the effect is not uniform; although in the center of the city, the ground rents are decreased, this is offset by an increase in ground rents at the periphery.

Netzer: I agree. There is a possibility that this could occur; there are possibilities for all sorts of situations other than forward shifting. All kinds of backward shifting could occur. And they are not fanciful cases.

Holland: So most of those statistical tables that have been used in the last several years for state tax policy purposes, say the New Jersey tables and the Connecticut tables, have incorporated in them assumptions about the distribution of the property tax that you would not find acceptable.

Netzer: There is an exception. Many of these tables refer solely to the residential tax component. They refer to the taxes on owner-occupied residential property: the ACIR studies, the special tabulations from the Residential Finance, and the Survey of the Census of Housing. This data can be taken at face value. They are a straightforward direct cross-tabulation between current money income and taxes paid.

Holland: And I suppose that other refinements, those relating to permanent income, we are not particularly concerned with at this time.

Business and Industrial Taxation

Richard Lindholm: I think that leads us to a point we came up with over and over again: the trend of policy decision in many states to shift more of the property tax away from residential property to business property. There is general agreement that this is going on over the whole country. I don't know whether we came to a decision, whether the policy move in this direction is something very bad or quite good. I wonder if some others would like to comment on this.

Vickrey: How many think it is bad?

Eli Schwartz: I think it is bad, since much of the property tax goes for education. If you believe in decentralization and some autonomy of control for local education and feel that the residents of the area will retain some of the benefit from good schools, then having the local residents contribute some of the funds to support the type of schools and the educational programs they want makes some sense. However, I can't think of any move that will change the way that education is financed sooner than to have the big shopping malls paying most of the local education tax. I don't see the justification for it or the equity.

John Shannon: I think the change is good to the extent that it reduces the shelter costs of low- and moderate-income home owners. The property tax now takes an extraordinary bite out of their current income. Secondly, housing is viewed from a social standpoint as somewhat different from other forms of expenditures. In the property tax field, we should give housing somewhat the same preferential treatment that we give the consumption items under the sales tax. It does have a special character, and is socially recognized as such. Harold Groves used to say that housing expenditures were especially meritorious, that society is well served by people who put relatively more of their budget into housing.

Holland: Up to some point.

Shannon: Up to some point. To the extent that these traditions and feelings are recognized explicitly in preferential tax treatment, especially for low- and moderate-income home owners, I think it is all to the good.

Schwartz: Nevertheless, why would you want to finance this subsidy for low-cost housing out of the taxes on shopping malls or new industrial construction, especially when the revenue goes largely to education? Moreover, you get the peculiar geographic subsidization. The shopping malls, for example, are scattering outside of the central cities onto open farm lands, wherever there is a crossroad of a major highway. Some township with a minimal population is subsidizing its school completely; some other more-populated area gets no break. I think this will eventually lead to a complete state taxation for the financing of schools or complete abolition of the local school districts. I am not sure I am in favor of that.

Shannon: Could I respond really briefly? Implicit in the idea of shifting some of the burden that is now borne by the low-income and moderate-income home owners is the growing strength of the state income and sales tax movement. The shift is to general taxes that are diffused more widely. I am not implying that the alternative is to sock business on the property tax.

Schwartz: That is the way the question was posed.

Netzer: But practically speaking, when the argument is made that we'll lower the share of the property taxes in the general state and local tax revenues, it is unlikely that the substitutes enacted will be entirely personal taxes. Legislatures do not adopt personal income taxes without enacting corporate income taxes that are more than equal. Therefore there is always some substitution of additional business taxes, be it the corporation tax or the sales tax.

Vickrey: I think that in policy, there is always a problem between the difference of the image and reality. For example, the property tax is assumed to fall heavily on the farmer. For a long time, the image of a farmer was the man behind a plow or picking grapes; however, the reality of a farmer, in terms of tax policy, is the man who lives in Omaha and drives out to his farm two or three times a year to do things to it. [laughter]

Netzer: This is a New Yorker's view of the farm. [laughter]

Vickrey: Well, at any rate, there is a difference between the image of the farm worker as a poor, hard-working man who needs some encouragement, and the reality of the person who actually benefits from all of the farm subsidies and tax breaks.

Lindholm: Maybe policy will change somewhat toward the farmer now that he has the high prices, assured markets, and expanding production. Some of the carry-over from the bad days of the thirties when the farmer was given special benefits are going to disappear, perhaps starting this year. We will get more revenues from agriculture.

Vickrey: We also have the image of the home owner as the widow in the cottage or the poor working man in his modest home somewhere, but the reality is that of a $20,000-a-year executive in Scarsdale.

Netzer: $20,000 a half-year.

Holland: That is after taxes.

Vickrey: I am a little dated, I guess.

Taxpayer Attitudes

Holland: One of the difficult areas that the conference touched upon was the policy makers' perception of what the taxpayers' perception is of what is going to happen to them. This seemed to be a common thread. Dick, for example, suggested that the American public doesn't seem to think that capital gains are true components of changes in wealth. For some not fathomable reason, this obvious change in ability to convert assets into cash is somehow not deemed real.

Netzer: Either capital gains or increases in the size of estates.

Holland: Yes. But nevertheless Americans have always shown a little bit more interest in capital than say their British counterparts. When we describe our millionaires, we walk about them as having ten million dollars. As the British describe their rich people, Mr. Darcey, in *Pride and Prejudice,* had ten thousand pounds a year. We have always shown a little more perception of wealth. [expletive deleted]

In fact, I wonder what people do think about taxes. For example, many feel that in the context of political tensions, the property tax has a number of advantages. One of them has to do with the generally slow nature of the rate changes. On the other hand, many people have pointed to other aspects of the property tax as being decisively against it. One is its obvious and potent reality as compared to other taxes. It might be useful to go out and learn more about what, in fact, people perceive about their taxes. If there is an educational job to be done, we can do that more intelligently if we know what the ogres are. However, I am afraid that when we get all finished, we'll find that the ogres seem to be higher taxes. And that everything else is an excuse.

Vickrey: How many people still pay their property tax once or two or three times a year in whopping big chunks.

Lindholm: That is generally the case—

Holland: In Oregon.

Lindholm: If you had an opinion poll, people's attitudes would be different during statement time.

Holland: That would be a bad opinion poll.

Schwartz: Most mortgages are amortized. The property tax is paid along with the monthly payment; it is another monthly charge. Of course, for income tax purposes, they send you a statement of the total property tax you paid.

Vickrey: Even when mortgages are amortized, very often you pay your taxes separately. Not everybody arranges for prepayment of their taxes. I wonder if anybody knows how prevalent the practice is.

Shannon: Our research indicates that somewhere between 55 percent and 60 percent of the single family home owners in the United States finance their property tax payments through the mortage houses. But even here, you have a curious announcement effect, because ordinarily the home owner has a flat debt service charge. The total of interest and principal are always the same. The one dynamic element in his monthly payment is the property tax. My wife remarks when our installment payments have risen, and she points to the property tax as the villain.

Netzer: Have you heard about fire insurance recently? Makes the property tax rise look picayune.

Shannon: Yes, another dynamic element. Nevertheless we just can't assume that because 55 or 60 percent of the home owners have a relatively painless pay-as-you-go arrangement, they are necessarily deadened to the tax increase.

Vickrey: Is this of all home owners or just those with mortgages?

Shannon: Of all. Sixty percent of the total.

Netzer: There are some partial studies of the arrangements of mortgages, and a very, very, large fraction of all mortgage financial houses have a tax payment plan. Ninety percent of all mortaged single-family houses have arrangements of this kind.

Lindholm: We should find out whether those who pay without realizing it have a different attitude toward the property tax than those who pay at the end of a year or six month period. We could see whether this is significant.

Netzer: Except I think that John's [Shannon] point is right. The property tax part of the payment does change from year to year. Moreover, conventional arrangements for adjusting the account, the total escrow payment, mean that at the end of the accounting period, if there has been a particularly large property tax increase, the mortgage service company demands a large cash payment. This could be quite substantial if they have miscalculated. Of course, if you have quarterly tax collections, you are not going to get that massive an adjustment.

Implementing Tax Changes

Holland: I wonder if we can also, because we want to get things into this summary—explore somewhat the problem you touched on in your paper, Dick [Netzer], of the best method of implementing some property tax changes. For example, a shift of land value taxation.

The problem of implementation of any change involves the necessity of providing a flow of information to the taxpayer. Are there methods of moderating the mechanism of implementation for those taxpayers who are really very severely affected? These may be a small number. Although it might be a windfall for some, there would be the relatively few taxpayers who would be particularly hurt.

Netzer: Here you have two stages, two aspects. One is the political or economic desirability of reducing the anguish of the first impact. The second is that during subsequent iterations to observe what will happen in fact. One must see how quickly the happy solutions of the kind Bill [Vickrey] has talked about will be forthcoming: those where there are only gainers, no losers. The problem of implementation does call for research.

Holland: However, the gains would appear in guise of the ephemeral and diaphanous attributes of a capital gain. But even the gainers would be faced with a very palpable and concrete increment in taxes. So the problem of appeasing the taxpayers is an exercise in very imaginative economic education.

Netzer: Yes. Well, of course, one device is the use of an iterative process. If you make the tax change small, clustering around a zero percentage change in liability for individuals, your problems are reduced.

You rule out extreme distributive changes as you make the tax change smaller. But the price you pay is that you don't get as much of the advantage of the tax reform.

Shannon: A bit back, in discussing the distributive changes, I may have raised the problem of the widely perceived hostility to capital gains taxation without qualification. The first qualification is very important: the difference between taxing unrealized capital gains as opposed to realized. Secondly, is the problem of the imposition of taxes on the unrealized capital gains of low-income people and small farmers. That is, as opposed to taxing the realized gains of the upper-income groups. There is a profound difference.

Holland: However I think we might start to think about ameliorating mechanisms. The property tax is often levied on persons of small income but of not inconsequential wealth. This wealth can serve as the basis for financing the tax or as a basis for postponement of the tax. The tax liability can be accumulated against that wealth, to be collected at some later date.

Shannon: But there is a third dimension to this issue, the type of the property. The tax on the capital gain on housing or a small farm may be contrasted to AT&T stock. The great mass of taxpayers in the low and moderate income are affected by an increase in taxes on the unrealized gains on homes and on farms. And this is where the fire really is to be found.

Holland: The fire is to be found there. I guess it is going to be an area of increasing severity. If we continue to have a brisk inflation, nevertheless, this group will be a relatively advantaged group compared to some other members of the community.

Shannon: And this is why those who are interested in the well-being of the property tax ought to say a little prayer every night that the national administration can check inflation. If there is one thing that can really tear public support from an ad valorum tax, it is a raging inflation.

Holland: Which is also the same thing that can tear public support out from underneath an income tax.

Shannon: To a lesser degree.

Lindholm: Well, with progressive rates.

Schwartz: We were talking at coffee break today; someone suggested that some of these problems may not be so much a tax problem as a finance problem. We could develop some imaginative financial devices, for example the proposed reverse mortgage for elderly people. These people could become life tenants of their property against its capital value. Perhaps elderly people should be able to go to some bank and borrow against their property to pay the tax. The tax could accumulate against the property. If plans of this type could be financed at normal interst rates, it would take a lot of the fire out of the problem.

The unrealized capital gain isn't such a bad problem if you don't have to pay cash. It is paying realized taxes on unrealized capital gains that hurts. If the taxes were unrealized too, accumulated against the unrealized gain, I don't think the crisis would be as acute.

Netzer: In other audiences, John [Shannon?] has been very eloquent in talking about the legislator's attitude toward any of these things. In effect, they amount to liens on the property of elderly people. Many of the people we are concerned about are elderly. They and I are very hostile to the present system because there are no liens. Nevertheless, I must admit, where there have been liens, they have been wildly unpopular.

Schwartz: It may be an educational problem. In other countries and in other societies, they have been worked out.

Holland: Are you assuming that, or can you cite some instances of it?

Schwartz: Professor Jack Guttentag is very strong for the reverse mortgage. He has a whole system—

Holland: That is Jack Guttentag country, but where else?

Schwartz: The only place I know of where it is quite common, according to my readings, is that something similar to the reverse mortgage has been used in France; unfortunately it has very detrimental social effects. [laughter] The elderly farmer sells his farm for a periodic cash payment to a younger adjoining farmer; he remains as a life tenant. This is a sort of reverse mortgage. Of course, the problem is that if the old farmer lives too long, it makes the young farmer, who eventually hopes to acquire the property, very unhappy.

Lindholm: We have the procedure through the state.

Holland: In Oregon.

Lindholm: Yes. Although no one uses it. And no one has been foreclosed. I mean, no one has spent so much that the government would have to say, "We are giving you more than your property is worth in tax relief." However, very few people use it. Even though it is not so complicated; perhaps it could be sold. No one put on a big campaign.

Holland: Is it very new, Dick [Lindholm]?

Lindholm: No, it is not new. It's been there quite awhile.

Schwartz: It is not advertised.

Lindholm: It was, when it was originally adopted; it came up last year again.

There is another point about the problems of explicit payments vs. implicit gains we have been talking about. Your tax payment is an explicit payment, while the rent or that interest you obtain from rising property values can be implicit. And therefore on one item, gains, one is paying out cash, whereas the other is a sort of accumulation. Therefore, there is a difference in attitude toward the two amounts.

Holland: There is a difference in attitude; however, there is always a difference in attitude even between explicit streams of different signs.

Netzer: The evidence in regard to the negative attitude toward liens or lien laws is most strongly found in another area. There has been an abandonment of the use of liens for recovery of old age assistance in all states. The negative attitude seems implausible. Here the people are on welfare, and the state places a lien on the house, not to be exercised until death. Nevertheless this is treated as sort of a denial of the American way of life. And it has been abandoned by the states.

Cal Skinner: Not by all of them.

Netzer: Most of them. But it is very hard to enforce. And the abolition of lien laws has been very narrowly beaten in Congress. Incidentally, there have been several efforts in Congress to have the Social Security Act amended to provide that if any state has a lien law, it's welfare plan would be decertified.

User Charges and Benefit Taxation

Holland: Several times during our discussions, the concept of user charges has come up. I wonder if this is just because the user charges are a good, logical, and rational method of finance. Is there a perception that increased use is being made of user charges? Or is there a perception that the opportunities for applying user's charges are more open than before? Is there anything new in user charges?

Skinner: There are notations.

Holland: Developer notations?

Skinner: Yes. It is just like a sewer charge. You apply them for use of the existing school system; just as charges are made for hooking onto the sewer system.

Lindholm: And the developer pays for it?

Skinner: The developer pays for it; however, to the extent he passes them on, the new owner pays.

John Riew: I read an article by Charles McClure.[2] He argues that local taxation, unlike federal tax, ought to be primarily a benefit tax for reasons of resource allocation. He argues that the property tax should be de-emphasized because it doesn't function very well as a benefit tax. Then he discussed different kinds of a user charge or benefit tax. One was a pollution control charge.

Moreover he argued for parental payments for the financing of the children's education. That appears to be a new thought, more or less;

however, I think it is beginning to be talked about more often. Other than these, I don't see really anything that we don't already have. Moreover, the user charge pertaining to school financing seems highly controversial.

Besides, isn't it true that the property tax might be a general proxy for user charge? If you have a large lot, you pay for the longer road extending to cover the entire length of the front foot. The cost of protection, police and fire, goes up with the property value. And there should be some correlation (even if weak) between the size of the house and size of the family, and some relationship between size of the family, the number of kids, and the cost of education. Indeed in general, the property tax could be considered as a benefit-oriented tax. To say that we ought to move toward benefit taxation and that the property tax should be dispensed with doesn't seem quite convincing to me.

Netzer: However, the property tax may not be very efficient as a resource allocator. The device you have to use should reflect costs, not benefits. It is not value of service as used in the economics of regulation, that concerns us—it is cost. I doubt if there is any significant public service at the local level whose cost has a high positive correlation with the value of individual parcels of property. This is what we are talking about.

Of course, if one has a highly homogeneous residential community, where virtually all parcels and houses are the same value, all parcels are about the same size, the people are roughly the same age distribution, and the family composition is similar, then they are all consuming about the same services. Essentially, in this case, the property tax is something like a head tax. It may be a reasonable proxy for the distribution of the average, not the marginal, costs of the package of public goods offered by the local government. But once you leave this case, there isn't much for which the assessed value of individual property (the property tax is not a tax on the size of the house, the frontage feet or the size of the lot, or the fire damage hazard) is a good proxy of the cost of service. The measure of the tax is assessed value, and I think the best relation you could get to costs of most services by simple correlation is a coefficient of 0.6. That is not very good.

Holland: 0.6 is not very good at all.

Schwartz: Yes, but if you look at it from another point of view, not as an allocation of cost but as a method of recapturing some of the benefts, there is some justification for the property tax. Surely the provision of public goods to different areas does affect the value of the property.

Vickrey: However, the attempt to recapture of benefits leads to inefficiency in resource allocation. That is the problem. Take the case of the fire protection. On the benefit basis, it is the burnable property that is being protected against fire and therefore ought to pay. However, if somebody insists on setting up tennis courts next door to the fire department, he is using up just as much of the land protected by that fire department as somebody who builds a house on it.

Schwartz: However, I still think that many of the services that local communities perform are still in the nature of public goods. They have a great deal of commonality, and it is very hard to separate out the various groups that benefit directly. Consider a general package of public goods and note that these raise the property values in the area. It raises the value of all parcels and then that of the tennis courts too. Taking back some of this value for the public fire department makes some equity sense to me.

Vickrey: If the tax were on the land value of the tennis courts, I would agree. However, the contribution of the ownership of that tennis court to the requirements for the fire department are pretty much the same, whether it remains a tennis court or whether somebody puts up a tenement.

Schwartz: Yes, that part is correct. Nevertheless, the value of the tennis court partly depends on the whole utility of living in the community and partly depends on the quality and amount of services provided.

Vickrey: I am not arguing that one shouldn't charge the tennis court. I am arguing that you should. However, this is not the normal concept of benefit applied to fire protection.

Schwartz: Because you just took fire protection as one—

Netzer: You're right. One does not apply the price analysis to public goods or to the public goods aspect of things that are impure public goods. One can't do it.

Then, we have to be concerned about tax finance and the rules to be used for tax finance. That is when we talk about tax price rather than price. Perhaps, for fire protection, I think we should be talking about the price, not the tax price. However for the public goods aspect, I think we should talk about tax prices and the problems of local decision making. Then the questions are the kind of taxes to be used and the equity and the efficiency characteristics of those taxes as taxes, not as prices for specific public goods. Because taxes don't make any sense that way.

I think that is really the problem. If you are dealing with prices, efficiency is what you are worried about in a conventional market sense; however, in dealing with taxes, you look at it a different way.

Weld Carter: If, in other words, your tax rate [tax price] were high enough, then that tennis court would undergo transformation and turn into a ten-story building.

Vickrey: Unless they are people who are willing to pay high rates for the use of the tennis courts, in that location.

Douglas Jones: Dan [Holland], I would be interested in this. Is there a feeling around the table that tax policy generally and particularly the property tax is a very useful device for accomplishing environmental control goals? Is anyone really pushing for that as a workable instrument?

Skinner: Illinois passed a special law to put part of the automobile, the catalytic converter, back on the tax rolls. Otherwise, we couldn't charge sales tax on it. It is unbelievable what some of these laws do.

Jones: On the plus side?

Skinner: Negative. My God, it is the biggest mess. Well, I am glad I wasn't there when they passed it.

Netzer: You know the conventional view about environmental control policy is that tax inducements to do the right thing are pure efficiency losses.

Skinner: Just tell them to do it.

Netzer: Or charge them for not doing it.

Lindholm: There are a large number of states that are giving property or income tax favors to the people who do install pollution control devices, and they have been quite successful in getting something done, whether you got your moneys worth or not. It did accomplish something. Now, could you have passed legislation—

However, personally I do favor the idea of ordering polluters to clean up and bear the cost themselves. Of course, the price of the goods that they produce would eventually include the cost of pollution control.

Vickrey: The trouble with the tax subsidy is that it assumes that there is one method of pollution control and that is the method that is given the tax privilege. Thus many times you get a subsidy for a large capital outlay in the guise of pollution control, when actually what you might really need is a change in the process that might have involved a relatively low cost.

Netzer: Or you could get a change in the product mix. A good example is paper. If you manufacture unbleached paper rather than bleached paper products, you drastically reduce the obnoxious effluence. If you put pollution on a charge basis, there is a fair probability that paper companies will start producing more unbleached products. They will spend money advertising unbleached products for pollution control process. They won't put in any pollution control equipment, but they will cut the effective pollution 90 percent by changing products.

Vickrey: Or they could shift the manufacture of the bleached product to the places where the pollution isn't so noxious. There may be some.

Holland: Time is up. Thank you very much for being with us at this conference.

Notes

1 "The Property Tax: An Excise or a Profits Tax?" *Journal of Public Economics* (April 1972), pp. 73-96.

2 *Public Policy,* Summer 1971.

Index

Aaron, Henry J., 33, 37n, 221n
Academic scribblers, 224
Accelerated depreciation, 183
Advisory Commission on Intergovernmental Relations (ACIR), 31, 37n, 217, 220, 221n
Alaska: committee for development of, 167; land use, 168-77; Bureau of Land Management budget, 170; native group protests, 170; North Slope oil discovery, 170; statehood act, 170; land freeze, 171; legislation on, 171-73, 176, 181; Department of Defense land holdings, 173; U.S. Forest Service land holdings, 173; classification of national interest lands, 175; Public Land Orders, 175; natural resources, 177-79; tourism and recreation, 178; property taxation, 179-82; Industrial Incentive Act, 180; pipeline taxation, 181-82
Alaska Native Claims Settlement Act, 184n
Almy, Richard R., 61
Althouse, Irvin H., 163n
Arthur D. Little Co.: study by, 189, 194n
Assessment: fragmentation of authority for assessment function, 10; fractional, 11, 13; inequities, 11, 66; inequalities contributing to political survival, 12-13; political obstacles, 20; equalization goal, 58-59; sales ratios, 59-60, 93, 96n; professionalization of personnel, 62-63; tools of, 64-65; preferential treatment of capital, 128
Attitudes: of taxpayers, 240-42

Back, Kenneth, 3, 57
Bailey, Martin J., 37n, 121, 164n
Barlow, Joel, 135, 166n
Barzel, Yoram, 148, 166n
Beck, Ralph A., 36n
Becker, Arthur P., 37n
Bendick, Marc, Jr., 233n
Benefit taxation, 245-48

Berndt, Ernst R., 163n
Berry, Albert, 115, 163n
Black, Duncan, 97n
Borcherding, T. E., 96n
Bosselman, Fred, 184n
Bossons, John, 35n
Boston, Massachusetts, 80-90
Bosworth, Barry, 148
Boulding, Kenneth, 166n
Brazer, Harvey E., 96n
Break, George F., 3, 23, 35n, 236
Brems, Hans, 164n
British Labour Party, 231
Brittain, John A., 35n
Brookings Institution: MERGE file, 30
Brown, Henry Gunnison, 224

Callies, David, 184n
Capital: limits of supply, 100; tax treatment of, 128; double-dipping, 130; tax subsidy to, 133; demand for, 136-38; replacement demand, 138; turnover, 143, 146; durable, 146; monument-building syndrome, 147; subsidies to, 149
Capital gains tax, 126, 152, 243
Carter, Weld, 247
Chicago, Illinois, 12, 21n. *See also* Cook County, Illinois
Circuit-breaker approach, 31, 200-205, 229-30, 233
Classification: of land for ad valorem tax purposes, viii
Condrell, William, 165n
Cook County, Illinois: classification of property, 12; de facto classification system, 19. *See also* Chicago, Illinois
Coons, John E., 55n
Counter-culture, 100
Cross-subsidies, 152

Dangerfield, Jeanne, 165n
Davis, Otto A., 96n

249

COMPOSED BY FOX VALLEY TYPESETTING, MENASHA, WISCONSIN
MANUFACTURED BY CUSHING MALLOY, INC., ANN ARBOR, MICHIGAN
TEXT IS SET IN TIMES ROMAN, DISPLAY LINES IN GOUDY AND TIMES ROMAN

Library of Congress Cataloging in Publication Data
Main entry under title:
Property taxation, land use & public policy.
(Publications of the Committee on Taxation,
Resources and Economic Development; 8)
Includes bibliographical references and index.
1. Real property tax—United States—Congresses.
2. Land—United States—Congresses. I. Lynn,
Arthur D., 1921-   II. Committee on Taxation,
Resources and Economic Development. III. Series:
Committee on Taxation, Resources and Economic
Development. Publications; 8.
HJ4181.P75   336.2'2'0973   75-12210
ISBN 0-299-06920-6

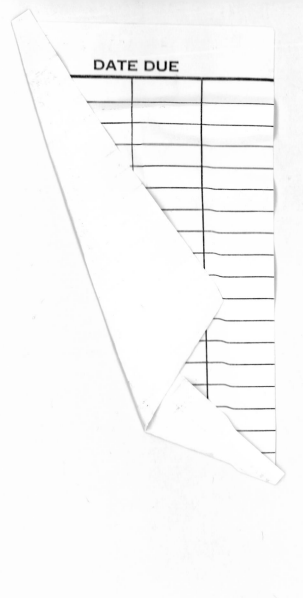

DATE DUE